BARTON REMEMBERED
1939 - 1945

Part Three

THOSE WHO CAME BACK

Researched and Written by

Geoffrey F. Bryant

Published by
Workers' Educational Association
Barton-on-Humber Branch
2000

Published 2000 by
Workers' Educational Association
Barton-on-Humber

Copyright © 2000
text and illustrations
author and owners of photographs
and the Workers' Educational Association
Barton-on-Humber Branch

ISBN 0 900959 15 0

British Library Cataloguing-in-Publication Data

A catalogue record for this book is available
from the British Library

Typesetting and photograph enhancement by Andy and Maggie Leitch
Printed by G.W. Belton of Gainsborough

Foreword and Acknowledgements

In 1997 the Barton-on-Humber Branch of the Workers' Educational Association published *Lest We Forget*, the first of what was intended to be a two part series entitled *Barton Remembered 1939 - 1945*. This gave short biographies of the 54 men and women from the town who lost their lives on active service or as a result of enemy bombing. Published in 1998, the second part - *The Home Front* - gave details of life in the town during the war years - The War Defence Services, Everyday Life, Leisure, Schooling and Industry. It was felt at the time that a third book was necessary to complete the story. This would give details of the experiences of those men and women who left the town to serve in the various branches of the armed forces and who returned afterwards to once again take up their lives in 'civvy street'. I started this task in 1999. The first requirement was a complete list of all the men and women who served in the army, navy, air force, and those other 'services' - the Land Army and 'Bevin Boys'. Most of the names on the list found below were recorded in the pages of the wartime editions of the *Barton-on-Humber Magazine*, a publication edited for most of the period by the Vicar of Barton, Canon W.E. Varah. His monthly lists were headed *Barton Men* [sic] *serving at the Front* and parishioners were asked to submit further names when appropriate. Clearly, he could only record those names that were given to him and one suspects that the service of a number of men and women went unmentioned. It also soon became clear that the numbers involved, (and the fact that many men and women had either died or left the town) meant that producing biographies of them all was going to be an impossible undertaking. As a result, this book contains the wartime biographies of those men and women who either came forward themselves and volunteered information or whose details were provided by living relatives and/or friends. I thank them all for the interest they have shown and for their patience in the face of my constant demands.

A further problem arose when it was discovered that many men and women who went into the services from their homes in Barton were not, in fact, born in the town. Should they be included? It was decided that they should because it is unlikely that their memories would ever be recorded in the town or village of their birth. If such a policy were not adopted, many men and women, born in Barton but resident in another place, when they were called up, would not come to the notice of the present writer and would not be remembered at their new addresses.

For particular help with preparation of this book, the author would like to thank Ernest Coulam, Dennis Houghton for his careful proof-reading of the text, David Lee Photography for the provision of the front cover, Andy and Maggie Leitch for the restoration of the photographs and the preparation of the book for publication, Freda Readhead, Nora Thompson, Margaret Usher and Charles Watkinson. If any reader is able to point out errors or omissions in the text could they please let the author know. It is hoped to publish these in future editions of *The Bartonian*.

In the preparation of the biographies and the accompanying inserts, I have found the following texts particularly useful -

Commager, H.S.,	*The Story of the Second World War*	Washington	1991
Elliot, P.,	*The Cross and the Ensign - a Naval History of Malta 1798 - 1979*	London	1982
Forty, G.,	*British Army Handbook 1939 - 1945*	Stroud	1998
Gilbert, M.,	*Second World War*	London	1989
Keegan, J., (Ed)	*Atlas of the Second World War*	London	1989
Man, J.,	*Atlas of D-Day*	London	1994
Mercer, D.,	*Chronicle of the Second World War*	London	1990
Ray, J.,	*The Second World War*	London	1999
Taylor, A.J.P.,	*The Second World War*	London	1975

Geoffrey F. Bryant
8 Queen Street'
Barton-on-Humber, DN18 5QP
March 2000

Chapter One

The Barton Men and Women who served in the Second World War

This chapter is a list of those men and women who left Barton during the years 1939 to 1945 to serve their country in the Armed Services, the Merchant Navy, the Land Army or as a Bevin Boy. The list is certainly incomplete and probably contains numerous errors. However, it is the result of some two years of searching and should provide future researchers with a body of information on which they can build.

Those names printed **bold** lost their lives during the war and their stories are recorded in *Barton Remembered 1939-1945; Part One, Lest We Forget*, with further details in Addendum chapters in Parts Two and Three of this series. Names which are underlined are those men and women whose biographies appear in Chapter Three of this volume. Where it has been possible to determine the particular service in which a man or women spent the war years this is shown after the name - A for Army, ATS for Auxiliary Territorial Service, RAF for Royal Air Force, WAAF for Women's Auxiliary Air Force, RN for Royal Navy, WRNS for Women's Royal Naval Service, MN for Merchant Navy, LA for Women's Land Army and BB for Bevin Boy. The letters POW follow the names of those men who were prisoners-of war.

Harry Adamson - A
Harry Adlard - A
Charles Akester - A
Harold Akester
Robert H. Akester - A
Henry Alcock
Stanley Alcock - RN
Harry Allenby
John Almond - A
Allan Altoft - ?RAF
Charles Altoft - ?A
Clifford Altoft - A
Walter Altoft
Tom Andrew - RAF
Kenneth Andrews
Walter Andrews
F.W. Eric Appleyard - A
G. Edward Appleyard - RN
Bernard Ashley - RN
John Ashley - A
Albert Ashton - A
Denis Ashton - A
Elsie Ashton - WAAF
Samuel Ashton - A
Alfred Atkin
Harry Atkin - RAF
Alan Atkinson - A- POW
Charles Atkinson A & RN
Jack Atkinson
Ralph Atkinson - RN
Stanley Atkinson - A
Dora Audas
Jack Austin - RN
James Austin - A
Norman Austin - A
William Avison - RN
Charles Ayres - A
James Ayres - A
George Bacon - A
John William Bacon - A
Robert Bacon
Stanley Bacon - A- POW
Steven Bacon - RAF - POW
Ben Baldwin - A
Eric Barber
Thomas Barker - A - POW
Arthur Barley - POW
Harold Barraclough - RN
Leonard H. Barraclough - RAF
Maurice Barraclough - RN
Reginald Barraclough - RN
Olive Barratt
Henry Barrett
Arthur Barton - A
Frederick Barton - A

Walter Barton - A
Arthur Barwick - A
Albert Baxter - A
Eric Baxter - A
Albert Beacock - A
Charles Beadle - A
Harold Bell - A
Frederick Benson - RN
Herbert Beverley
John Bilton - A
Frederick Bingham - A
Frank Bird - A
Robert Birkett - RN
Arthur Birks - ?A
Arthur Allen Birkett - RM
Thomas Birkett - A
David Birtwhistle - A
Denys Birtwhistle - RN
John Birtwhistle RAF
George Blackburn
John Blades
Geoffrey Blakeborough - A
Leonard Blogg
Ernest Blyth - A
Leslie Blyth - A
Fred Blythe
Harold Blythe - A
Robert Blythe - A
Alan Bolton
Eric Bones
G. Edward Bones- A
Alec Booth - RAF
Dennis Booth - A
Philip Booth - RAF
George Boyce
Samuel Joseph Boyd - ?RN
Alfred Boyes
Christopher Braithwaite - A
Harold Braithwaite - A
Frederick W. Brameld - RN - POW
Mavis Brameld - ATS
Roland Brameld -
Charles Broddley - A
Jack Broddley - A
Alan Bromfield - A
Jack Bromfield - A
James Bromfield - RAF
John William Bromfield - A
Dorothy Brooks (nee Varah)
Geoffrey Brooks - A
George Brooks - A
Alfred Douglas Brown - ?A
Bessie Brown (later Graves) - WAAF

Harold Brown
John Brown
Kenneth Brown - A
Leonard Brown - A
Hilary Brumpton (later Firth) - ATS
John Bullivant - RAF
Thomas Burfoot - A
Joseph Burke - A
Keith Burman - BB
George Burton - A
Harold Burton - RN
Norman Button
Bernard Cammack - RAF
Eric Cammack - A
George Cammack
Harry Cammack - A
Leonard A. Cammack - A
Horace Campbell - A
Peter Campbell
Frank T. Cant - A
Albert Cantrell - RN
Arthur Cantrell - A - POW
Charles Cantrell - RN
David Canty - RAF
Granville Canty - RAF
Frank Carlile
Kenneth Carter - RN
Norman Carter - A
Thomas Carter
Jack Cartledge - RN
Cecil Chafer - A
Harry Chafer - A
John William Chafer - A
Joan Chant (later Bruntlett) - LA
William E. Chant - A
Arthur Chapman - A
Fred Chapman - A - POW
George A. Chapman - RN
Harry Chapman - A
John Chapman - A
Walter Chapman - A
Frederick Chapman - A
Arthur Chappell - A
Harold Chappell - RAF
Percy J. Chappell - A
Clifford Clapson
Jack Clapson - A
Eric Clark - RAF
George Clark - A
William Clark
Joseph Clark - A
John Clarke
Peggy Clay
Albert Clayton

Jim Clayton - RN
John Clayton - A
W. Ronald Clayton - RN
Roland Clayton - RAF
Dennis Clipson - RN
Bernard Clipson - RAF
George Clipson - A
John Hugh Clipson - A
John William Clipson - A
Stanley Clipson - A
Haydn Cocking - A
Archibald Codd - A
Beatrice Codd
(later Cooper) - WRNS
Percy Codd - RN
Stanley Codd - A
Walter Codd - A
Wilfred Codd - RAF
Charles Cole - A
Donald Cole RM
John Cole - RAF
Maurice Cole - A
Ruby Cole - LA
Stanley Cole
Harry Colley - A
Betty Collingwood - WAAF
Cyril Combes - A
Leslie Conway - A
Donald Cook - ?A
Eric Cook - A
Ernest Cook - A
Leslie Cook - RN
Norman Cook - A
Ronald Cook - A
Gladys Cooper - ATS
Peter Cooper
Michael Costello
Ernest Coulam - A
Emily Coupland - WAAF
Georges W. Coupland - RN
Henry Coupland
John Coupland
Theodore Coupland - A
Mary Coupland - ATS
Victor Coupland - A
Ruby Cowell (later Cole) - LA
Alice Cowton (later Owen) -
WAAF
Arthur H. Cowton - RAF
Barbara Cowton - (later Instone) -
WAAF
John Bertram Cowton - RAF
Albert Cox - A
Alfred Cox - A
George Cox

Ken Cox - A
Kenneth Cox - RAF
Ralph Cox - RAF
Stanley Cox
Thomas Cox - RN
Walter Cox - A
Norman Credland - A
Aubrey W. Cressey - A
Leslie G. Cressey - A
Beatrice Croft
William Cross - A
Albert Crow - A
Henry Crowther - A
William Crowther - A
Barry Curtis
Charles Danson - A
Edgar Dawson - RN
John Dean - A
William Dean - A
Herbert Dent - A
John Dent - A
Frank Dewey - A
Wilfred Dickens - A
Stanley Dickinson
Charles Dimoline - A
Jack Dimoline - A
George Dixon - A
Nora Dixon - WAAF
Vera Dixon (later Nurse) - WAAF
Albert Doughty
Corney Doughty - RN
Frederick H. Doughty - A
George Doughty - A
Harry Doughty
William Doughty
Eileen Draby
Francis Draby
Alfred Drury - A
J.F. Cyril Drury - A
Henry Drury - A
John W. Drury - A
Denis Ducker - RAF
Gerald Ducker - MN
Henry Dunderdale
Clarke Dunn - MBE, DFC - RAF
Edwin Noel Dunn - A
Mary Dunn
James Durham - A
Kenneth Grainger Eaton
Raymond Eayres - RAF
Wilfred Eayres - A
Norman Ebbaston - A
Wilfred Ebbaston - RN
Harry Eden - POW
George Edwards - RN

Eric Ellerby
Grace Evelyn Ellerby - ATS
Stanley Ellerby - A
Geoffrey Elm - RAF
Cecil Elwood - A
George Emperingham - A
James Espin - RAF
Madge Espin - WRNS
Dorothy Fairbank - WAAF
Edward Fairbank - A
Robert Fairbank - A
Arthur Wallace Farr - A
Clifford Farr - A
Eric Raymond Farr - A
Harry Farr - A
George Farr - A
Noel Farr - RN
Peter Farr - A
Frederick Farrow
George Ferriby - A
Edward Field - RAF
Alec Fisher - A
Harold Fisher - A
Jim Fletcher - A
Stanley Fletcher - RM
Albert Foster - RAF
Clifford Foster - A
Frank Foster - A
Henry Foster - A
John W. Foster - RN
Roy Foster - A
Stanley Foster - A
Walter Foster - RAF
Cyril Franklin - A
Edward Franklin - A
George Franklin - A
Percy Franklin - A
Robert Franklin - A
Sylvia Franklin - ATS
Winifred Franklin
T. James C. French - RAF
John French - RAF
Peter F. G. French - RAF
Reginald French - RAF
Harry Furniss - A
Arthur Gadie - A
Frederick Gadie
Lionel Mervyn Gardiner
Winston Garfoot - A
Stanley Gilfoy - A
Reginald Gill - A
Henry Gilliatt - A
George A. Gilmour - A
Arthur Glover
Kenneth Glover - RAF

Alison Goddard
James W. Goddard - RAF
Elsie Goodhand - (later Hastings) - WRAF
Ernest F. Goodhand - MN
Ernest Goodhand - POW - RAF
Jack Goodhand - RN
Joyce Goodhand - (later Barker) - ATS
Mary Goodhand - (later Thurlby) - WAAF
Peter Gooseman - A
Ronald Gossop - RN
Doreen Goulding - WAAF
Ernest Goulding - A
Harold Goulding - A
Harry Goulding - RN
James Goulding - A
Norman H. Goulding - RN
Arthur M. Gouldthorpe DSM - RN
Cyril Gouldthorpe - A
Donald Gouldthorpe - A
Charles Gouldthorpe - A
George Gouldthorpe - A
Walter Gouldthorpe
James H. Gowshall - MN
John Grasby
Norman Grassby - A
Thomas Grassby - A
William Grassby - A
Clifford Graves
Donald Graves - A
Donald Graves - A
Geoffrey Graves
George Graves - RAF
Harry Graves
James Graves - A
Norman Graves
Ernest Greaves - RAF
George Grebby - A
David Green - BB - A
Russell Green - RN
Thomas Green - A
Geoffrey Greenfield - A
George Greenwood - A
Robert Greenwood - A
Alfred Griffiths - A
Harry S. Griffiths - A
Arthur Grimbleby - RN
Betsy Grimbleby - ATS
Brian Grimbleby - A
Clarence Grimbleby - RN
John Grimbleby - RAF
Norman Grimbleby - RN

Ralph Grimbleby - RN
Walter Denis Guy - RN
Harry Hall - A
Charles Hamilton - RN
Jack Hamilton - RN
John Hamilton - A
Robert Hamilton - RN
Eric Handley - A
Frank Handson - RN
Phyllis Handson - WAAF
William Handstock - A
George Hare - A
Philip Hare - A
Ernest Harness
Walter Harness
Arthur J. Harrison - A
Robert T. Harrison - A
Leslie Harvey - RN
Edward Hastings - RAF
Kenneth Hastings - BB
Frederick Havercroft
John Havercroft - A
Nellie Havercroft
Walter C. Havercroft - RAF
Joyce Headley
Robert Heath - A
Arthur Hedley - A - POW
Enid Hedley - ATS
Jack Hedley - RN
Joyce Hedley - WAAF
Beryl Hewitt - WAAF
Donald Hewitt - ?RAF
Edward Hewitt
Frank Hewitt
Gerald Hewitt - A
Ralf Hewitt - RAF
Roland Hildreth
Arthur Hill - RAF
James Hill
Kathleen Holland
Ernest Hoodless
George Hoodless - A
Frank Hopper - RAF
Walter Horne - A
William Horne - RAF- POW
William Horsfall
Norman Horsewood - A
Arthur Houghton - A
Albert Reginald Houghton
Geoffrey Houghton
Kenneth H.L. Houghton DFM - RAF
Margery Houghton
Dorothy Howell - ATS
Frank Howell

George Howell - A
Frank Howsam
Victor Howson
Walter Howson - A
R. T. Anthony Hudson - RAF
Henry Hunsley
Alan Hunt
Ruth Hutchinson (later Prestwell) - ATS
Frederick Hyke
Geoffrey Jacklin
Jack Jackson
Victor Jackson - A
Wilfred Jackson - A
William Jarvill - A
Charles Jenney - RN
Cyril Jennings
John Jennings
Alfred Jickells - A
Eric Jickells - A
George W. Jickells - A
James Jickells - A
John Jickells - A
Renold Jickells - A
Zena Jickells - ATS
Alan Wilfred Johnson
Albert Johnson
Arthur Johnson
Douglas Johnson - A
Frank Johnson MM - A
Harold Johnson - A
Keith Johnson - RN
Norman Johnson
Stanley Johnson - RN
Walter Johnson - POW
John Johnston
Ronald Jones
Charles Kent
Reginald Kent - A
Dorothy Kerridge - WRNS
Elsie Kerridge - WAAF
Ernest Kerridge - A
Haves Kerridge - RN
James Kerridge - MN
Herbert Kerridge - RN
Thomas Kerridge - A
Bessie King - ATS
Edward King - A
Eric King - A
Frederick King- A
Gerald King - RAF
Henry King
James King - A
Leslie King - A - POW
George Kirby

Norman Kirby
Raymond Kirby - RN
Fred Kirk - A
J.S. Kirk - A - POW
Charles Kirkland - A
Frederick Kitchen - A
John Kitchen - A
Sidney Kitchen
Frank Kitching - A
Noel (later John) Kitching - A
Arthur Knight - A
Donald Lacey - A
Ernest A. Lacey - A
George Lacey - A
Herman Lacey - A
Albert Lait - A
Maurice A. Lakeman - A
Joseph Langley -A
Masie Langley - ATS
Ronald Langley - RN
Charles Laughton
Betty Lawrence - WAAF
Jack Lawrence - A
Jim Lawrence - RN
Joseph Lawrence - RN
Marjorie Lawrence - WRNS
Dennis Lawtey - A
Frank Lawtey - A
George Lawtey
Hector Lawtey - A
Norman Lawtey
Stanley Lawtey MM - A
Walter Leeman - A
Harold Lees - RN
John Lindley - RAF
Gordon Linley - RAF
Brenda Llewellyn - WAAF
Arthur Lowery - A
Charles Lowery - A - POW
Verdun Lunt - A
John Manton
George Marriot - A
Peter Marsden
Eunice Marsh (later Whiteley) -
WRNS
Ronald E. Marsh - RN
Wilfrid Marshall-Ducker - RAF
Roland Mason
Olive Matthews - WAAF
Beulah Mellors (later Hammond) -
WAAF
Robert Mellors - RN
Clifford Metcalfe - A
Fred Metcalfe - A
Joyce Metcalfe - WAAF

Peter Metcalfe
Ernest Millson - RN
Frank Milner - A
Kenneth Milner - RAF
Kenneth Moffatt - A
Leslie Moor
Oswald Moor
Cyril Moss - RAF
John Moss
Jean Mounser - WAAF
Joan Mounser - ATS
Charles Mumby
Cyril Naylor - RN
Ronald Naylor A
Thomas Naylor - RN
Donald Nelthorpe - A
Arthur Newbitt - RN
Donald Newbitt - RAF
Ethel Newbitt - WAAF
George Newbitt - A
Gordon Newbitt - BB and NAAFI
Roy Newbitt - A
Thomas Newbitt - A
**William Ernest Newbitt DSM -
RN**
William B. Newbitt
- POW - A
John Newbown - RN
Henry Newmarch
Charles H. Newton - A
Ronald J. Newton - RN
William Newton
Gilbert Hugh Nowell - **RN**
Douglas Nurse - RAF
John Nurse
Arthur Oldridge - A
Geoffrey Oldridge - A
George Oldridge - A
Olga Oldridge
Sidney Oldridge - A
Stanley Oldridge - RN
Walter Oliver - A
Arthur Osgerby - A
Joseph Osgerby - A
Ralph Pape - A
Elsie Pack - ATS
Arthur Parks - A
Harold Parks - A
William Parks - A
Arthur Parsons - A
Ernest Parsons
Betty Paul (later Sidell) - ATS
Walter Paul - RAF
Clifford Peck - A
Harold Peck - RN

Richard Pettit - A - POW
George Leonard Platt
Mark Pickard - RM
Mary Pickard
Robert Pickard - A
Winifred Pickard
Alfred Pike - A - POW
W. Ernest Pike - RN
Wilfred Pike - A
George Pilkington - RAF
Denis Pinchbeck - RAF
Peter Pinchbeck
Percy Portess
George Plaskitt - RN
Arthur Proctor
Frank Proctor
Harold Proctor MM - A
Herbert Proctor
George Quickfall - MN
Cyril Rayton
Walter Readhead - A
Charles Redman - A
Edward Reed
Edward Richardson - A
Walter Richardson - RN
George Richmond
James Richmand - A
Ralph Richmond - RAF
Roy Richmond - A
Jack Rickwood - RAF
Frank L. Riggall
Arthur Robinson - A
Clarence Robinson - A
Frederick W. Robinson - A
Joyce Robinson - ATS
Kenneth Robinson - A
Victor Robinson - RN
William Robinson - A
Vincent Rogers
Geoffrey Rose - RN
John Ross
Horace Rowntree - A
Henry Rowson - A
John Rushby
Frank Salter - A
Ethel Salter - WAAF
Edward Sanderson - A
Lot Sanderson - A
Thompson Sanderson
Geoffrey Sandvig - A
George Sergeant
Albert E. Seddon - RM
Arthur Seddon - RN
Frank Seddon
Robert Seddon - RM

Walter Seddon - RN
George Seeley - A
Kenneth Sempers - A
Walter Sempers - RN
Barratt Sewell
Francis N. Shakesby - RAF
Fred Sharpe - RAF
Leonard Sharpe - RN
Joan Shaw
Arthur Shepherd
Christopher Shepherd - RN
Edith Shepherd
Jeremy Shepherd
Roland Shephardson - A
Beryl Shields - WRAF
Jack Showler - A
Albert Shucksmith - A
Edward Shucksmith - RN
Harold Shucksmith - A
Rowson Shucksmith - A
Albert Simons - A
Frederick Simpson
Audrey Skinner - WAAF
Charles Skinner - RN
Alan Smith - A
Alex Smith - A
Alfred Smith - RN
Cyril Smith
George Smith - A- POW
Richard Smith - A
Roland Smith - A
Reginald A. Snelling - RN
Byron Snow - A
Arthur Sobey - A - POW
Eric Sobey - A
Fred Sobey - RN
James Sobey - A
Leonard Sobey - A
George Southall MBE - A
Henry Southall - A
Joseph Southall
William Southall
Arthur Sparks
Ernest Sparks - A
George Sparks
Arthur Spence - A
Jack Spencer - RAF
James Spencer - RAF
John Spencer
Sidney Spencer - A
Bessie Spittlehouse
Claude Spittlehouse - RM
Clarence Stamp

George Stamp - A
Verdun Stamp - A
Arthur Stead - A
George Stead - A
Jack Stead - A
William Stead
Patricia Stevenson - ATS
Clifford Stockdale - A
George Stockdale - A
Marjorie Stockdale - ATS
Charles Storey - RAF
William A. Storey - A
Peter Stow - A
Wilson Straw - A
Albert Stuffins - A
George Stuffins
Peggy Stuffins - WAAF
Charles Such - RAF
Sidney Such - A
Thomas Tate - A
Leonard Taylor - A
Albert Thompson - RN
Allen Thompson - A
Arthur Thompson - A
Arthur Thompson - A
Dennis Thompson - RAF
Edward Thompson
Ernest Thompson - RAF
Harry Thompson - A
John Thompson
Philip Thompson - A
William H. Thompson - A
Lily Thurlby - WAAF
Nellie Thurlby - WRNS
Wilfred Tindall - ?RAF
Herbert Tink - A
Sidney Todd
Stanley Todd - A
David Tong - A
Allan Towle - RAF
Joan Towle - WAAF
Wilfred Towle - RN
Emily Trought - WAAF
Ernest Turner
Frederick Turner - A
Joseph Turner
William Turner - A
Henry Unsworth
Arthur Vanderstock - RAF
Audrey M. Varah (later Walton) -
ATS
Oswald Varah - A
William O. Varah MC - A

W. Edmund Varah - A
Cyril Vause - A
Harold Vernon
Horace Vickers - RN
Sylvia Vickers - WAAF
Kenneth Waddingham - RN
Jack Walker
John Walker - A
Joseph Walker - RM
Thomas Walker - A
Douglas H. Watson - A- POW
John Watson - A
Lewis Watson - RAF
David Wall
Ralph Watkin - RAF
Charles H. Watkinson - RAF
D. Watson - A - POW
Eric Welch - A
Harold Welch - A - POW
Ronald Welch - A
Derek Wells - POW
Geoffrey Welsh - A
Geoffrey West - RAF
James West - A
Margaret West (later Gouldthorpe)
- ATS
Albert Weston - RN
Norman Weston - A
George Whiles
Charles Wilson
Reginald Wilson
Albert Windle - RN
Edmund H. Windle - RN
Kenneth Winn
Arthur Winship - RN
C. Frederick Winship - RN
Clifford Winship - RN
Ernest Winship - RN
James Harold Winship - RN
Roy Winship - RAF - MN
Albert Wood - A
Frank Wood - A
Vera Woodcock
Bernard Wrack - ?A
Harold Wray
Harold Wrigglesworth
Arthur Wright
George W. Wright - A
Maurice Wright - A
William Wright - A
Basil F. Wrightson - RAF
Ernest Young

Chapter Two

Bartonians and Wartime Events: 1935-1945

The tables in this chapter give outline details of those events which took place during the years 1939-1945 at which Barton men and women were either present or associated. Further details will be found in their individual biographies or in the shaded inserts which are to be found throughout Chapter Three.

1939	
The attack on Poland on 1 September 1939 provoked Britain and France to declare war on Germany on 3 September. A small **British Expeditionary Force** was moved to the Continent. For some six months - October 1939 to April 1940 - a 'phoney war' persisted as the Germans failed to launch their expected attack into Northwest Europe.	Bones, Hedley, Hector Lawtey
The **Barton 'Terriers'** moved to the Waltham area and set up their searchlights.	Harold Braithwaite, Brown, John Clipson, Stamp Burton, Ron Newton
On 10 September 1939, a German **magnetic mine** sank the *SS Magdepur*.	
1940	
The period of quiet in western Europe was not to last as the Germans first struck into **Scandinavia** (April 1940) and then into **Belgium, Holland and France** (May 1940). In Britain, Chamberlain's government fell from power and **Winston Churchill** became leader of an all-party coalition. The presence of superior German forces caused the Allies to retire from both theatres of war - the evacuation of the British army from **Dunkirk** (26 May-4 June) being little short of miraculous.	David Birtwhistle, Bones, Garfoot, Hector Lawtey
In late June 1940 the French surrendered and the **Italians entered the war** on the Axis side. A German invasion of Britain seemed imminent but the Luftwaffe's inability to win the **Battle of Britain** (August-September 1940) or to force the country to surrender with its bomber **Blitz** (September 1940-May 1941) meant that Hitler's plans had to be shelved. In both of these battles the radar screen along the south coast was vitally important for the RAF fighters and the anti-aircraft defences. The RAF retaliated with bomber attacks on German towns.	Coulam, Dimoline, Horne
At the same time Hitler's **U-boat and long-range bomber offensive** was aiming to starve Britain into submission and losses of war and merchant ships crossing the North Atlantic mounted alarmingly.	Appleyard
In April 1940 **British troops landed at Namsos** in Norway.	Jack Clapson
In May 1940 a British force was sent to occupy **Iceland** and prevent its falling into German hands to be used as a U-boat base.	Jack Clapson
In October 1940 **Mussolini invaded Greece** but with RAF assistance the Greeks took the offensive.	
On 11 November 1940 many Italian warships were sunk in **Taranto** harbour. On that same day it was announced that 24,000 women had enrolled in the **ATS** (Auxiliary Territorial service], 8,800 in the **WAAF** (Women's Auxiliary Air Force), 3,400 in the **WRNS** (Women's Royal Naval Service) and 25,000 in the **Women's Land Army**.	
Between December 1940 and February 1941, British and Commonwealth troops had stunning **victories against the Italians** in North Africa, Sudan, Kenya and Italian East Africa.	Codd, Dunn
1941	
Whilst events in Western Europe proved increasingly difficult for Britain, the army in **North Africa**, aided by Commonwealth forces, routed the Italians and drove them out of Egypt and Cyrenaica. Some British troops were	

transferred to the **Balkans** in an attempt to stop the German advance there but this proved fruitless and by April 1941 the British Force withdrew.	
In February 1941 the German *Afrika Corps* under General **Rommel** began to arrive in North Africa.	
On 4 March a British force landed on the **Lofoten Islands**	Jack Austin
On 29 March, the Royal Navy inflicted considerable damage to the remnants of the Italian fleet at **Cape Matapan**.	Dunn
During April 1941, German and Italian troops drove the Allies out of Cyrenaica although Tobruk held out. In the Balkans the Allies, aided by a small contingent of British troops, sent over from North Africa, were defeated and had to be rescued by the Royal Navy in a Dunkirk-style operation.	
The Battle in the Atlantic took a dramatic turn in May 1941 when the great German battleship - the *Bismarck* - sailed into the Atlantic to attack allied shipping. The pride of the British fleet *HMS Hood* was sent against her but was quickly sunk by a salvo from the German ship. However, action by other ships and planes from the carrier *Ark Royal* succeeded in first crippling the ship which, on 27 May, was finally destroyed.	Jack Austin
The **bombing** of industrial and civilian targets in Britain and Germany continued to intensify and losses of men, women and aircraft mounted on both sides. Britain's radar stations played an important part in the defence of the country.	Betsy Grimbleby, Joyce Robinson, West
Between November 1941 and January 1942, the Allies again advanced in the western desert of North Africa and for a second time overran **Cyrenaica**. However, when troops had to withdraw to aid in the defence of the East against the Japanese, part of the newly occupied ground had to be given up.	Codd, King, Noel Kitching, Wilf Pike
On 7 December 1941, the Japanese entered the war and struck the American Navy a devastating blow at **Pearl Harbor**. At the same time, her troops began the systematic conquest of South-east Asia and what British troops there were in the area were soon in headlong retreat.	
Hong Kong surrendered on 25 December after 18 days of fighting.	
1942	
On 12 January the capital of Malaya, **Kuala Lumpur**, fell to the Japanese army. In late January the Allied forces in North Africa were forced to retreat in the face of a new German offensive.	
On 15 February **Singapore** surrendered to the Japanese and a similar fate befell **Rangoon** on 9 March.	Alf Pike
On 1 April 1942 PQ13, the first convoy to sail for Russia, arrived somewhat battered at Murmansk.	Appleyard, Austin, Newbown
On 16 April King George VI awarded the George Cross to the island of **Malta**. Later in the month the Germans started their **Baedeker raids** on British historic towns and cities.	
Operation *Ironclad,* the **invasion of Madagascar** began on 5 May.	Garfoot
The first of the RAF's **'thousand-bomber' raids** dropped 1,455 tons of bombs on Cologne in 31 May 1942.	Glover
By May 1942, the Japanese army had advanced through Burma and although it was positioned to invade India, had decided that such a move was impracticable. Throughout the rest of 1942 and much of 1943, the Japanese remained inactive in northern Burma whilst the Allies built up their strength in India in preparation for an offensive.	

9

In 1942 German U-boats began successfully hunting in 'packs'. During the year Britain lost eight million tons of shipping and built only seven million.	Jim Clayton, Coupland, Ducker
On 21 June **Tobruk** fell to Rommel's advancing *Afrika Corps* and by early July the German and Italian troops were halted at El Alamein, only 60 miles from Alexandria.	Hewitt, King, Noel Kitching
4-5 July - the Admiralty ordered **Convoy PQ17** bound for Russia to scatter. In the next days 100,000 tons of cargo went to the seabed in 23 merchantmen.	Austin
Lieutenant-General Bernard **Montgomery** took command of the British 8th Army in North Africa.	
The Axis campaigns in North Africa were handicapped by their inability to take the British strategic base of **Malta** and the island was bombed mercilessly during 1942. In August 1942 an allied convoy of merchantmen and warships - **Operation** *Pedestal* - got vital supplies through to the besieged island.	Appleyard, Austin
By September 1942 there were 40,000 enrolled in the **Women's Land Army.**	Chant
On 24 October Montgomery launched his great offensive at **El Alamein** which put Rommel into headlong retreat.	Altoft, Codd, Wilf Pike, Shephardson
On 7 November **Operation** *Torch*, the Allied landings in Morocco and Algeria, was launched with General Eisenhower in command.	Chris Braithwaite, Bones, Chappell, Jack Clipson, Eayres, Elwood, Hector and Stan Lawtey, Arthur Sobey, Eyres, Elwood, Hector Lawty, Stan Lawty, Arthur Sobey

1943

On 13 May 1943 Allied troops striking from both east and west accepted the **surrender of all the Axis forces in North Africa.**	Noel Kitching, Arthur Sobey
The war at sea (where the U-boats' menace was being defeated with the help of radar-assisted reconnaissance aircraft) and the bombing raids over German towns, industrial targets and ports, continued unabated and enemy losses and casualties mounted.	Glover, Watkinson
By mid-1943 the Allies were able to cross from North Africa and strike at **Sicily - Operation** *Husky* (10 July 1943) and mainland Italy itself (3 September 1943).	Blakeborough, Cartledge, Drury, Eayres, Noel Kitching, Arthur Sobey
On 9 September 1943, **Operation** *Avalanche*, the landings at **Salerno** - took place.	Altoft, Bones, Alan Bromfield, Chappell, Jack Clipson, Hector Lawtey, Arthur Sobey
In July 1943 **Mussolini fell from power** and in September the Italians joined the Allied side in the war.	
On 1 October 1943 the Allies entered **Naples**.	Elwood
Throughout the later years of the war an uninterrupted **Allied bombing campaign** was aimed at German industrial and civilian targets.	William Horne
In mid-October the British, with Portuguese permission, established a base on the **Azores** from where they could mount aerial protection flights over the Atlantic convoys.	Austin
From December 1943 until May 1944, the Allies fought a series of desperate battles to take the heavily fortified hill on which Monte Cassino monastery stood and so open the way for the advance on Rome.	Chris Braithwaite, Hector Lawtey
In December 1943 the system of balloting for **'Bevin Boys'** was begun.	Burman

1944

22 January 1944 - Allied landings at **Anzio**. The advance northwards in Italy continued during early 1944. Now only German troops barred the Allied advance.	Harold Braithwaite, Cox, Dent, Greenwood, Shephardson
In March 1944, the Japanese launched an offensive across the Indian border aiming to capture Chittagong and Imphal. **Imphal** and **Kohima** were soon surrounded but held out against ferocious Japanese attacks.	Burton, Kerridge, Kirk
By April 1944 a **civil war was raging in Greece**.	Jack Clipson
On 18 May **Monte Cassino** finally fell to the Allies and on 26 May they entered **Rome**.	
In the Far East, the **war against Japan** began to favour the Allies as American troops began the reconquest of the Pacific Islands and British and Commonwealth forces turned the tide in North-east India and Burma. In July, General Slim began the Allied advance into Burma. Conditions in Japanese prisoner-of-war camps were inhuman and the death rate very high.	Brown, Ron Clayton, Philip Thompson
On 6 June 1944, **D-Day**, an Allied invasion force under US General Eisenhower landed on the Normandy beaches and the liberation of Western Europe began.	Atkinson, Jim Austin, Broddley, Jack Bromfield, Burton, Jack Clapson, Codd, Fairbank, Ferriby, Gouldthorpe, Brian Grimbleby, Horne, Jickells, Frank Kitching, Knight, Charles Newton, Wilf Pike, Readhead, Fred Sobey, Welch, Wright
The first **V-1 pilotless flying bomb** landed on London on 13 June.	Bernard Clipson, Dimoline, Betsy Grimbleby, Marsh
In August **PLUTO** (Pipe-Line Under the Ocean) was laid between England and France to supply 700 tons of petrol per day to the allied troops.	Griffiths
In early August, the right flank of the Allied army in Normandy, Patton's 3rd Army, **broke out from the beachhead**. On 15 August the US 7th Army and Free French Forces mounted **Operation _Anvil_,** the landings on the French Riviera.	Altoft
Paris was liberated on 25 August 1944 and on the same day the Allied army began its advance towards the **Gothic Line** in northern Italy.	Bones
By September, the Allies had fought their way onto German territory and it was clear to all that the end of the war was now in sight.	Sempers
On 8 September 1944, the first **V-2 rocket** landed at Chiswick in west London.	
Operation _Market Garden_ - the parachute landings at **Arnhem** - was launched on 17 September. This bold move to capture vital bridges and open the way onto the North German Plain proved to be a costly failure.	Linley, Arthur Sobey
On 12 November the **Tirpitz** was finally sunk by Lancaster bombers from 9 and 617 Squadrons.	Andrew
On 3 December 1944 the **Greek communists attacked Athens**.	
In December 1944 the Germans launched their counter-offensive in the **Ardennes**.	
On 24 December **Kalewa** in north Burma fell to the Allies.	Broddley

1945

In January the British mounted an amphibious **invasion onto the Greek mainland** to rescue Greek and British forces from the communist attack.	Ken Cox, Hector Lawtey
On the night of 13/14 February, Allied bombers devastated **Dresden.**	King
The Allied armies finally crossed the Rhine in April 1945 and on the 25th of that month **American and Russian forces** met on the River Elbe.	Frank Kitching, Bill Varah
Bologna in northern Italy fell to the allies on 21 April and the Germans fled across the Po valley. On the 29th the **German army in Italy surrendered** unconditionally.	
During the early months of 1945, the Allied armies began their great advance southwards into Burma. On 20 March **Mandalay** fell, **Rangoon** on 3 May. The Japanese were defeated and only mopping up was to follow.	Ron Clayton, Cocking, Foster, Gouldthorpe, Harrison
On 8 May 1945, **VE Day**, German resistance finally ended and the war in Europe was over. The Royal Family and Winston Churchill appeared on the balcony at Buckingham Palace.	
6 August 1945 - first **atomic bomb** dropped on **Hiroshima** and three days later a second one fell on **Nagasaki.**	Norman Grimbleby
On 14 August the Japanese surrendered unconditionally and the war was over. The following day was celebrated as **VJ Day.**	Appleyard

Chapter Three

The Biographies

This chapter comprises the biographies of some 104 men and eight women who left Barton during the years 1939 to 1945 to serve in either the Army, the Navy, the Air Force, the Merchant Navy, the Land Army or as a Bevin Boy. Interspersed amongst these and in roughly chronological order are a number of shaded inserts which give details of particular events and campaigns in which Bartonians featured. Whenever a **bold,** bracketed number or numbers - **(6)** or **(6,10)** - appears in a biography this indicates that further information is contained in the appropriately numbered insert.

Cliff Altoft

Sapper, 6020310
Royal Engineers
Mine Clearance and Bailey Bridge Construction

Clifford Douglas Altoft was born in 1917, the son of Mr George and Mrs Annie Altoft of School Lane, South Ferriby. He attended the school and sang in the choir at South Ferriby. He played for the village football team. On leaving school, he worked variously at Frank's Brickyard in South Ferriby, as 'second chap' looking after horses for 'Squire' Barton at Saxby-All-Saints and, from 1937, as a piling contactor in the building of the chemical works at Flixborough. In 1937 he married Elsie Coulwill at Holy Trinity church, Barrow-on-Humber and the couple took up residence in Barton.

On 15 February 1940 Cliff was conscripted into the army and reported for initial training with the Royal Fusiliers at Blandford. From there he was sent, at a time when a German invasion was felt to be imminent, to the north-east of England to help build the coastal defences - pill boxes and barbed wire entanglements - on the coast between Newbiggin and Amble. After this task was completed, he spent periods at Throckley near Newcastle and at Monmouth in Wales undergoing extensive training. Having displayed his practical skills in defence building, he was transferred into the Royal Engineers and posted to Barton Stacey in Hampshire where he was trained in mine clearance.

Following 10 days embarkation leave, he travelled to Greenock where he boarded the *Queen Mary* bound for the Middle East. He landed at Port Said and in mid-1942, after a journey inland by lorry, he joined No 573 Royal Engineers Army Field Company - part of 10 Corps RE in the 8th Army. By now the advance of the Axis powers in North Africa had reached its furthest point east and Allied preparations were under way for the Battle of El Alamein **(7)**. Cliff's first job had been to lay minefields in the Alam Halfa area to prevent any further enemy advance towards Alexandria and Cairo.

At 9.15 pm on 23 October 1942, the day on which Montgomery launched his 8th Army against Rommel's German and Italian divisions, Cliff found himself in the front line with the 2nd New Zealand Division clearing safe paths through the enemy minefields. The mine clearance parties were out in the open in full view of the enemy so all along they worked under enemy fire. Cliff and a colleague manned a mine detector. One of them moved forward with the detector and would hear a sharp whistle through his earphones when they passed over a mine. His partner following behind then had to make the mine harmless. That night Cliff estimates that his two-man team cleared some 100 mines, both the *Tela* anti-tank mines and the anti-personnel *S-mines*. These latter consisted of a canister full of ball bearings and, when detonated, the canister

jumped into the air and spread its lethal projectiles far and wide amongst the advancing infantry. The cleared tracks through the minefield were bordered on either side with white tape so that the advancing infantry and armour could easily pick out the safe paths.

At about 10.00 pm, the shells fired by the 1,000 guns of the British artillery and those fired in response by the enemy began to whistle over the heads of the mine-clearing parties. Cliff and his companions had to work just behind the Allied creeping barrage. Following the success at El Alamein, Cliff's unit proceeded to advance all the way across North Africa and in May 1943, he was in one of the first parties to reach Tunis. All the time he was busy clearing minefields and helping to open roads and passes which had been obstructed by the retreating enemy. No 573 Company travelled in small lorries and survived on a diet which mainly consisted of hard biscuits and corned beef. Bread was a rare luxury.

Following the Axis surrender at Tunis, Cliff, thinking that he was about to return to the UK, was moved back to Tripoli. It quickly became clear that he had assumed incorrectly and on 9 September 1943, after a voyage from Tripoli in an invasion barge, he found

Cliff Altoft with his wife and daughter taken on his embarkation leave in 1942.

Cliff Altoft (in centre) clearing mines at El Alamein.

Work with the Americans largely consisted of clearing mines, unblocking roads and mountain passes and building bridges over the many Italian rivers which had to be crossed as the Allies moved northwards. Cliff particularly remembers building British Bailey bridges over the Volturno and Gorigliano rivers on the approach before the great battle to take Monte Cassino.

When Cliff's unit got a well-earned break from the front line, he spent some time clearing mines from Italian vineyards, work which usually resulted in the grateful Italian farmers making available copious supplies of their best wines. Finally No 573 Army Field Company reached the River Po and Cliff's Italian campaign came to an end. His unit was pulled out of the front line and sent to Leghorn where, in August 1944, it became part of the force which mounted Operation *Anvil*, the invasion of southern France. The force quickly advanced up the Rhone valley and Cliff undertook little mine clearance. Eventually he arrived in the Low Countries and there he was actively engaged along the canal and river network building new bridges and clearing ones which had been destroyed or damaged. VE-Day found him at Oldenberg in Germany and from there he was granted 10 days leave - his first return home after three

himself landed with the American Rangers and the British Commandos on the northern sector of the Salerno beach **(12)**. As usual, his job was to clear paths through the minefields for the Allied tanks. The force was pinned on the beach for some 10 days and, because of the fierce enemy resistance, re-embarkation and retreat was, for a time, a possible outcome. However, the Allies prevailed and the break-out from the beachhead got under way. The 10 Corps of the Royal Engineers was at this time, and for the rest of the Italian campaign, attached to the American 5th Army. Cliff immediately noticed a significant improvement in the quality of his rations!

1. The British Army in the Second World War

In April 1939 the British army totalled some 645,000 men under arms. Of these 224,000 were Regulars - many of these stationed in India and other overseas garrisons; 325,000 were in the Territorial Army Field Force; and 96,000 in the Territorial Army anti-aircraft units.

In March 1939 the government had decided to double the numbers in the Territorial Army and on 27 April, the Military Training Act was passed which re-introduced some conscription.

In June 1939, 200,000 men aged between 20 and 21 were registered in 'the Militia'. They could choose to join either the army, the navy or the air force. See - Walt Cox, Robert Fairbank and Arthur Sobey

Also recalled were some 150,000 men in the Army Reserve who had recently completed a period of service in the Regular Army. See - Fred Kirk

By 3 September, the army strength had been increased to 1,065,000 men under arms and on that same day, the National Service (Armed Forces) Act passed through Parliament. This stipulated that all men between the ages of 18 and 41, unless in a reserved occupation, were liable to be conscripted for military service. (In 1939 an infantryman's uniform, consisting of some 80 items, cost the nation £20.)

By December 1939, 727,000 men had registered for service and by 1940 the army had some 4,000,000 men under arms. By D-Day one third of the entire male population of the United Kingdom of working ages were in the forces. In April 1945, just under 5 million persons were under arms - some 3 million of these in the army. By that date the British army consisted of 34 infantry divisions, 11 armoured divisions and 2 airborne divisions.

Information from Forty, G, *British Army Handbook,* Stroud 1998.

years and three months overseas.

On his return to Europe, he was employed looking after Germans who were rebuilding bridges in their shattered country. Eventually his unit was disbanded and he was finally demobbed from Strensall on 4 March 1946.

Information from

Cliff Altoft

Tom Andrew

HM Auxiliary Unit 1940-1942
Warrant Officer, 1623715
No 9 Squadron, Royal Air Force
Flight Engineer

Thomas Raithby Andrew was born at Elsham but moved with his parents to live at Grange Farm, Barton-on-Humber in 1936. He attended Brigg Grammar School and his hobbies were riding, shooting, cycling, swimming and athletics. On leaving school in 1939, he started an apprenticeship at Atkinson's Garage on Barrow Road.

In 1940 he joined his father as a member of the local

Tom Andrew.

'Sugar Loaf' Patrol of HM Auxiliary Unit based at Grange Farm (see *Barton Remembered 1939-1945; Part Two, The Home Front,* pp 21-22).

In February 1942, he went to the recruiting office in Lincoln and joined the RAF Volunteer Reserve to become a pilot. He was, however, asked to remuster to train as a flight engineer for the new four-engined bombers which were then coming into service. After completing his training, mainly at St. Athan in Wales, (and gaining his brevet or 'half wing') he joined 'B' Flight of No 9 Squadron flying Lancasters from Bardney. A wartime Lancaster squadron comprised two flights, 'A Flight' and 'B Flight', with nine or ten aeroplanes each. The seven-man crew consisted of (from front to rear) a bomb aimer/front gunner, a pilot, a flight engineer (who in emergency was qualified to act as second pilot), a wireless operator, a navigator, a mid-upper gunner and a rear gunner.

No 9 Squadron's flights were mainly aimed at military targets in Germany and France and they sometimes carried the earthquake 12,000-pound bomb designed by Barnes Wallis known as 'Tallboy'. Targets included Karlsruhe and Stuttgart (a round flight of 7 hours 55 minutes) in Germany, two daylight raids on the port of Brest, and raids on V1 launch sites at Bois-de-Cassen, Trossy, Etaples and Lorient.

In September 1944, he flew to Yagodnik near Archangel in northern Russia from where he was to have taken part in an attack on Germany's largest and most powerful battleship, the 46,000 ton *Tirpitz*, then anchored in Kaa Fiord in northern Norway (6). (Although the fire-power of the *Tirpitz* was greater than any British ship, she spent most of the war at anchor in Norwegian fjords watched over by numerous British battleships and aircraft carriers in case she did put to sea and attempt to attack the convoys taking vital war supplies to Russia. Such an attack could have been catastrophic as the *Tirpitz* was easily capable of sinking every ship in a convoy.) Twenty-eight Lancasters took part in the raid, 20 carrying 'Tallboys'. One of these bombs went straight through the ship's forecastle.

He did, however, fly on a later attack on the *Tirpitz*, this time from Lossiemouth in Scotland. *Tirpitz* was then at anchor at Tromso which could be reached by Lancasters carrying 'Tallboys' with their mid and rear gun turrets removed and fitted with extra fuel tanks. Even so, the planes took off with the heaviest load ever carried by a Lancaster and the crews feared that they might never get off the ground. Flying towards the target at 12,000 feet Tom sighted the ship, 'briefly looking like a large silver pencil.' Unfortunately cloud soon obscured the target and the bomb aimers, only able to roughly calculate the position of the target, failed to score any direct hits. The complete trip took 12 hours 20 minutes - the longest ever bombing operation by Lancasters. On the flight home, Tom celebrated his 21st birthday!

By then he had done 31 operations (flying some 218 hours) and had finished his tour of operations, so he was not on the attack on 12 November 1944 which finally sank the German battleship. (In this final raid, 30 aircraft from Nos 9 and 617 Squadrons again flew from Lossiemouth to Tromso Fiord. In perfect visibility they dropped their 'Tallboys' from 14,000 feet. Two bombs penetrated the ship and caused the magazine to blow up. The ship capsized and about half of the 1,900 crew were trapped in the upturned hull.)

On leaving No 9 Squadron, Tom went to Wigsley (Notts) as an instructor. His final months in the RAF were spent doing various desk jobs before he was demobbed in early 1947.

Information from

Tom Andrew

Ted Appleyard.

Ted Appleyard

Petty Officer, PLX 22200
Royal Navy
Captain's Valet/Ship's Duties

George Edward Appleyard was born in 1917, the son of Mr George Edward and Mrs Sarah Ann Appleyard of 10 Newport, Barton-on-Humber. He was educated at the Church School in Queen Street School and, on leaving, was employed as a stake lad at the ropeworks. From there he went to work in the Export Department at Hopper's Cycle Works making crates for the export of bicycles. Whilst stencilling the names of exotic destinations on the crates, he was inspired to travel and so decided to join the navy.

In May 1937 he travelled to Derby to enlist in the Royal Navy. In June 1937 he joined *HMS Victory*, the training barracks in Portsmouth and, though he found this hard going, he did gain his first experience of comradeship. On finishing his training, he joined the training ship *HMS Hawkins* as a leading hand and then in mid-1938 was transferred to the battleship *HMS Nelson*. This ship sailed for the Mediterranean and during a courtesy call at Gibraltar, Ted took his first steps on foreign soil. From Gibraltar the ship sailed on, first to Cadiz and then to Malta - the main base for combined manoeuvres with the Mediterranean Fleet. Later visits were made to Alexandria and Italy.

In early 1939 his ship returned to the UK and Ted was transferred to a shore establishment - *HMS Ganges* at Ipswich. There he became part of the administration staff responsible for the training of boys aged 14-16 years. It was on a Sunday morning tea break (3 September 1939) during his stay at Ipswich that he heard Neville Chamberlain announce on the radio the

declaration of war against Germany. He was quickly sent back to *HMS Victory* at Portsmouth and was then assigned as a petty officer on one of the navy's oldest aircraft carriers, *HMS Courageous*. The ship was engaged in training for submarine spotting in the English Channel and the North Sea and it was during this period that he met Bill Weatherley, the brother of Madge, his future wife.

Later he was sent to do minesweeping duty on *HMS Speedy* (a minesweeping sloop with a crew of about 75 men and armed with 4-inch guns, an Oerlikon and multiple pom-pom anti-aircraft armament). Whilst working on this ship, he heard of the sinking of *HMS Courageous* on 17 September 1939 with the loss of some 500 men.

Following the evacuation from Dunkirk, he did several convoy duty trips (6) across the Atlantic from Greenock on the Clyde to the seas off Newfoundland. Later, *HMS Speedy* was involved as an escort to the convoys which sailed with war materials from Britain to northern Russia and brought back pit props. (For more about the Russian convoys see the biography of Jack Austin.) During these horrendous voyages, the ship would become covered in ice and those who had to do lookout duty in the crow's nest could only tolerate the cold for about half an hour before they had to come down to be thawed out. At Murmansk, the British sailors would exchange cigarettes and rum for Russian furs and china to bring home. On the last trip he made, the ship was iced in for two months until a channel was cleared by the Russian icebreaker *Lenin*. When the British ships left harbour, the crew would wave to Russian children who skated on the ice which immediately formed behind the vessel's stern.

In 1942 the *Speedy* went back to the Mediterranean on mine-sweeping and convoy escort duties. In August it took part in the epic convoy - Operation *Pedestal* - which brought the oil tanker *USS Ohio* and four merchantmen into Grand Harbour, in Malta **(10)**. The *Speedy* arrived with the merchantmen and then returned to sea at night to locate the struggling *Ohio*. On 15 August, along with another minesweeper, *HMS Hebe*, and the destroyer *HMS Matchless,* the *Speedy* towed the American tanker some 40 miles at a speed of two knots before she reached safety in harbour. Her whole superstructure had been destroyed by enemy bombs. On the voyage from Gibraltar, Ted's ship's crew subsisted on a diet of tea, brought up from below in a bucket, and corned beef sandwiches. There was never an opportunity to go below for a proper meal or a decent sleep. Ted spent the whole voyage manning one of the Oerlikons on the ship's bridge. This convoy relieved the island which had been for months under constant German air attack and, owing to lack of food and oil, would otherwise have had to surrender. As the ships entered Grand Harbour, it seemed that the whole of the population of the island, all cheering, had turned out to greet them. For their efforts, every member of the ship's company received the Maltese George Cross.

From Malta, Ted flew to Egypt to join the frigate, *HMS Petard.* Whilst there and by chance, he met fellow Bartonians Ron Clayton (see *Barton Remembered 1939-1945; Part 1, Lest We Forget*, pp 24-25) and Clarry Grimbleby (see *Barton Remembered 1939-1945; Part 1, Lest We Forget,* pp 41-42) at the ice-cream counter in 'Groppy's' hotel. There they heard 'ships' recall' and all three, in different ships, sailed to the Dodecanese islands off Turkey's western coast to intercept German ships which were launching attacks there.

Ted's ship was hit by a German radio-controlled glider bomb (known by the British as a 'Chase-me-Charlie') which entered one side of the vessel, took away the main bulkhead of the ammunition locker, exited the other side and exploded. The ship was run aground in Turkey. The Turks gave the crew three days to repair the ship and set sail. The holes were plugged using copper plates taken from the sick bay and horsehair from the hammock beds. A British destroyer came and towed the *Petard* all the way back to Alexandria. During this voyage, the ships were attacked by German bombers but the timely arrival of a squadron of American Lightning fighters drove the Germans off. On leaving the ship in Alexandria harbour, Ted was greeted by the army guard, Bartonian Tom Green, who exclaimed, 'You lucky devil, getting back in that thing!' One of the ship's two engines was repaired and this allowed the *Petard* to return to England.

He next joined *SS Queen Elizabeth* at Greenock and,

after sailing across the Atlantic, he travelled by train to Vancouver and joined *HMS Berryhead* (a British ship built by the Canadians as part of their contribution to the war effort). From there he sailed to San Francisco and then across the Pacific to Hawaii to join the American fleet which was involved in recapturing a number of islands from the Japanese.

From there the *Berryhead* sailed to Hong Kong and was amongst the first five ships to dock in that port after the Japanese surrender. After six months in Hong Kong, the ship sailed back to the UK where it became part of the reserve fleet in Portsmouth.

Ted was eventually demobbed in 1949.

Information from

Ted Appleyard

Denis Ashton

Private, 14873910
Royal Army Service Corps, Army Catering Corps
Driver/Dispatch Rider, Cook

Denis Keith Ashton was born in 1926 the son of Mr

Denis Ashton.

Samuel and Mrs Edith Ashton of 69 Fleetgate, Barton-on-Humber. He was educated at the Church School in Queen Street and, on leaving, worked in the Press Shop at Hopper's Cycle Works. He attended St. Mary's and St. Peter's churches and was very interested in photography.

In November 1944 he was conscripted into the army and went to Shorncliffe in Kent for initial training. From there he was posted - first to the RASC depot at Alfreton in Derbyshire where he trained to be a driver/dispatch rider and then to Oulton Park in Cheshire for training on 15 cwt Bedford trucks. By this time, the war was coming to an end and VE Day found Denis at Ossett in Yorkshire attending a cook's course as his services as a driver were no longer required.

In late 1945 - still in the RASC - he moved to Norfolk and cooked at a large camp which received troops returning from the war in Europe and awaited demobilisation. From there - by now in the Army Catering Corps - he was moved to the Headingley Cricket Ground in Leeds where he cooked for ATS ladies billeted in the surrounding area.

In February 1948 he was demobbed from Aldershot.

Information from

Denis Ashton

Elsie Ashton and David Rennison on their wedding day - 14 October 1941.

Elsie Ashton (later Rennison)

ACW (Aircraftswoman)
Women's Auxiliary Air Force
General Duties

Elsie Stella Ashton was born at Hendon near London in 1920, the daughter of Mr Samuel and Mrs Edith Ashton. The family moved to this area when Elsie was a few months old and lived in Pasture Road, Barton-on-Humber.

She was educated at the Church School and she attended St. Mary's and St. Peter's churches. On leaving school she was employed in the Erection Department at Hopper's Cycle Works.

In 1939 she joined the ARP in Barton and, on hearing the air-raid siren, was obliged to don her uniform and report for duty at the nearest air-raid shelter (usually the one opposite Cob Hall in Priestgate). Here she was to give any help which might be required.

In 1940 she volunteered to join the Women's Auxiliary Air Force and was sent to Bridgenorth for initial training. She was subsequently posted to the RAF fighter base at Usworth, near Durham and there did general duties in the Cookhouse. She was there for almost two years and has very happy memories of her service.

On 14 October 1941 she married David Rennison (see *Barton Remembered 1939-1945; Part Two, The Home Front*, p 54) and in 1942 she was demobbed and returned to Barton.

Information from

Elsie Rennison

Charlie Atkinson

Private, 1760918
Royal Artillery
Petty Officer, CJX332882
Royal Navy

Charles Atkinson was born on 11 June 1915, the son of Mr William and Mrs Edith Atkinson. In his youth they lived in one of the houses at Blyth's Brickyard. He was educated at the County School in Castledyke where one of his duties was to ring the school bell. He had seven brothers and three sisters. One of his earliest memories is walking every morning from his home to Poor Farm to collect the family's milk. He left school when he was 14 and went to work at Blyth's. Quite soon he was ordered to join the crew of the yard's sloop - the *Iona* - where he became the mate. Sometime later he joined the crew of the sloop *Marfleet,* which was based at Market Weighton. After two years on the *Marfleet,* he went first as mate on the 140-ton *Alva S* owned by Jack Simpson of Barton, next on the *Proto* with captain Tom Hoodless, and then back onto the *Alva S.* By now it was 1940 and in January of that year, Charlie and the *Alva S* were frozen into the Trent at Flixborough.

Soon afterwards, Charlie's call-up papers arrived and he became Private Atkinson C. After a period of initial training at Buxton in Derbyshire, he became a member of No 553 Seachlight Battery in Belfast. However, after some 150 days as a soldier, he got a class B release and returned to the *Alva S* running cargoes up and down the Humber. In early 1942 the Royal Navy found itself short of men with Charlie's experience on smallish craft and offered £5 per week to any volunteers who would join for six months service. As this was more than Charlie was earning on the river, he jumped at the opportunity. For him that six months service did, in fact, last until the end of the war!

By then the invasion of Europe - codenamed Operation *Overlord* - was being planned and Charlie (along with fellow Barton boatmen George Ayres, Fred Winship, Walter and Arthur Seddon) was employed handling the small craft - mainly modified Thames lighters - which, with engines mounted, were to be used to carry essential supplies to the invasion forces. By now, Petty Officer Charlie Atkinson was in command of a former Cory's coal lighter of 300 tons capacity with a crew of two motormen ('stokers' in RN parlance) and two able seamen.

The initial training for beach landing was carried out at Tenby in South Wales before they moved back to the Isle of Wight. Here Charlie found himself in command of his lighter which, on D-Day + 2 (8 June 1944), landed 300 tons of ammunition on the Utah Beach on the Cherbourg peninsular **(15)**. This was the landing place for the American 1st Army and he recalls the beach being a shambles of wrecked vehicles. Charlie stayed with the Americans off-loading their large Liberty ships which had to anchor in deep water offshore.

When Cherbourg was eventually captured, the small lighters became redundant and Charlie's boat was eventually moored in Barfleur harbour and left. He returned to Poole in England where he helped to prepare LCGs (landing craft guns) for use in the campaigns in the Pacific. He took one to Lamlash on Arran Island but the war ended soon afterwards and his services were no longer required.

He was demobbed from Rosneath in Scotland though on his way home he had to call at York to pick up his 'civvies'.

Information from

Charles Atkinson

The Slabline - Journal of the Humber Keel and Sloop Preservation Society, 48, (1998) pp 2-9.

Jack Austin

**Leading Coder, P/JX 220285
Royal Navy
Coder**

Jack Austin, the brother of James Austin, (qv) was born in 1918, the son of Mr James Harry (who was killed in the First World War in which he was awarded the Military Medal and bar) and Mrs Edith Annie (later Naylor) Austin of Soutergate, Barton-on-Humber. He attended the Church School in Queen Street and was a member of the choir and server at St. Peter's and St. Mary's churches. He was also a member of the Barton Boys' Club. After leaving school, aged 14, he was employed in the Enamelling Department at Hopper's Cycle Works.

Jack Austin.

He received his call-up papers in September 1940 and, on the advice of his girlfriends father, he decided to join the Royal Navy. His initial nine weeks of training took place at *HMS Collingwood* at Fareham near Portsmouth. From there he was posted to a former hospital, *HMS Wellesley*, in Liverpool where he began his training as a coder. This involved working with a ship's telegraphist coding messages to be transmitted and decoding messages received. The work had previously been done by the telegraphist but it had been found that overwork slowed down the transmission and receipt of vital messages. If the code work was performed by a specialist, often vital minutes could be saved. Different codes were used when ships were in different oceans.

At Christmas 1940, he was given seven days leave during which he was married to Doreen Stamp at St. Mary's church. At the end of his leave, he reported to the naval barracks at Portsmouth awaiting a draft. When this came through he travelled, with two other coders (each of the three would cover a ship's watch), to Rosyth where they joined the Tribal Class destroyer *HMS Somali*. This ship, of some 1750 tons, had a crew of some 250 men and was armed with six 4.7-inch guns, two 4-inch guns, torpedo tubes, pom-poms and depth charges. This was to be Jack's home for the next two years.

Two days after Jack arrived on the ship, it sailed to Scapa Flow escorting the aircraft carrier *HMS Courageous* and a cruiser. Jack was violently seasick!

The *Somali* undertook a variety of tasks during the time Jack was aboard. On one occasion she escorted two troopships full of commandoes who were landed on the Lofoten Islands in northern Norway to destroy a number of factories there. Later she sailed to capture a German weather-reporting trawler in the Arctic Ocean. These reports aided the Germans to disrupt Allied shipping in the North Atlantic though the 'real' target was the trawler's *Enigma* enciphering/deciphering machine and its settings. The trawler was towed back to Scapa Flow. Later the *Somali*, along with another destroyer, was detailed to escort the battleship *HMS Rodney* across the Atlantic **(6)** on her way to a refit in the United States. During the voyage, a message was received informing the *Rodney* that the German battleship *Bismarck* was at large in the Atlantic and had sunk the British battle-cruiser *HMS Hood*. The *Rodney* was ordered to turn round and engage the enemy. When the *Rodney* sighted the *Bismarck,* she had already been attacked by Swordfish torpedo planes from *HMS Ark Royal* which had damaged her rudder to such an extent that she could do no more than sail around in circles. The *Rodney* and the *King George V* bombarded the damaged ship which was eventually sunk by torpedoes from *HMS Dorsetshire*. Meanwhile the *Somali* had run low on fuel and had had to retire to the Loch Foyle base in Northern Ireland to refuel.

On four occasions, *HMS Somali* escorted convoys of merchant ships taking supplies to the Russians. These convoys began in 1942 and the first 12 reached their destination without loss. However, Hitler became convinced that these were merely a prelude to an Allied invasion of Norway and he ordered the German navy to station a force of warships there to counter this supposed threat. The battleship *Tirpitz* and the battle-cruisers *Scharnhorst* and *Gneisenau* were duly dispatched to Norway and, though the Allied landing never took place, these great ships posed a continuing threat to the Russian bound convoys. These convoys of 20 to 30 merchant ships had a surrounding escort of some 10 to 12 destroyers. Sailing behind the convoys were a number of trawlers whose job was to pick up any survivors who had managed to escape from vessels, some of which were always sunk by the enemy. These pick-ups had to be accomplished very speedily for the chances of a sailor surviving long in the freezing water were not good. The convoys largely lacked air cover and because of the danger of giving their position away to nearby U-boats, no radio transmissions were allowed. Jack's job was merely to decode all the incoming messages which were received. Transmissions between the ships in the convoy was by Aldis lamp or semaphore flags. The convoys were frequently shadowed by large German Focke-Wulf Condor reconnaissance planes which continually transmitted in Morse code the letter A - dot-dash. U-boats and bombers based in Norway could pick up this signal and use it to find their way to the convoys. The destroyers would escort a convoy to the safety of Russian waters (these outward convoys were prefixed PQ + number) and then pick up a homeward bound convoy (prefixed QP) which they accompanied into British home waters.

Jack and *HMS Somali* were part of the escort which, in June/July 1942, accompanied the ill-fated convoy of some 35 merchant ships - the PQ17. This convoy left Reykjavik on 27 June 1942 bound for Archangel. Summer convoys, undertaken in months with very long days and few hours of darkness, were particularly dangerous but Churchill insisted that PQ17 should sail. On reaching the waters off northern Norway, Jack was on watch on 4 July when a part-coded message was received from the Admiralty. The message read: 'OWING TO THREAT FROM [ENEMY] SURFACE SHIPS CONVOY IS TO DISPERSE AND PROCEED TO RUSSIAN PORTS.'

Thirteen minutes after this message was received from the admiralty, another one, now headed 'SECRET MOST URGENT' read: 'CONVOY IS TO SCATTER.'

The merchant ships then attempted to make their own way to a Russian port but not before the Captain of *HMS Keppel*, senior officer of the close escort, signalled to his commodore: 'SORRY TO LEAVE YOU LIKE THIS. GOODBYE AND GOOD LUCK. IT LOOKS LIKE A BLOODY BUSINESS.'

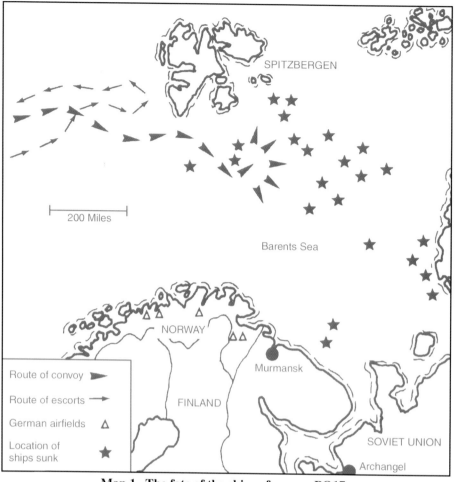

Map 1. The fate of the ships of convoy PQ17.

apparently much of the material sent never left the Archangel docks. A by far larger amount was sent through Persia - a route which the Germans could not threaten.)

In July, soon after this awful experience, the *Somali* was ordered to sail to the Mediterranean where it became one of the escorting warships involved in Operation *Pedestal* - the relief of the island of Malta **(10)**. Jack vividly describes this experience as his 'Voyage of Terror'. Constantly under attack, the *Somali* completed its task and in mid-August enough supplies of food and fuel were delivered to the beleaguered island to ensure that it did not have to surrender. However, as the *Somali* was making its way back to Gibraltar a lone enemy bomber attacked the ship. A stick of bombs exploded so close to the vessel that the engines were stopped and she sprang a number of leaks. Good work by the engine room staff got the ship under way again and she limped into Gibraltar where she was patched up prior to her return to Scapa Flow and duty on the Russian convoys.

The close escorts had previously received a SECRET MOST IMMEDIATE order to 'WITHDRAW TO WESTWARD AT HIGH SPEED' and so they left the convoy to its fate.

It transpired that the Admiralty, having (wrongly) decided that the *Tirpitz* had left the safety of the Norwegian fiords to attack PQ17, had sent out these fateful orders. In fact the *Tirpitz* had not moved but now the unguarded convoy was at the mercy of nearby U-boats and German bombers. Twenty-four of the thirty-five merchant ships were sunk and down to the bottom went some 100,000 tons of vitally needed supplies, including 430 tanks, 210 aircraft and 3,350 vehicles. Jack and the crew of the *Somali* were devastated when they heard the awful news. The fleeing escort force made no contact with the enemy. Churchill subsequently referred to these tragic events as 'one of the most melancholy naval episodes in the whole of the war.'

(Following the PQ17 debacle, only two other convoys sailed in 1942 and none were attempted during the summer months of 1943. In total, 40 convoys sailed to Russia and some 100 ships were lost. Though they may have made some modest contribution to the Russian war effort and showed that the British and Americans were prepared to help their struggling ally,

On 20 September 1942, Jack was on duty in a room below the bridge when he heard through the speaking-tube (which attached the telegraphists and coders to the bridge) a seaman's voice shouting, 'Torpedo approaching, port side!' Avoiding action proved impossible and the torpedo struck the *Somali* in her engine room. All of the engine room crew lost their lives and the ship began to list and sink. Half the ship's company were ordered to abandon ship and Jack's watch was transferred to the accompanying trawler the *Lord Middleton*. Another tribal class destroyer, HMS *Ashanti*, took the *Somali* in tow and managed to keep her moving towards home for about a day. However, the weather broke and in the ensuing storm the *Somali* broke her back and went down taking the crew remaining on board, some 100 men, to their deaths.

Jack landed back in Scotland and was put on a train for transfer back to Portsmouth. He vividly remembers the WVS ladies on York station supplying him with splendid corned beef sandwiches and tea, and he later stayed for a night - in a bed for once - at the Union Jack Club in London. On arrival back in Hampshire he was first re-kitted as he had lost all his gear when the *Somali* went down. He was drafted to Portsdown Hill and spent some nine months there learning how a shore base was run before he returned to Portsmouth.

By now it was mid-1943 and still the German U-boats were menacing Allied shipping as it crossed the mid-Atlantic out of range of spotter aeroplanes. In the middle of the Atlantic lie the Azores Islands which belong to Portugal, a nation then friendly to the Allies. The Americans and the British received permission to establish an airfield and shore base on the islands and this facility would ensure that the Germans did not have free range in the middle of the Atlantic. Jack was to be on the staff of this shore base and as part of a British army, navy and air force contingent he sailed to the Azores aboard the *Franconia*. On the island he joined the crew of *HMS Lusitania* and along with the American personnel stationed there helped plot the position of, and attack, any U-boats operating in the area. This work proved highly successful and helped to reduce shipping losses. Jack stayed on the Azores for the rest of the war.

In July 1945 he was flown back to England and in October 1945 he was demobilised.

Information from

Jack Austin

Taylor, A.J.P., *The Second World War; an illustrated history*, Penguin 1976, pp 140-141.

Broome, J., *Convoy is to Scatter*, London 1972.

Jim Austin

Sergeant
Norfolk Regiment

James Austin was born in 1916 the brother of Jack Austin (qv).

He took part in the D-Day landings **(15)** and later lost an arm in the fighting around Caen.

Information from

Jack Austin (brother)

Walter Barton

Private, 14258981
Royal Army Medical Corps
Nursing Orderly

Walter Barton was born in 1923, the son of Mr William and Mrs Mary Ann Barton of 1 Victoria Terrace, Barton-on-Humber. He was educated at the County School and on leaving was employed at Stephenson's Brickyard. During the early years of the war this, and all Barton's brick and tile works, were producing bricks and tiles badly needed in Britain's bombed towns and cities. He was a member of the Barton Boys' Club.

He was conscripted in August 1942 and reported to Maryhill Barracks in Glasgow for initial training.

---

2. The British Expeditionary Force (BEF)

At the start of the war, the government ordered that an expeditionary force of four regular army divisions (158,000 men and 25,000 vehicles) was to be made ready to cross to France. This force, to be commanded by General Lord Gort VC, would be reinforced by other divisions as they became available. Ten squadrons of Fairey Battle light bombers were also sent to France. On 11 October, it was reported to parliament that 158,000 British troops had arrived in France. The winter passed peacefully and the BEF slumbered in its Flanders trenches.

When the Germans launched their assault on the Western Europe on 10 May 1940, the BEF had a strength of 10 divisions. Its first move was to advance into neutral Belgium to meet what was thought to be the Germans' main thrust in the north. There were no prepared defences in the Low Countries and by the time a defensive line was agreed upon, Guderain's panzers were flooding out of the Ardennes to the south and threatening to encircle the British and French from the rear. By the 14th, the Germans were over the 'impassable' river Meuse at Sedan.

On 13 May 1940 Churchill, the newly-appointed British Prime Minister, delivered his 'blood, toil, tears and sweat' speech to the House of Commons. By 25 May the Allied position was desperate. A small British force was desperately defending Calais in the hope that the Germans would concentrate their main efforts on its capture and thus relieve the pressure on Dunkirk through which it was hoped to evacuate at least a part of the BEF. Churchill ordered the Royal Navy to prepare ships for the evacuation.

At the point when a complete debacle seemed certain, the German panzers were halted within sight of Dunkirk - and the rest is history!

See - Ted Bones, Arthur Hedley and Hector Lawtey

Following this he was posted to the RAMC depot at Beckett's Park in Leeds where he started about three months of medical training.

From there he was posted to a field ambulance at Stenigot near Louth in Lincolnshire. Here he underwent more training in medical techniques. After about six months, the field ambulance was disbanded and transformed into two casualty clearing stations (CCSs). Walter's station went to Morpeth in Northumberland and from there he was posted to a holding depot in Leeds prior to embarkation.

He travelled to Greenock where on his birthday, 11 September 1943, he boarded the troopship *Moultan* - a former passenger liner of about 20,000 tons. The ship joined a convoy at the mouth of the Clyde and, after a wide sweep into the Atlantic, docked at Gibraltar. From there they sailed through the Mediterranean, calling at Port Said, and on to Bombay. He reported to the RAMC Depot at Deolali from where he was sent back to the Military Hospital in Bombay where he worked on the venereal disease ward treating British and later some American servicemen.

In early 1944 he was transferred, as part of a field unit, across country by train and paddle steamer towards the front line in Assam and Burma. He finally arrived at Dimapur and from there moved on towards Imphal **(18)**. However, the road was blocked at Kohima where a Scottish regiment was surrounded by Japanese troops. Eventually Kohima was relieved and Walter was able to move on to Imphal where he joined the 33 Corps HQ. From Imphal he travelled up the Tamu road following the retreating Japanese army. Again, on his birthday, 11 September 1944, he crossed the border between Assam and Burma.

Any soldier wounded in the front line was treated by the battalion or regimental medical staff on hand. He would then move back to the nearest CCS (Walter's unit) where the casualty was made ready for the journey back to the field hospital some miles in the rear.

In late 1944, he came home on leave and on 28 February 1945, he was married to Kathleen Datlin at Reading. He eventually returned to Bombay from where he was again posted to his old unit which was now near Meiktila, south of Mandalay. From there he was sent by air to join the 5th Indian Division at Rangoon. The Division was training for a proposed amphibious landing at Singapore. However, before the assault could take place, the Japanese surrendered. The 5th Division did sail to Singapore and occupied the port.

He was eventually demobbed in early 1946.

Information from

Walter Barton

David Birtwhistle

Captain
Royal Artillery
Gunner

David Alexander Birtwhistle was born in 1918. He and his twin brother Denys (qv) were the sons of Dr Percy and Mrs Ella Birtwhistle of Priestgate, Barton-on-Humber. He was educated at Monkton Combe School, Bath and subsequently was articled to Stephenson, Smart and Co, accountants of Brigg whose senior partner was Colonel Hart of Redbourne, the commanding officer of the North Lincolnshire Territorials. He expected all his male staff to join the 'Terriers', and in July 1938 David duly joined the Barton force - an anti-aircraft searchlight unit - with the rank of second lieutenant.

He was called up in August 1938 in the 'Phoney War' period of that year when the Barton 'Terriers' were sent to defend Immingham Docks. They took their searchlight and were also given a German WWI field gun for which they had no ammunition! After a few months they were stood down and returned to civilian life.

The Territorials were again called up in early September 1939. They began as searchlight operators in North Lindsey coastal area defending Hull. In 1940 he went with the BEF to France **(2)**. However, shortly after landing they had to retreat and David was one of

David Birtwhistle.

the last men to be taken off the Dunkirk beaches **(4 - 5)**. On reaching England, he was dispatched to Tenby in Wales and, on reporting to his commanding officer, found that he was just in time to prevent the posting of a letter to his parents notifying them that their son was 'Missing believed killed.'

His next move was to Hornsea were his unit manned a naval gun in an emplacement to defend the East Yorkshire coast. His next posting, in 1942, was to the 2nd Indian Field Regiment, Royal Artillery in which he became a gun position officer.

In August 1943 he was sent to serve in Persia and Iraq. From May 1944 he was in a field and anti-tank artillery unit based at Muttra in Western India.

On 5 November 1945 he began his journey home by sea and was finally demobbed in April 1946.

Information from

John Birtwhistle (brother)

Anne Birtwhistle (widow)

Denys Birtwhistle

Lieutenant
Royal Navy
Dental Surgeon

Denys Birtwhistle.

Thomas Denys Birtwhistle was born in 1918, the son of Dr Percy and Mrs Ella Birtwhistle of Priestgate, Barton-on-Humber. He was educated at Monkton Combe School, Bath and Guy's Hospital Dental School in London.

In 1941, he joined the Royal Navy as a dental surgeon and served at *HMS Royal Arthur* (formerly Butlin's Holiday Camp at Skegness) from 1941 to 1944. Following this he served on *HMS Patroller* - a merchant ship which had been converted into an aircraft carrier sailing mostly in the Indian, Southern and Pacific Oceans. The ship returned to the UK bringing back prisoners-of-war and troops.

He was demobbed in 1946 and returned to dentistry in Reading.

Information from

John Birtwhistle (brother)

Valerie Birtwhistle (widow)

John Birtwhistle

Flight Lieutenant, 160629
Royal Air Force
Pilot

John Frederick Birtwhistle was born in 1916, the son of Dr Percy and Mrs Ella Birtwhistle of Priestgate, Barton-on-Humber. He was educated at Monkton Combe School, Bath and Edinburgh University Veterinary School. He attended both St. Mary's and St. Peter's churches. Whilst at university (1935-1938), he was a member of the Senior Officers' Training Corps attached to the various cavalry regiments stationed in Edinburgh.

In 1940, he qualified as a veterinary surgeon and applied to join the Royal Army Veterinary Corps. However, he was informed that 'owing to the paucity of vacancies' it was suggested that he did locum jobs until he was called up. During this time he served in the Edinburgh LDV and later, when in Barton, was a member of the town's Home Guard unit. Having not been called up 12 months later, he decided to apply for another service but found that veterinary surgeons were all in a reserved occupation. He later found that as all aircrew members were volunteers, he would be able to join the RAF to train as a pilot.

In late 1941 he was summoned to RAF Cardington, Bedfordshire where he was enrolled as a trainee pilot. Sometime later he travelled to Lord's Cricket Ground in London which was the Air Crew Receiving Centre. From there he went to the Grand Hotel, Torquay which housed No 13 Initial Training Wing. On finishing his

John Birtwhistle (centre) and the crew of Lancaster LE - K for King of No 630 Squadron in 1945.

course there, he went to Greenock where he boarded the *MV Letitia* and sailed to Halifax, Nova Scotia. From there he went onward by train to RCAF Pierce at the foot of the Rockies in Alberta, a base of the Commonwealth Air Training Scheme. Here he started his flying training on Stearmans. From there he moved to RCAF Medicine Hat which was a senior flying training school where, flying Harvards, he received his 'wings'.

His next move, in early 1943, was back to England where he reported to RAF Shawbury in Shropshire for advanced flying training in European conditions, so unlike those encountered in sunny North America. His previous experience with the army encouraged him to volunteer for an army co-operation squadron. As a result, he was posted to various army and navy anti-aircraft co-operation squadrons at Detling in Kent, Hutton Cranswick in Yorkshire, Cardiff, Shobden in Herefordshire, Eastchurch, the Isle of Sheppey and others. Here he flew in Oxfords, Hurricanes and Martinets. The work involved target towing, aerial reconnaissance and anti-aircraft training for both the army and the navy. He stayed with the army co-operation squadrons until after D-Day when all of them were disbanded.

Subsequently, he asked to be transferred to a Mosquito photo reconnaissance unit but owing to an administrative blunder, he ended up at RAF Morton-

in-the-Marsh. This was an all-Australian station where, as a 'Pommie', his services were not welcome! From there he was posted to Lossiemouth in northern Scotland which was a Wellington OTU (operational training unit) for bomber crews. There he picked up six 18-year old boys who formed the rest of his crew. After completing training, they flew to RAF Bottesford in Leicestershire where they were converted to flying Lancasters. From there, just before VE Day, they reported to No 630 Squadron at RAF East Kirkby, in Lincolnshire. There they trained for a week or two with the intention that the squadron should join 'Pye Force' in Burma. However, VJ Day arrived before they were posted and No 630 Squadron was disbanded.

Three crew members were posted away and John was posted to No 1 Ferry Unit at Pershore in Worcestershire where he flew new Lancasters to squadrons in Egypt. The four-man crew - pilot, navigator, flight engineer and wireless operator - no longer included gunners or bomb aimer. The route taken was via RAF St. Mawgan in Cornwall, Bordeaux, over the Pyrenees, Marseilles and Tunis, where they stayed for a night. The flight onward landed at various airfields in Egypt.

On 10 March 1946 he was demobbed at Uxbridge after flying for 1124 hours and 35 minutes.

Information from

John Birtwhistle

Geoff Blakeborough

Lance Corporal, 1562081
Royal Artillery
Gunner

Geoffrey Shuttleworth Blakeborough was born in 1907, the son of Mr Walter and Mrs Emma (née Shuttleworth) Blakeborough of Brighouse, Yorkshire. He was educated at Bootham School, York and the University of Sheffield where, in April 1931, he qualified as a solicitor. He subsequently moved to Barton and was employed in that capacity at the solicitors' practice headed by Gilbert Nowell in his premises at 33 Whitecross Street. He lived at 22 High Street in Barton. He later became a partner in the firm of Nowell and Blakeborough at the same address.

At Lincoln in May 1940 he enlisted in the army and joined No 207 Anti-Aircraft Training Regiment of the Royal Artillery with the rank of gunner. He was later posted first to No 336 Heavy Anti-Aircraft Battery (August 1940-July 1943) and then to No 104 Heavy Anti-Aircraft Regiment (July 1943-September 1944). He served in North Africa and Sicily between June 1943 and October 1945.

His army records show that his service with the Royal Artillery ended in September 1944 and that from that date until his demobilisation in January 1946, he was serving in the 4th (November 1944-March 1945) and 6th Battalions (September 1944-November 1944 and March 1945-January 1946) of the Sherwood Foresters. In September 1945 he was promoted to the rank of unpaid lance corporal. A medical inspection report issued at the Eugenio Barracks (?somewhere in Sicily or Italy) and dated 1 October 1945 describes him as being 'fit for journey to UK.' His testimonial reads, 'Whilst in this unit Lance [Corporal] Blakeborough has been employed as Company clerk and his conduct and work have been exemplary.'

Information from

Joan Blakeborough (widow)

Geoff Blakeborough.

Ted (Eddie) Bones

Private, 4804360
6th Battalion, Lincolnshire Regiment
Intelligence Section

George Edward Bones was born in 1919 at 30 Butts Road, Barton-on-Humber, the elder son of Mr Joseph and Mrs Sarah Anne Bones. He attended the County School in Castledyke and the Primitive Methodist Sunday School and Chapel in Queen Street. For most of the prewar years he lived in Maltkiln Lane.

He left school aged 14 and began work as an office boy in the Brigg Road offices of Hopper's Cycle Works. He was soon promoted to the Accounts Department.

In October 1939 he was 'called up' into the 6th Battalion of the Lincolnshire Regiment and, after initial training at Grantham, joined the office staff of the Battalion's 'C' rifle company then based at Scunthorpe. In April 1940 the Battalion moved to Southampton prior to sailing to France and eventually joining the British Expeditionary Force near Douai **(2)**. After a short stay there the order was received to retreat - 'For three days and nights we plodded wearily towards Dunkirk passing abandoned vehicles, bloated dead horses and refugees. We had little sleep during this period ...' Ted Bones reached the Dunkirk beaches on Saturday 1 June 1940 and eventually boarded a destroyer which brought him back to Dover early on the following Monday morning **(4-5)**.

For the next two and a half years, the Regiment was based at numerous camps up and down the British Isles. In late 1941, whilst based near Dymchurch, Ted passed a course which enabled him to join the Intelligence Section at Battalion HQ. After a period of

27

Ted Bones

intensive training in late 1942, the Battalion moved to Greenock, embarked on the *MV Sobieski* and, after sailing half way across the Atlantic in a decoy move, turned east and steamed into the Mediterranean Sea. On 17 January 1943, the Battalion landed in Algiers **(11)**. During its time in North Africa, the Battalion was engaged in a four-day battle to hold the vital road and rail junction at Sedjenane against an enemy force five times superior in numbers. Later information showed that the Germans were convinced that they had fought against 'specialised troops' rather than 'an ordinary county regiment from Lincolnshire'.

By May 1943, the conquest of North Africa was completed, the *Afrika Corps* surrendered and 250,000 prisoners were taken. After a brief look at Tunis, the Battalion was required to guard 55,000 Italian and 10,000 German prisoners in POW cages at Oued Zarga.

In due course the Battalion was returned to full strength and underwent another period of training (which included amphibious exercises) to equip it to take part in Operation *Avalanche* - the landings at Salerno **(12)**. The landing, early on 9 September 1943, was fiercely resisted but as Ted was placed in charge of the Battalion's most precious mail from home, he was not directly engaged in the battle which was fought to establish the bridgehead. Eventually Salerno was secured and the advance northwards began. During

a rest period, a visit to Pompeii was enjoyed.

Once north of Naples, the Battalion was engaged in the crossings of the rivers Volturno and Garigliano and, early in 1944, the minor battles at the River Peccia, the Sujo Valley and the capture of Mount Faito. By March 1944, the Battalion had suffered many casualties and withdrew from the line to take a well-earned rest. However, on 16 March it was put aboard the *MV Batori* and sailed to Egypt where a period of leave in Cairo was organised. Ted visited the Pyramids and the Sphinx.

The Battalion next moved into a camp in Palestine from where leave visits to Tel Aviv, Haifa, Jerusalem and Bethlehem were enjoyed. After a spell in Syria, the Battalion prepared to return to Italy.

The campaign in Italy was by then well advanced, and by August 1944 the Allies were preparing to breach the heavily defended German positions on the *Gothic Line* which ran across the peninsular from just south of La Spezia on the west coast to Rimini on the east. Ted was with the 8th Army on the east and was told that the ultimate objective was Vienna. Whilst advancing he crossed the Rubicon (which brought back school day memories of Julius Caesar) and went into the small state of San Marino.

In the Apennines to the north-west of San Marino, Ted witnessed the death of the Battalion's Intelligence Officer, Captain Brunt, VC, MC, who was hit by a shell when trying to recover a wounded comrade laying in no-man's-land. Shortly afterwards the Battalion, having been engaged in heavy fighting for some time, was pulled out of the front line for a Christmas break. During this period Ted travelled to Florence where he visited the opera for a performance of *The Barber of Seville*. After Christmas the Lincolns returned to the front and were engaged in heavy fighting for some three months. When it came its turn to retire for a rest, Ted's section was shelled as it made a dash for safety. A German shell grazed Ted's helmet and fell at his feet. Amazingly it failed to explode and Ted had another of his numerous escapes. This was the last action involving the Lincolns which proceeded to Taranto at the foot of Italy and there embarked for 'special duties' in Greece which was in the throes of civil war. After landing at Patros, the Intelligence Section was housed in a villa beside the Mediterranean. From there it moved to Pirgos but was, in fact, soon returned first to Patros and from there back to Italy.

Arriving once more (late April 1945) in northern Italy, the Lincolns were held in reserve for the final push. Though they could hear the sounds of battle they were never called to fight and heard that by early May the Germans had finally been driven out of Italy.

When VE day was announced, Ted was somewhere on the border between Italy, Austria and Yugoslavia.

3. The Menace of the Magnetic Mine

On 10 September 1939, only seven days after war had been declared, the first British ship to be sunk by a mine - the *SS Magdepur* - foundered off the east coast of England. In the following months, more ships suffered the same fate and it became known that the Germans were laying magnetic mines in coastal waters, initially from some of their submarines and later from aeroplanes. The mines which were either moored just below the surface or laid on the sea bottom were detonated when the magnetic field of a ship which passed over them triggered a detonator. In November and December 1939, some 200,000 tons of Allied shipping was lost to this awesome weapon.

On 14 November 1939, Winston Churchill, First Lord of the Admiralty, informed the War Cabinet of the losses being wrought by this most dangerous weapon which could not be destroyed by the usual techniques used by British minesweepers. The magnetic mine was not, as Hitler boasted, a new German 'secret weapon' since it had been used by the Royal Navy in the First World War and in 1939, the British Mine Experimental Department knew of the existence of the German magnetic mines and was developing one of its own.

Early British attempts to sweep these mines using magnetic bars attached to a wire pulled along between two vessels were not a great success. What was crucially needed was the recovery of an unexploded mine so that its mechanism could be examined. The breakthrough came on the morning of 23 November when an intact mine, dropped from an aeroplane, was defused and later recovered from the beach off Shoeburyness in Kent by Lieutenant Commander John Ouvry and Chief Petty Officer Baldwin. After two days of intense activity at the shore station *HMS Vernon*, the secrets of the mine were laid bare. It was found that it had a mechanism which was activated when the polarity of a vessel passing above caused a detonating needle to move from an east-west to a north-south orientation. In order to clear them from our waterways, the mine sweepers involved needed to create a magnetic field which would move the mine's needle to the north-south position and thus trigger the detonator attached to the 660lb explosive charge. Good results were soon being achieved.

Systems were also necessary to protect all other metal vessels from the mine's menace. This could be achieved by providing every ship with a 'degaussing girdle - a length of energised wire which was fastened round the ship's hull at the level of the upper deck. This effectively neutralised the ship's magnetism so that she did not move the needle of a magnetic mine. Thousands of miles of wire were soon being used to provide this protection - even on ships as big as the *Queen Elizabeth*. It is somewhat ironic to recall that the degaussing technique was named after a German scientist, Carl Frederick Gauss (1777-1855)!

The mines could also be detonated by the strong magnetic field emanating from an energised dural hoop attached to the underside of an aircraft flying over them.

See - Harold Burton and Ron Newton

Celebrations were muted as the soldiers thought they may be required to go to the Far East and fight the Japanese or stay in Europe and sort out 'the Russian problem'. Ted took a walk in the nearby hills and, whilst admiring the glowworms, wondered if they had put on a special show for this momentous day.

After VE Day, the Battalion was moved to occupy the German barracks in the small village of Wolfsberg in Austria. Here the task was to deal with Yugoslav refugees. Following this, Ted left the 6th Lincolnshires and moved back to Army HQ at Caserta in Italy to undertake clerical duties. Once there it was soon discovered that Ted was interested in accountancy so he was moved to the Army Pay Corps at Cento Celle on the outskirts of Rome where he worked checking copy invoices of supplies sent to various units and to the NAAFI. He remained there for eight months until he was transferred to Aldershot for release in February 1946.

At Aldershot he exchanged his army uniform for a demob-suit and his boots for shoes. On payment of 35 shillings (£1.75p), he was allowed to keep his army greatcoat.

Ted's memories of his war were many and varied. He remembers a show in which the 'Soldier's Sweetheart', singer Vera Lynn, gave to the troops in the desert. Of this he particularly remembers the efforts of a fatigue party which was required to dig her own private latrine! He remembers concerts he attended whilst in Rome, particularly those in which the great Italian tenor Gigli sang and that given by our own Gracie Fields. He remembers occasional cinema shows - one held during a sand storm - and his visits to Pompeii, Naples, Rome and Florence. He recalls the improvement in the quality of food provided to the forces in the Middle East compared with the bully beef and hard biscuits which were their rations in France in the early part of the war. He remembers 'compo' rations - wooden boxes which held sufficient food to feed a given number of men for one day. Most of it was in tins - bacon slices, stews, milk puddings, plum duff, fruit, jam, sardines and cheese but also included was tea, milk, sugar, cigarettes, chocolate and boiled sweets. Each man had his own mess tin in which to heat food warmed over the ignited methylated spirit blocks which were provided. The men always tried to shave and wash every day though this might be done using a bucket full of cold water which had to be shared by 30 men. Whenever they retired from the front line, showers were usually available. Each man washed his own clothes whenever possible but they could not be ironed and repairs were carried out using the 'housewife' with which each man was provided.

The 6th Lincolnshire's padre, Rev. Peter Laurence, was a well-liked man who held services whenever he could; looked to the dead and wounded; and, in less hectic times, organised activities such as quizzes.

Ted does not remember ever receiving 'comforts' from home but feels that in his circumstances, they were not necessary. He is of the opinion that his diet and clothing were probably better than that of the civilians back in England.

Although Ted went to live and work in Scunthorpe after the war, he did return to Barton in the 1950s when, for a time, he was the Accounting Officer for the Gas Board in its Dam Road premises.

Information from

Ted Bones

Alec Booth

Corporal, 3060997
Royal Air Force
Carpenter

Alec Wright Booth was born in 1925, the son of Mr Arthur and Mrs Lizzie Booth of 43 Waterside Road, Barton-on-Humber. He attended both the County and the Grammar School in Barton and on leaving was employed at Clapson's Shipyard in Waterside working on the building of wooden motor minesweepers (see *Barton Remembered 1939-1945; Part Two, The Home Front*, pp 143-146). In 1942 he went to Loughborough Training College where, after two years work, he qualified as a school teacher.

He was conscripted into the Royal Air Force in August 1944 and did his initial training at Hednesford. He worked as a joiner, first at RAF Thorney Island and later at RAF Gibraltar. He was demobbed in August 1946.

Information from

Philip Booth (brother)

Dennis Booth

Sergeant, 7359070
Royal Army Medical Corps
Clerk

Dennis Arthur Booth was born in 1919 - the brother of Alec (qv). He attended the County School and on leaving was employed as a clerk by the solicitors Brown, Hudson and Hudson. He worshipped at St. Chad's church. He was conscripted into the army as part of the 'First Militia' in September 1939 and did his initial training at Boundary Park in Leeds. He subsequently worked as a clerk in the RAMC.

In 1940 he was posted to India but on his way there, he was dropped off at Basrah and stayed there for some years. He later served in No 1 General Hospital at El Kantarah in Egypt **(7)** and whilst there in 1944 he had a meeting with his brother Philip. He came back to England for demobilisation in 1946.

Information from

Philip Booth (brother)

Dennis Booth.

Philip Booth

LAC, 1145417
Royal Air Force
Fitter IIE

Philip William Booth was born in 1925, the brother of Alec and Dennis (qv). He attended the County School and on leaving worked as a driver for Woolley's Bakery in Barrow. He was a member of the Barton Boys' Club and attended St. Chad's Church.

On 6 April 1941, he volunteered to join the Royal Air Force and reported for initial training at No 9 Receiving Centre at Blackpool. From there he was posted to RAF Kirkham near Preston for training as a flight mechanic and then took the Fitter IIE (E for 'engines') course. In December 1941, he was posted to RAF Kenley in Surrey and somewhat later sent abroad to No 107 MU (Maintenance Unit) at RAF Kasfareet in Egypt **(7)**. There he worked on the repair and servicing of the engines of Baltimore twin-engined bombers and Tomahawk and Kittihawk single-engined fighters. These planes were in action with the 8th Army in its push to Tunis and later in the campaign in Italy. There were about 500 personnel at this unit - airframe fitters, engine fitters, repair and recovery sections, motor maintenance units, cooks and clerks. A number of Egyptians were also employed at the base. Whilst in

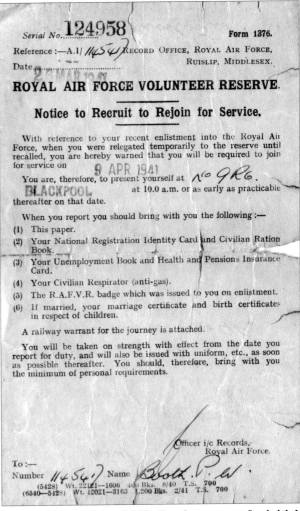

Form 1376 requiring Philip Booth to report for initial training at No 9 Receiving Centre at Blackpool.

Egypt, Philip was able to use his leaves to visit Port Suez, Ismailia, Port Said, Cairo, Alexandria, the Pyramids and the Sphinx.

Between June and September 1945, he was detached to RAF Nicosia which was at that time being closed down. From there he returned to Kasfareet. In January 1946, he travelled back to England. He was finally demobbed from Uxbridge in mid-1946.

Information from

Philip Booth

Philip Booth.

Chris Braithwaite

Corporal, 14252292
Royal Army Medical Corps
Operating Theatre Attendant

Christopher William Braithwaite was born in 1923, the son of Mr Harold and Mrs Beatrice Braithwaite of 15 Marsh Lane, Barton-on-Humber. He was educated at the Church of England school and on leaving was employed as an office boy at Hopper's Cycle Works, in the market garden run by Ken Ducker in Pasture Road and in 1939 took a job as engine cleaner with the LNER on the Humber Ferry. He was a member of the St. John's Ambulance Brigade in Barton.

On 2 August 1942 he was conscripted into the army and reported to the General Service Corps Depot at Beckett's Park in Leeds for his initial training. Having found that he held a Home Nursing Certificate from the St. John's Ambulance Brigade, he was transferred into the RAMC and underwent a further six weeks training at York Military Hospital. He was soon put on night duty as a nursing orderly and spent the next nine weeks working in that capacity. At the end of that period, he applied for a weekend's leave but was soon informed that he could have not a weekend but 10 days leave. The snag was that it was 10 days embarkation leave!

That completed, he travelled back to York and from there was moved to the docks at Glasgow where he boarded a Norwegian troopship which took him to Algiers in North Africa **(11)**. From there he moved to a 50-bedded camp reception station (CRS) which was part of 100 General Hospital. The CRS dealt with casualties from the front who were delivered in field ambulances. After treatment at the CRS, they might then be transferred some 20 miles to the 92 General Hospital at Bougie some 110 miles east of Algiers. Whilst Chris was at this CRS, it was increased in size from 50 to 500 beds, mostly under canvas.

Soon the North African campaign was over and the troops were now training for the invasions of Sicily and Italy. Many of the patients to be treated had been struck down with malaria and much of the work at the CRS involved the treatment of men suffering the worst stages of an attack. Chris particularly remembers one soldier who had been badly burnt by a phosphorous grenade being used in a training exercise. The man was speedily operated upon but, notwithstanding Chris' constant care, he unfortunately died of his injuries.

After some time, Chris was transferred to a garrison company at Djidjelli (a little way to the east of Bougie) where he served in the medical inspection room. This was based in a commandeered hotel. From there men went out into the countryside spraying anti-mosquito chemicals into nearby streams, drains and ponds in an attempt to cut down the numbers being struck down with malaria. Even so, everyone by now slept under a mosquito net for safety. Whilst he was at Djidjelli, he met fellow Bartonian Ken Cox who was serving in the RAF and had reported sick.

In March, 1944 Chris celebrated his 21st birthday at Djidjelli. For some time he had saved his weekly ration of beer and, along with more alcohol and a cake supplied by the local NAAFI girls and some officers he knew, they had as good a night as could be

Chris and Sally Braithwaite in Rome in 1945.

expected under the circumstances. The very next morning, Chris moved out of Djidjelli bound for the Italian mainland.

He landed at Naples as the battle for Monte Cassino was at its height **(12)**. The 100 General Hospital erected four large marquees, each capable of accommodating about 100 beds. A smaller, centrally-placed tent housed the doctors and nursing sisters. The noise from the nearby battle could clearly be heard at the field hospital.

Following the fall of Monte Cassino in May, Chris' unit, just behind the front line, made its way slowly up Italy through Rome, Perugia, Arezzo and Florence. Whilst he was in Florence, Chris was promoted to the rank of corporal and was mentioned in dispatches.

He was stationed in Perugia when he met the lady who was to become his wife. Sally was a nurse serving with the ATSP (Auxiliary Territorial Service Palestine) - an ATS unit raised by the Jewish settlers in what was then Palestine to help the Allied war effort. Their decision somewhat later to get married caused some initial problems for the military authorities, which, being the couple's guardians, decided that the ceremony could not go ahead without the permission of both sets of parents. After this was eventually obtained it was further decided that each of them should be interviewed by their respective padres - Chris by a Church of England priest and Sally by a Jewish rabbi. The nearest rabbi was found to be in Milan and so they both travelled there. When they arrived the rabbi was away in the country so they spent a night waiting for his return. During this wait they met Chris's brother, Harold, and had a pleasant night out with him. At the meeting on the following day, the rabbi was not very encouraging - he felt they might last a year together. (In fact, they celebrated their Golden Wedding in 1995!) The couple were married in Bologna on 12 December 1945. The reception took place in the hospital; the honeymoon, first in a nearby bed and breakfast hotel, and later in Rome.

Whilst in Rome, Chris was contacted by the army authorities who informed him that if he wished to be home for Christmas, he should report back to his unit as quickly as possible. Unfortunately, when he reached Milan on his return journey, he found that it was impossible to proceed any further and he spent Christmas 1945 there. His leave over, he returned to Italy and whilst finishing his service there he was put in charge of the operating theatre at the hospital - a job he found most satisfying.

His overseas service completed, he was sent back to England and had a leave in Barton where he was re-united with Sally. After his period of leave, he was posted to the Military Hospital in Chester where he served out the rest of his service before he was demobbed in early 1947.

Information from

Chris Braithwaite

Harold Braithwaite (left) with his brother Chris in Italy in 1945.

Subsequently, like the rest of the 'Terriers', he was transferred into the Royal Engineers and then into the Royal Artillery. (For the story of the Barton 'Terriers' between 1939 and 1944 see the biography of John Clipson [qv]).

When the Barton unit was finally broken up in mid-1944, Harold (like John Clipson) was transferred into the Royal Army Service Corps. There he joined No 733 Company, a pack transport unit which specialised in moving supplies through rough terrain using horses. He was moved back to Scotland and was stationed at Ballater where he undertook mountain training.

After about six months there, he was drafted to Italy and his unit landed at Naples **(12)**. Here he joined No 266 Company 'Italian Pack Transport' which used mules to move supplies and Harold and his companions were put in charge of Italians who looked after the mules. The unit was used to move supplies up to units engaged fighting the enemy in areas inaccessible to motor vehicles. When they neared the font line positions, there was always a guide waiting to escort them on the last and most dangerous part of the journey. Harold was up in the lines when the war ended.

Again his unit was broken up and its members transferred to different stations. This time Harold was moved to a mechanical unit - No 34 Company RASC (General Transport) based near Athens in Greece where he drove a lorry transporting supplies to other units in the area.

Harold Braithwaite

Private/Sapper/Gunner, 2061077
Lincolnshire Regiment, Royal Engineers, Royal Artillery and Royal Army Service Corps
Anti-aircraft Unit and Pack Transport

Harold Skelding Braithwaite was born in 1921, the son of Mr Harold and Mrs Beatrice Braithwaite of 15 Marsh Lane, Barton-on-Humber. He was educated first at the Church School and later at the school in Elsham. Before the war he variously worked on farms, in Blyth's Brick and Tile Yard, at Earl's Cement Works and finally at Ferriby Chalk Quarry. He attended both St. Peter's and St. Mary's churches and in 1938 he became a member of the Barton Territorial Army unit based at the drill hall in Butts Road.

Along with the rest of the Barton 'Terriers', Harold was called up for service just before war was declared. The unit was moved to the New Waltham area and he was in one of the bell tents in which they slept when he heard Neville Chamberlain's momentous broadcast informing the nation that it was to be war with Germany.

It was from there that he was sent back to Aldershot for demobilisation and he arrived back in Barton on 28 April 1946.

Information from

Harold Braithwaite

Jack Broddley

Bombardier, 819280
133 Field Regiment, Royal Artillery
HQ Regimental Transport

Jack Broddley was born in 1914, the son of Mr George and Mrs Emily Broddley of 99 Ings Lane, Barton-on-Humber. He attended the County School and on leaving was employed by Harry King, builder, of Holydyke.

In 1932 he reported at Woolwich and enlisted for six years in the Royal Artillery. From there he was moved to Longmoor in Hampshire where he underwent training on 18lb guns before being transferred to Spike Island near Queenstown (now Cobh), near Cork in Southern Ireland where the British had a coastal defence battery of 6-inch fixed guns. There were a number of such British bases in Ireland at this time though these were later handed over to the Eire government.

In 1935 Mussolini invaded Abyssinia and so, fearing for its interests in the Mediterranean and North Africa, Britain strengthened her defences in the region. Jack was posted to Tigne Fort at Valetta in Malta as apart of the garrison manning the fixed 6-inch guns there.

In 1936 he was sent back to Woolwich from where he

Jack Broddley, Kempen in Germany in 1945.

was sent to Formby, near Liverpool where the battery of guns was part of the North-West Fixed Defences and he stayed there until 1938 by which time he had completed his six years of service and he was demobilised.

He came back to Barton and found work at the Admiralty tanks at Killingholme. His civilian life did not last long for on 19 June 1939, he was called back for two months service preparing a tented camp at Kinmel Park in North Wales which was to be used by those men to be called up in 'The First Militia'. On 19 August he was released - but not for long!

On 6 September, he was again called back and reported to Sandown Racecourse from where he was posted to 133 Field Regiment at Tenby in South Wales where they still manned old-fashioned 18lb guns. Jack joined the Headquarters' staff and was to serve there for the rest of the war. His job was involved with the Regiment's transport of guns, ammunition, food and other supplies.

In spring 1940, the Regiment moved to Portadown in Northern Ireland where it became part of 160 Brigade and was so to remain for the rest of the war. Here it was armed with the new 25lb field guns. (An artillery field regiment, commanded by a colonel, consisted of three batteries each with eight guns. Each battery had a major or captain in charge. A gun was crewed by four men - a sergeant in charge, a layer who was in control of both elevation and traverse, and two men who handed up ammunition and loaded the gun. A 25lb gun would fire a shell some two miles. Orders to fire and instructions regarding targets would come from brigade HQ and out in front of the guns would be observation posts, usually manned by officers, which would report back to the guns on the accuracy of their fire.)

In late October 1941, the Regiment was moved to Newcastle and underwent training which included firing on the ranges at Sennibridge. There followed moves to Monmouth and Builth Wells in Wales and Sittingbourne and Herne Bay in Kent where it undertook training in preparation for its role in the invasion of Europe. In June 1944 the Regiment moved to London and boarded the ships which were to take it across the Channel. It spent seven days at the mouth of the Thames waiting for good weather on the Normandy beaches, all the time being shelled by German long-range guns. Eventually, it sailed and landed on the Arromanches Beach on D + 21 **(15)**.

Jack's first six days in France were spent waiting in a cornfield before his unit was sent to relieve a division near Caen. From there he moved to the Falaise area where a large body of German troops was surrounded and then surrendered. Prior to the surrender, the Regiment had shelled Falaise for three weeks and after the surrender Jack was amazed: 'I have never seen so many bodies and dead animals in my life. The

4. The Miracle at Dunkirk

On 1 September 1939, Hitler's army and air forces invaded Poland and three days later the British Prime Minister, Neville Chamberlain, in a broadcast to the nation and the world, announced that as a result Britain was at war with Germany.

The Poles were quickly defeated and their country was divided between Germany and her ally Russia.

Hitler, fearing a Franco-British thrust into his country's industrial heartland in the Ruhr, ordered his generals to prepare an early offensive in the west, a course of action at that time unplanned and which would involve the German army facing numerically superior French, British and Belgian forces.

The plan *Yellow* originally proposed by Hitler's General Staff involved a campaign very similar to that mounted in 1914. The German army would take to field in three Groups -

- in the north, the strongest Group 'B', commanded by Field Marshal Bock, would drive through the Low Countries. Bock would have under his command the bulk of Germany's panzer divisions.

- in the centre, facing the Ardennes would be Field Marshal Rundstedt's Group 'A' which would act in a secondary role and support Bock's left flank.

- in the south, Group 'C' under Field Marshal Leeb would hold down the French armies on the Maginot Line.

For two main reasons - bad weather and an aeroplane accident which gave the British and French sight of the German battle plan - the order to proceed was postponed time and again during late 1939 and early 1940. By that time it had become clear to the Germans that the reinforced British Expeditionary Force (BEF) and the cream of the French army was facing Boch's front in the north and the all-out victory envisaged there would be difficult if not impossible.

An alternative plan, *Sicklestroke*, worked out by Field Marshal von Manstein, was subsequently adopted. This moved the main German thrust to the Group 'A' area. A mass of tanks would move through the Ardennes (considered 'untankable' by the British and French), cross the Meuse, and then advance at speed across the open north French plain to the sea, thus encircling the Allied forces in the north and cutting their lines of communication and supply.

On 10 May 1940, 136 army divisions began Germany's assault to the west. An initial attack in the north involving airborne and land troops aided by the *Luftwaffe* seemed to confirm to the Allies that the predicted repeat of the 1914 campaign was unfolding. However, by 12 May Rundstedt's advance through the Ardennes was completed and his tanks had crossed the French frontier. On 20 May the Germans reached the Channel coast encircling the BEF and the French First Army Group and by the 23rd they were overlooking Dunkirk, the last port through which the BEF could withdraw.

Amazingly, at this juncture Hitler ordered his panzer divisions to halt their *Blitzkrieg*. For three days they were forced to watch as the British improved the defences of the port and began the 'miraculous' evacuation for which Dunkirk will for ever be remembered. The Board of the Admiralty hoped 30,000 troops would get away but by 4 June, when that port finally fell to the Germans, some 338,000 soldiers (including 114,000 Frenchmen) had been rescued and shipped back to England. Losses were however substantial as all the equipment which had been mobilised for the Battle of France, including some 700 tanks, had to be left behind and fell into German hands. Numerous reasons have been given for Hitler's hesitation before Dunkirk. Suffice to say that his hesitation was of enormous benefit to Britain at a most dire moment in her history.

See - David Birtwhistle, Ted Bones, Winston Garfoot, Hector Lawtey

stench was terrible. Bulldozers came to clear a way down the road and push the bodies into the ditches.'

Following this action his unit moved over the Seine and went through Antwerp and Nijmegen in Holland, and Bruges in Belgium before spending the early winter of 1944 at Liege. During this period the Regiment took part in the action of the 53rd Welsh Division to stem the German counter-offensive through the Ardennes. Eventually the enemy was surrounded and surrendered on Boxing Day 1944.

In 1945 he moved through the Reichwald Forest to the banks of the Rhine. Winston Churchill, the British Prime Minister visited the Regiment and Jack saw him fire what was supposed to be the first shell across the Rhine. Jack says that Churchill was deceived - they had already fired thousands of shells over the river!

During the following two days, Royal Engineers completed a pontoon bridge and Jack's regiment crossed into Germany the next day.

After crossing the river his unit moved to Hamburg just before the end of hostilities in May 1945.

Jack was later moved to Dusseldorf where he undertook police duties before he travelled back to Aldershot for demobilisation in November 1945.

Information from

Jack Broddley

Carlisle. In January 1943 he passed the army driving test. He subsequently served as a driver in Africa, Italy, Egypt and Palestine. He took part in the landings at Salerno **(12)**. He finally saw service as part of the army of occupation in Austria.

In early 1946 he attended a basic cooks' course and qualified as a class II cook. He was transferred into the Army Catering Corps on 28 February 1946.

He was demobilised in July 1946.

Information from

Enid Bromfield (widow)

Alan Bromfield

Private, 14339237
Royal Engineers/Army Catering Corps
Driver/Cook

Alan Bromfield was born in 1914, the son of Mr John William and Mrs Sarah Bromfield of Westfield Road, Barton-on-Humber. He attended the County School, St. Chad's Church and was a member of the Oddfellows' Friendly Society. He was a founder member of the 1st Barton Scout Troop.

He was trained as a bricklayer by Pickard's Builders of Barton but during the early years of the war he was employed by Phillips of Brigg as a builder in a reserved occupation.

He was called up in November 1942 and enlisted at

Jack Bromfield

Private, 4806890
2nd Battalion, Lincolnshire Regiment
Rifleman/Signalman

Jack Bromfield was born in 1915, the son of Mr Robert and Mrs Sarah Bromfield of 14 East Acridge, Barton-on-Humber. He was educated at the County School and on leaving worked at Barraclough's Tileyard.

He was conscripted into the army on 24 June 1940 and on 17 August that year married Doris Newmarch at St. Mary's church. At the height of the blitz in December 1940, he was released to the reserve 'for civilian employment as a tiler'. There was a desperate shortage of roof tiles in London and other towns and cities which were being blitzed by the German

A group of North Lincolnshire men photographed during their initial training at Burton Road Barracks in Lincoln in 1940. Left to right: George Blakey (Grimsby), Ernest Cook (Barton), Jack Bromfield (Barton), Harry Haddock (Barrow Haven), Walter Smith (Barrow) and 'Tut' Herring (Ulceby).

Alan Bromfield.

bombers.

He rejoined the colours in February 1941 and, in September of that year, was posted to 2nd Battalion of the Lincolnshire Regiment where he served as a rifleman/signalman having to learn Morse code and semaphore. (For the wartime activities of 2nd Battalion see under Ren Jickells, [qv].)

Jack landed on Sword Beach on D-Day **(15)** and fought throughout the early part of the campaign to liberate north-western Europe. Whilst on service in France he was injured when a cooking stove exploded and he spent a considerable time in hospital at Derby and Chesterfield. Once again, towards the end of the war, his skill as a tilemaker was recognised and he was demobbed 'for civilian employment' to help produce the vast quantities of roofing tiles needed to repair wartime damage and build new houses for the returning soldiers.

Information from

Doris Bromfield (widow)

Geoff Bromfield (son)

Leonard Brown

Acting Lance Corporal, 2062060
Royal Army Service Corps
Waterman/Coxswain, small craft

Leonard Brown.

Leonard Victor Brown was the son of Mr Leonard and Mrs Caroline Brown of Garden Village, Tofts Road, Barton-on-Humber. He was educated at the County School and subsequently worked at Raby's Farm in Tofts Road.

In 1938 he joined the Territorial Army in Barton and was part of the searchlight unit stationed at the drill hall in Butts Road. On 24 August 1939 he was called away from his work on the farm on Horkstow Road and told to report to the drill hall with enough food to last for 24 hours. From there he was transferred to Grimsby and the searchlight was set up at New Waltham. (See biography of John Clipson, [qv].)

Late in the war he was posted to Burma before finally being demobbed in 1946.

Information from

Dorothy Sobey (sister)

Keith Burman

Bevin Boy

Keith Burman was born in 1926, the son of Mr Ernest and Mrs Lillian Burman of 5 Victoria Terrace, Barton-on-Humber. He attended the County School and on leaving was employed at the quarry on Ferriby Cliff.

In October 1944 he was called to a medical at Lincoln. Shortly after arriving home he received a letter requiring him to report to a mining training centre at Cresswell in Derbyshire. Here he spent about six weeks preparing for work in a colliery as a Bevin Boy **(14)**. Periods underground, classroom training and spells of physical education (including running through the streets of Cresswell in shorts) prepared Keith for his future work. On the last day, all the trainees were allocated a place of work and Keith was sent to Alfreton in Derbyshire.

Here he was accommodated in a specially built miners' hostel which held some 250 Bevin Boys recruited from all over the country. The 'Boys' were employed at mines over a wide area and Keith was sent to Pinxton Colliery where he worked until his release in February 1948. A bus was provided to get the boys to work. His work, along with three other Bevin Boys, was largely involved with ponies which were used to move the coal from the coal face. This old colliery still had no conveyor belts. The miners at the coal face filled tubs and Keith's job was to attach his pony - Ben - to some four or five tubs and lead them along the roadway rails. When he reached the main gallery the tubs were attached to a wire which pulled them to the bottom of the shaft. There the tubs were put into a cage for transport to the mine surface.

5. The Miracle of the BEF's Return

(From a report by E.A. Montague in the Manchester Guardian, 1 June 1940)

In the grey chill of dawn today in a South-eastern port war correspondents watch with incredulous joy the happening of a miracle. By every canon of military science the B.E.F. has been doomed for the last four or five days. Completely out-numbered, out-gunned, out-planned, all but surrounded, it had seemed certain to be cut off from its last channel of escape. Yet for several hours this morning we saw ship after ship come into harbour and discharge thousands of British soldiers safe and sound on British soil.

We went down to our reception port last night by a train which took more than twice the usual time to cover the distance. The reason was easy to see. Again and again we stopped outside a station while the dim shape of a troop train shot past us northward bound.

When at last we reached the port in the small hours, the chief hotel was packed and every armchair in the lounge held its sleeping soldier or sailor, huddled beneath overcoat or groundsheet. Most of us lay down for a couple of sleepless hours on the floor, and were proud to do it.

As the rising sun was turning the grey clouds to burnished copper the first destroyer of the day slid swiftly into harbour, its silhouette bristling with the heads of the men who stood packed shoulder to shoulder on its decks. As it slowed down and drifted towards the dock side the soldiers on board shouted cheerful ribaldries to us who stood watching them with a mixture of pride and pity. They at any rate did not regard themselves as the central figures of a tragic drama. The gangways were in position in no time - on these ships all ceremony had been waived for the time being - and the unconscious heroes began to clamber upwards towards the soil of England.

One watched with pride that became almost pain as one cheerful, patient figure succeeded another. They had passed through nights and days of hunger, weariness, and fear, but nearly every man still had his rifle and a clip or two of ammunition: nearly all had brought away their full kit with them - and what an agony its weight must have been at times; most of them had shaved, and quite a number were carrying the extra burden of a Lewis gun or a Bren gun. Their eyes were red with weariness above dark bags of tired skin, but they were still soldiers and still in good heart.

The wonder of their self-discipline became all the greater when one heard their stories. They were of all units and ranks. Some were in the position of the gunners whose battery had been shelled out of existence near Oudenarde, because our overworked fighter 'planes had had no time to deal with the German reconnaissance 'planes. Their battery commander had told them to do the best they could for themselves now that their usefulness had gone, and they had walked thirty miles to Dunkirk, there to take their chance on the Dunkirk beach, which will become as famous in history as the beaches of Gallipoli.

All the stories of the men skirt inarticulately round the beach at Dunkirk. It was, and is, the place to which the isolated but unbroken men came to wait their turn for the ships which came through shell fire and bombing to rescue them. It is a stretch of level sand backed by dunes. The sea in front of it is shallow for some way out, so that ships cannot come close in, and successive sand-banks parallel to the shore catch at the keels of the rowing-boats which come in at low tide.

Many of the men have spent two or three or four days on this beach, hiding in hollows scratched in the sand or in command dug-outs in the dunes from German 'planes which have scourged them with bomb and machine-gun. Their nights have been sleepless, and they have lived only on biscuits and water. Yet even their discipline holds. Units have been told off to look after 'beach organisation' and to detail men for embarkation whenever one of the gallant destroyers moors beside a jetty.

At other times the various craft, which are risking their lives to rescue the soldiers, cannot come near the shore. When that happens the men must row themselves out in the small boats or swim to the waiting ships. I met a Staff officer to-day who had spent the last twelve hours before his embarkation in the sea, continuously in water up to his waist, helping to push off the boats which had grounded on the sand-banks. For a large part of the time he was under fire.

Even when the men had embarked their danger was not over. Every now and then among the men who climbed the gangplank into England one sees stretcher-bearers carrying a still form, its face bloodless and remote in some dream of pain, its bandages white and brilliantly stained. It is a man who has been hit by one of the shells from the German shore batteries, or by a bomb from the 'planes which on occasion have pursued the ships to within a few miles of the British coast. Yet they survive in their tens of thousands and are able to joke and sing as they march ashore.

Their condition is astonishingly good. Perhaps one man in a thousand is shaking with nerves and obviously fit for nothing but hospital. The rest are clearly tired, hungry, and in some cases footsore. They walk stiffly, and some of them obviously find it painful to walk at all.

But there is nothing wrong with them which a few days' rest and good feeding will not put right, and their fighting spirit is quite unweakened. Men who were really exhausted would not be able to talk to reporters; these men can and apparently enjoy doing it, and without bombast they make it clear that they are still as good soldiers as they ever were. They are most comforting to see and hear. Their only bitterness is about the lack of R.A.F. 'Planes to defend them from bombers and that, alas! Is no news to us'.

The long string of steel-helmeted men passes steadily but swiftly up the gang-plank and away into the station, where they will be put into trains, fed, and dispatched to depots, where they can be re-organised and rested. A few stretcher cases are hoisted out of the ship in slings, the litter of forgotten kit is cleared away into sorting sheds, and in no time the ship is ready to return to Dunkirk.

But long before it is ready another has drawn up alongside, and as often as not the men on the second ship are being unloaded across the decks of the first.

British ships and French and Dutch, warships, drifters, trawlers, yachts, barges, they bring back their loads across hostile Channel and then go back undaunted into the inferno, where Navy and Air force and Army are fighting furiously to keep open the last loophole of escape for our men. All the selfless courage of two nations is being thrown into the resistance at Dunkirk, and it looks as if it will not be spent in vain.   June 1, 1940

He started work at 0730 and finished at 1500, five days each week. As there were no pit baths at Pinxton at that time, the Bevin Boys had to travel back to Alfreton before they could wash. For the return journey, no transport was provided and the 'Boys' had to return - black as soot - on the normal service bus. They were paid the same rate as the miners. Accommodation at the hostel cost 30 shillings per week. They were provided with breakfast, packed lunch and an evening meal.

On Saturdays and Sundays, the 'Boys' could enjoy themselves and the hostel had its own football

Keith Burman (front row, 2nd from left) with fellow Bevin Boys.

team - The 'Alfreton Miners' Hostel Football Team' - in which Keith played right-half. He also played cricket against nearby miners' welfare teams. In the hostel there was a snooker table and dances were organised at regular intervals.

Keith got back to Barton regularly - he could come home every weekend if he wished. For a number of visits he was given a free rail pass - further visits had to be paid for out of his wages. His journey home

involved bus rides from Alfreton to Mansfield and Mansfield to Worksop where he caught a train to Brigg. A bus took him from Brigg Station to Barton.

Keith met his wife whilst he was at Alfreton and they were married at Chesterfield soon after his release.

Information from

Keith Burman

Harold Burton

Stoker First Class, KX 154786
Royal Navy
Diesel Stoker

Harold Burton was born in 1921, the son of Mr Ernest and Mrs Ruth Burton of Winterton. In 1935 he moved to Barton to live with his grandparents Mr and Mrs Todds of Westfield Road (respectively caretaker and cook at Barton Grammar School). He was variously employed as errand boy at Dewey's shop in George Street, engine boy at Leggot's quarry and finally, before being called up, was employed on the building of the airfield at Elsham. He played football for the Boys' Club and tennis in Baysgarth Park.

He was conscripted into the Royal Navy in May 1942 and enlisted at *HMS Duke* at Malvern where he did his initial training. From there he was posted to *HMS Europa* at Lowestoft for further training which included work on diesel engines. He next moved to *HMS St. Tudno* near Sheerness from where he joined the ex-trawler-turned-minesweeper *HMS Delphinus* as a diesel stoker.

A specially built, steel compartment on this boat held two five-cylinder diesel engines which generated electricity. Harold's job was to look after these engines. The electricity which they produced was passed down two wires which ran from the back to the front of the boat. The current, passing through the water, would explode any magnetic mines over which the boat sailed. The ship itself was degaussed **(3)** at Sheerness prior to sailing and was armed with two machine guns, one on either side of the ship's bridge. A crew of about 20 manned the vessel.

His boat swept the area between Sheerness and Dover at night. Other minesweepers swept during daylight hours. When they were in the Dover area, they could see the flashes from the big guns which were firing

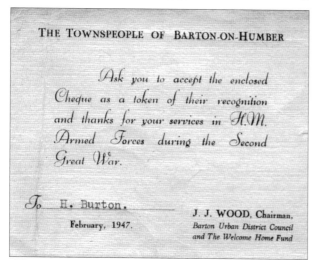

The record of Barton's 'Thank You Cheque' given to all returning servicemen and women.

Harold Burton.

across the Channel and could hear the 'swush' of the shells flying overhead.

In December 1942, he was sent back to Lowestoft where he was put in the main guard at *HMS St. Luke*, a former hospital which had become the main training establishment for Royal Navy stokers. In July 1943 he was posted to *HMS Alafoss* at Grimsby. Again, this was another ex-trawler converted into a minesweeper and formed one of a group of four which swept together. Three boats sailed abreast some 200 yards apart with their wires trailing behind. The fourth boat sailed astern ready to take up position in the front row if required. This small flotilla swept the shipping channels between the Humber and Lowestoft and the Humber and Whitby. Each voyage took seven days after which the minesweepers spent three days in Grimsby before sailing again. At the start of a voyage, each minesweeper picked up a barrage balloon from one of the old Humber ferries which were based at the Bull Fort boom at the mouth of the river. The balloons, flying over the flotilla, were intended to deter German dive-bombers.

In 1944, prior to the invasion of Europe, the flotilla was moved to Portsmouth from where it swept the sea lanes which were to be used on D-Day **(15)**. It sailed from Portsmouth and only turned round when it was about a mile off the French coast.

In November 1944, Harold was sent back to Lowestoft where he helped in the kitchen of a grand hotel which was being used as quarters for officers based at *HMS St. Luke*. In February 1945, he was posted to Glasgow to commission *ZZ3,* an experimental wooden sweeper which was to be used in the dykes in Holland. The boat sailed to Sheerness with a destroyer escort but soon afterwards Harold was sent to Yarmouth to join *MMS* (Motor Minesweeper) *1023* which swept the channels off the East Anglian coast.

In May 1946 he was demobbed from Lowestoft.

Information from

Harold Burton

Bernard Cammack

Sergeant 980794
Royal Air Force
Air Target Operator, Flight Engineer

Bernard Cammack, the son of Richard Arthur and Beatrice Cammack, was born in Rotherham in 1919 but moved to Barton when he was six weeks old. His father, a Bartonian, had been directed to work at the steel works in Rotherham during the First World War. Bernard attended the Church School in Queen Street and worshipped at St. Mary's church in Barton. He was a member of the local Cub, Boy Scout and Rover Scout troops. He was a keen cyclist and member of Barton Wheelers. On leaving school, aged 14, he worked as a lorry boy with Anglo-American Oil (later

Bernard Cammack.

The menu for Christmas Dinner at RAF Leeming in 1942.

Esso) at its depot in Soutergate. This closed in 1938 when the business moved to Brigg. Prior to being called up, he lived at 28 High Street, Barton from where his parents ran a fruit and vegetable business.

He served in the Royal Air Force from March 1940 until March 1946. After initial training at Padgate and Bridgenorth, he qualified first (October 1941 to May 1942) as an air target operator with 1482 Flight at West Raynham, later (May 1942) as a flight engineer with 405 Conversion Flight at Pocklington, and finally as a fitter IIE (E for engines) at Halton, Bucks in May 1943.

His flying logbook shows that he also spent time variously stationed at Blackpool, Cambridge, Sawbridgeworth, Leeming, Topcliffe, Swanton Morley, and St. Athan. During the later months of the war, most of his time seems to have been spent flying on the air tests of aircraft before going on or resuming operations. Entries in his log record: 'Engine-change' - a 45 minutes flight in a Mosquito to 10,000 feet with 'two rolls', 'Installed new engine on Mitchell FL215 - Very successful', and most dramatically as a passenger in a Halifax in July 1942 -'Circuits & Bumps - Crash Landed'! He flew a total of 105 hours 35 minutes in Lysanders, Bostons, Defiants, Halifaxes, Martinets, Venturas, Mitchells, and Mosquitoes.

Bernard's brother, Leonard, died in Italy in July 1944 (see *Barton Remembered 1939-1945; Part One, Lest We Forget,* pp 18-19).

Information from

Joyce Cammack (widow) of Beverley

Jack Cartledge

Able Seaman, PJX322341
ML232, Royal Navy
Gunner

Jack Cartledge was born in Barton in 1922 and brought up by Mr Robert and Mrs Anne Farr (grandparents) of 2 Victoria Terrace, Barton-on-Humber. He was educated at the County School and on leaving worked in the Tube Department at Hopper's Cycle Works. In 1939, he went to work at the Farmer's Company and from there in November 1941 he volunteered to join the Royal Navy. He reported first to Lincoln and from there was posted to *HMS Collingwood* at Fareham, near Portsmouth where he did his initial training.

Following this he was transferred to a camp at Fort William from where he undertook general training on various motor launches (MLs) and motor torpedo boats (MTBs) on nearby Scottish lochs. From there he went to *HMS Excellent* at Portsmouth where he underwent gunnery training. He worked on all types of small anti-aircraft guns.

His next move was to *HMS Iron Duke* (a base ship) at Scapa Flow where he was detailed to join *ML232*. This was a wooden ship, 110 feet long, with a crew of 17-18 men. It had a 3lb gun forward, twin Lewis guns either side of the bridge and Oerlikons midships and aft. The ship also carried depth charges and was equipped with an ASDIC listening mechanism. The ship did dawn to dusk patrols out into the Atlantic looking for enemy aircraft, ships or submarines which might have threatened the Scapa Flow base **(6)**.

In early 1943 *ML232* was ordered to the Mediterranean. Extra large petrol tanks were fitted to the ship's deck to provide fuel for the long voyage. The only stop between Scapa and Gibraltar was at Milford Haven where the ship was re-stocked. From Gibraltar the ship moved on to Algiers where it started patrolling the North African coastline. The ASDIC was continually in use searching for signs of German U-boats.

From Algiers, the boat was sent to Malta and from there *ML232* took part in the invasions of both Sicily and Italy. The ship also patrolled the harbours used by the invasion force and would periodically drop small charges into the water to deter the activities of the enemy's small two-man submarines and frogmen.

When the ship was based at Manfredonia on the east coast of Italy, it was frequently sent on patrols to the coast of Yugoslavia again looking for E-boats (the German equivalent of the MTB).

Jack's next move, in 1944, was to the Isle of Ischia, in the Bay of Naples, where the ship was fitted with mine-sweeping equipment. From there it sailed to Greece and took part in mine-sweeping activities round the

Jack Cartledge.

coastline. During this period they located and destroyed a large number of enemy floating mines. One day, whilst sweeping near Piraeus, the ship was shelled by German gunners onshore - they missed!

When the war in Greece ended, Jack's ship was handed over to the Greek Navy which carried on using it for mine-sweeping activities. The crew was transferred to another British motor launch and sent to Alexandria in Egypt where it waited for a ship to bring the members back to the UK. A French troop carrier finally landed Jack at Toulon from where he travelled by train to Dieppe. A British ferry took him to Portsmouth from where he was sent back to Scapa Flow to join an old mine-laying vessel, *HMS Ringdove*. The ship sailed to Newcastle from where Jack was demobbed in May 1946.

Information from

Jack Cartledge

Joan Chant (later Bruntlett)

Women's Land Army

Joan Lillian Chant was born in 1922, the daughter of Mr William Edward and Mrs Violet May Chant of Ings Lane, Waterside Road, Barton-on-Humber. She attended the County School and after leaving was employed in domestic service by Mr and Mrs A. Stow

6. The Battle of Britain, the *Blitz* and the Battle of the Atlantic

After having completed the occupation of Holland, Belgium and France by June 1940, the next German objective was to be the defeat of Britain. Many felt that such an outcome was inevitable and Hitler believed that at this point the war was more or less over and then the British would accept the peace terms which he was prepared to offer. In this he underestimated the resolve of Churchill and the people he led and whilst Hitler was preparing his Operation *Sea Lion* - the invasion of Britain fixed for 15 September - the British forces were preparing to resist. It was calculated that if the Royal Navy and Royal Air Force could keep Hitler at bay until late 1940, the worsening winter weather would prevent Hitler's seaborne invasion and allow an ever-stronger Britain to fight on into 1941.

The Germans clearly saw that a successful sea-borne invasion could only come after the *Luftwaffe* had gained complete mastery of the air and thus began the Battle of Britain which lasted from early July to early September 1940. Having failed in his initial intention to destroy Britain's fighter aircraft force and its airfields, the *Luftwaffe* leader, Herman Göring, began (in early September) the daylight bomber blitz aimed particularly at London. By mid-September both strategies had been frustrated, the first through the skill of the British fighter pilots in their radar-guided Spitfires and Hurricanes, the second through the obstinate resolution of the ordinary men and women 'in the street' who would not be subdued under the rain of German bombs. On 17 September Hitler postponed Operation *Sea Lion* 'until further notice' and on 12 October for the winter. The *blitz*, increasingly involving night-time raids as German bomber losses incurred during daylight raids proved to be unsustainable, continued until mid-1941. No longer was London the sole target and cities and towns all over the United Kingdom were hit with high explosive and incendiary bombs. Some 40,000 civilians were killed and hundreds of thousands of homes and factories were destroyed or damaged. Many men were sent back to Barton to produce the tiles needed for the repair of these buildings.

In mid-May 1941 the *blitz* eased as Hitler prepared for the invasion of Russia and moved aircraft across to the eastern front. The growing strength of the RAF's night-fighter force and British anti-aircraft defences, the poor German bombing strategy which flitted from target to target rather than hitting one particular target night after night, and the *Luftwaffe's* failure to develop a truly heavy bomber saved the day for the United Kingdom.

The *Luftwaffe's* failure to subdue Britain provoked a new strategy. The German air force and navy would, in the Battle of the Atlantic, enforce a total blockade of Britain. This would reduce her population to starvation and prevent supplies of arms and raw materials reaching her shores. The particular targets would be the merchant ships plying across the North Atlantic between Britain and North America. These would be attacked by long-range Condor aircraft which would either bomb the vessels or report their positions to lurking U-boats which were by now based in pens which stretched along the whole Atlantic coastline from Norway to southern France.

Initially the strategy appeared to be working very successfully and losses of British merchant vessels rose alarmingly in 1941. In the two months from 31 March to 31 May 1941, German U-boats sank 142 and the *Luftwaffe* 179 Allied ships. It is probably true to say that it was at this moment that Britain came nearest to losing the war. However, the organisation of escorted convoys of merchants ships, the sinking of the great German battleship, the *Bismarck*, the switching of many Condors to the eastern front and the increasing role played by the United States in the battle did much to bring relief to the beleaguered island of Britain.

See - Ted Appleyard, Jack Austin, Jack Clapson, Ernest Coulam, Jack Dimoline, Betsy Grimbleby, Walter Horne, Joyce Robinson

of Highfield House, Westfield Road. Mr Stow was manager of Hopper's Cycle Works. She spent most of her spare time working at home and looking after pigs, chickens, ducks, rabbits and helping with the gardening and greenhouse.

She was a member of the Salvation Army where she sang in the Junior Singing Company and was also in the local Girl Guides.

In March 1942 she joined the Women's Land Army following an interview with an official of the organisation at a house in South Ferriby. Although she stated that

she would prefer to be employed in horticulture or arable farming rather than on a diary farm, she was placed on a mixed farm. In June 1942 was sent to Shepherd's Farm at Goltho near Wragby.

She was given no initial training and on arrival at the farm at 4.00 pm she was shocked to be told to milk a cow - she was more than a little scared of them. On being told that this particular cow was very quiet and wouldn't kick, she sat down on the milking stool and, with trembling hands, set to work. After a few moments the quiet cow kicked over the bucket and sent the new milkmaid flying across the room. Harry, the farmer's

Joan Chant.

son, told her to get up and start again. This she did, now determined not to be beaten by a cow. Eventually she got the hang of it.

She received her uniform through the post - one greatcoat, one hat, two pairs of brace overalls, two Aertex short-sleeved shirts, two pairs of socks, one pair of shoes, one pair of cord trousers, and one green, V-necked jumper. Her milking coat overalls arrived later. One other Land Army girl worked on Shepherd's Farm - Jessie Hendry, a Scot by birth but then living in Grimsby. There were two other Land Army girls on nearby farms, another working as a dairymaid in Wragby and two forestry girls were billeted in a cottage close to Shepherd's Farm.

On Shepherd's Farm, there were three working horses which had to be fed and groomed, harnessed and taken to the fields. The work might be ploughing in winter or bringing-in the harvest in summer. It was all hard, physical work which Joan enjoyed. Later the farm was equipped with a Ford Standard tractor and a new plough and this made life a lot easier.

The farm kept pigs and sheep as well as the cows and calves and a huge bull. Some sugar beet was grown and this was all hand-worked and lifted. Other crops included potatoes, swedes, kale and mangolds for cow food. Other arable crops included barley,

wheat, oats and tic beans. A harvest of hay was always essential for the animals.

On 11 December 1943, she married the farmer's only son and as a result had to resign from the Land Army and hand in her uniform.

She still lives at Shepherd's Farm, Goltho. Her brother Ted was killed in action in 1943 - see *Barton Remembered 1939-1945; Part One, Lest We Forget, p 22.*

Information from

Joan Bruntlett

Percy Chappell

Private, 4806671
6 Battalion, Lincolnshire Regiment
Driver, Stretcher Bearer

Percy John Chappell was born in 1914, the son of Mr Charles William and Mrs Lucy Chappell of Townside, East Halton. He was educated at East Halton School and, following his family's move to Barton, at the County School in Castledyke. On leaving school, he was employed as a grocer's assistant by Hunt Brothers of George Street, Barton (now the Co-op premises). He attended the Primitive Methodist Chapel in Queen Street.

He was called up in June 1940 and reported for initial training with the Lincolnshire Regiment at Burton Road, Lincoln. Later whilst there, he served as a driving instructor. In 1941 he was posted to the 6th Battalion at Brandon in Suffolk where he worked as a driver. From there the Battalion was moved to Folkestone in Kent where it served as part of the front line defences against a possible German attack across the Channel. His job was to keep the Battalion supplied with food, clothing, bedding and ammunition.

In late 1942 the Battalion moved to Surrey prior to being transferred to North Africa. It sailed on the *SS Sobiesci* from Greenock to Algiers where the Battalion joined the 46th Division of the 1st Army **(11)**. From there it moved into Tunisia and took part in the fighting which eventually came to an end at the fall of Tunis. Percy's job as a driver was to keep up the supplies to the troops in the front line.

From Tunis the Battalion moved to nearby Bizerta where it waited for its next call into action. On 9 September 1943, Percy landed with the 46th Division - now part of American general Mark Clark's 5th Army at Salerno **(12)**. The Battalion was moved to Italy by the US Navy on a number of tank landing ships. The initial landing there did not go very well and the

Wedding photograph of Percy and Dora Chappell in October 1940.

American ships remained offshore in case of a withdrawal. Eventually the landing proved successful and the troops moved north towards Naples. From Naples the Battalion moved inland into the mountains and made its way north towards Monte Cassino. It was held in reserve at this battle.

After the fall of Monte Cassino the Battalion moved to Rome and was then sent to Taranto prior to sailing on to Greece where it spent a spell keeping the peace after the civil war.

From Greece the Battalion was moved for service in Egypt and Palestine. Whilst there it was decided that all A1 drivers were to be transferred back into general duties and Percy volunteered to join the Battalion's stretcher bearers and he served in this capacity for the rest of the war.

The Battalion's next move was back to Italy and it continued to fight its way up the peninsular until the war ended. On a number of occasions Percy was required to enter no-man's-land to bring back wounded comrades. This was very dangerous work and after the war ended, Percy was honoured by being

mentioned in dispatches in the London Gazette.

At this point the Battalion was moved into Austria where it served as part of the peacekeeping force. After about a year in Austria, Percy was sent back to England and in June 1946 he was demobilized from Dover.

Information from

Percy Chappell

Jack Clapson

Private, 4804554
4th Battalion, Lincolnshire Regiment
Infantryman, Driver

Jack Clapson was born in 1919, the son of Mr Tom and Mrs Mary Clapson of 25 Holydyke, Barton-on-Humber. He was educated at the County School and on leaving was employed at Cornhill Farm.

In September 1939, he was conscripted into the army and after initial training at Lincoln joined the 4th Battalion of the Lincolnshire Regiment where he became the driver of a tracked vehicle which pulled a 6lb anti-tank gun.

Jack was with the Battalion at Ripon in early 1940 when it was put on 'stand by' and a move to Finland seemed

Jack Clapson.

imminent. However, that order was cancelled and in April it moved first to Rosyth and then to Gourock where it boarded the *Empress of Australia* bound for Norway. The Battalion, part of 146 Brigade, landed at Namsos on 14 April 1940 and soon found itself in defensive positions facing a German advance from Trondheim. The only weapons available were rifles, Bren guns and one 3-inch mortar - the force had no machine guns, anti-tank weapons, artillery or air support. The Battalion's position soon proved untenable and in early May it arrived back in Namsos for the voyage back to Scapa Flow which was reached on 5 May 1940.

All Norwegian resistance ended early in June.

In June 1940, following the German occupation of Denmark, the Battalion was moved to Iceland and stayed there for some two years. The British decided to occupy that island to prevent it falling into the hands of the Germans who, it was feared, would use it as a U-boat and aircraft base threatening further our Atlantic convoys **(6)**. Eventually, the Battalion was moved back to England to prepare for Operation *Overlord* - the invasion of Europe.

On 10 June 1944 (D-Day + 4) Jack landed with his Battalion in Normandy as part of the 49th Division **(15)**. Subsequently he saw action throughout the campaign to free north-western Europe. He was wounded in Holland and returned to England for treatment at the Nottingham Hospital. On his return to the continent, he became part of the army of occupation in Germany before he was finally demobilised.

Information from

Jack Clapson

No author, *A Short History of the Lincolnshire Regiment*, Goslar (Germany) 1954

Jim Clayton

Able Seaman, PJX 314161
Royal Navy
DEMS gunner

Roy Clayton was born in 1922, the son of Mr Jack Wright and Mrs Elsie Eva Clayton of Humber Terrace, Barton-on-Humber. He was educated at St. Chad's School and on leaving worked at Hoe Hill Brick and Tile Yard and in the Frame Shop at Hopper's Cycle Works.

He was conscripted into the Royal Navy on 4 December 1941 and reported for training at *HMS Glendower* (Butlins holiday camp) at Pwllheli in North Wales. From there he moved to *HMS Wellesley* at Liverpool for a further one month's training to become

Jim Clayton.

a DEMS (defensively equipped merchant ship) gunner. Following a week's leave he was, like all the other DEMS gunners, posted to the port nearest to his home town. This proved to be Hull and he reported to the Ettal Reeda Hostel in George Street to await posting to a ship.

After four days he was put abroad the recently-built, 3,000 ton, coal-fired merchant ship *SS Winkleigh*. This was a thin-plated ship capable of some 8/9 knots whose home port was Cardiff. She was capable of carrying some 11,000 tons of general cargo. She was about to make only her third voyage and had a crew of about 40 men, including nine DEMS gunners who manned one 4-inch quick-fire gun of WW1 vintage, one breach-loading 4-inch gun, two Oerlikons and four Lewis guns. The ship sailed to Middlesbrough and was

loaded with ammunition and a deck cargo of aeroplanes in wooden cases. She sailed south through the Bay of Biscay in convoy and then made her way alone round the Cape of Good Hope and on to Mauritius. There she off-loaded her cargo but, as there was nothing available to carry back to England (the expected cargo was sugar), she was ordered to sail for the United States. Once again she rounded the Cape and sailed across the South Atlantic to Trinidad where she was to pick up coal for her boilers. At this time the Caribbean was a paradise for German U-boats. They could be refuelled and supplied in friendly

7. The War in North Africa

The Italian fascist dictator Benito Mussolini came to power in 1922. His dream was to create an Italian Empire and make the Mediterranean an 'Italian Lake'. In 1935 he attacked Abyssinia, the only large country on that continent still ruled by Africans. Half-hearted attempts to apply sanctions against Italy failed and in 1937, she left the League of Nations. Meanwhile some 100,000 Italians were sent to help Franco in his ultimately successful revolt (1936-1939) against the Spanish Republic. In the spring of 1939, following Hitler's lead in the annexation of Austria (1938) and Czechoslovakia (1939), Mussolini invaded and annexed Albania. In June 1940, he formerly entered the war as an ally of Hitler.

Britain, reeling from the recent defeat of the BEF and the escape from Dunkirk, faced enormous problems in the Mediterranean. What could she do to protect the link through that sea with her far-eastern empire? How could she safeguard her oil supplies from the Gulf? The Italian fleet, which included some 100 submarines, dominated the Mediterranean. Her control of Libya and Ethiopia threatened the British in Egypt and control of the Suez Canal. Italy had friendly relations with Franco's Spain. France had recently been defeated and the fate of her Mediterranean fleet was undecided.

Decisive action was clearly required and it was not long in coming. In November 1940, Operation *Judgement* was launched against the Italian fleet in Taranto. Planes of the Fleet Air Arm mounted a highly successful torpedo attack and seven ships were severely damaged, including three battleships. Italian naval domination in the Mediterranean was no more and in March 1941, her fleet suffered another crushing defeat at the Battle of Matapan (also see insert 8).

Meanwhile military activity in North Africa was escalating. Here Italy had some 500,000 men facing a British force of only 100,000 strong and fighting some 2,000 miles from home. In September 1940 the Italians began their planned two-pronged attack on Egypt - one force pushing eastward from Libya (see map 2), the other driving north from its base in Abyssinia. Both were decisively defeated. In North Africa, O'Connor's 30,000 troops drove the Italian force of 80,000 men back to El Agheila in Cyrenacia (east Libya) and took both Tobruk and Benghazi along with 130,000 Italian prisoners, 1,300 guns and 400 tanks. A massive victory, the capture of the port of Tripoli and the removal of the Italians from the whole of Libya, seemed in sight.

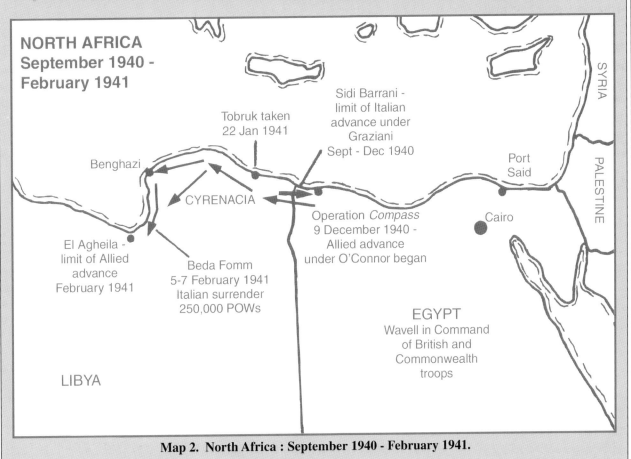

Map 2. North Africa : September 1940 - February 1941.

47

At that point Churchill made a fateful and ultimately futile decision. The Italian invasion of Greece in October 1940 met with spirited resistance and in the hope that the enemy's advance into the Balkans (?and eventually into the Middle East) could be halted he ordered some 60,000 Australian, New Zealand and British troops to be transferred from O'Connor's force in North Africa to aid the Greeks. As a result by February 1941 the advance of O'Connor's now much weakened force had come to a halt and a great opportunity had been lost. In that same month the arrival in Tripoli of Erwin Rommel and detachments of the *Wehrmacht* - to be known as the *Afrika Corps* - would, for a period, transform the military situation.

Meanwhile, the Italian forces in East Africa, outnumbering the allies seven to one were crushed. By May the Italian East African Empire had ceased to exist, the Italian commander surrendered on the 19th and the whole area was in Allied hands. Here was a much needed boost for morale - at this time victory was a novelty but obviously very welcome.

On 31 March Rommel and the *Afrika Corps* began their dramatic advance from their front line at Sirte (see map 3). This soon had the Allied forces in full scale retreat to the Egyptian frontier. The only Allied troops left in Libya were a small force of mainly Australian soldiers surrounded in Tobruk. The spirited resistance of the 'Rats of Tobruk' (who were later replaced by British and Polish detachments), lasted from April until November and kept that important supply port out of Rommel's hands. O'Connor was taken prisoner.

In May and June 1941 the Allied commander, Wavell, launched an series of unsuccessful offensives aimed at throwing Rommel out of Egypt and relieving the Tobruk garrison. These failures resulted in him being sent to India and his replacement, General Auchinleck, set about the task of building up his renamed 8th Army. On 18 November Auchinleck opened his long-awaited offensive - Operation *Crusader*; Tobruk was relieved in December and Rommel was pushed out of Cyrenaica. The Allied success was short-lived for in January 1942, Rommel once again took the offensive, caught the 8th Army unprepared, and recaptured much of the ground so recently lost. In another German attack in late May with numerically inferior forces, Rommel used superb skill when manoeuvring his armoured detachments and thus ensured victory. On 21 June Tobruk fell and 38,000 prisoners fell into enemy hands. Rommel continued to advance into Egypt but by mid-July his depleted and tired forces were forced to halt in the face of new Allied defensive positions running inland from El Alamein. The stage was set for a great battle. Rommel's long lines of communication contrasted markedly with the short haul along which the Allies needed to bring supplies from the Nile Delta.

Once again the Allies brought in new leadership - Alexander replaced Auchinleck and Bernard Montgomery took over command of the 8th Army. Montgomery, addicted to 'efficiency, determination and training' quickly endeared himself to the soldiers. Here, at last, was a man the equal if not superior of Rommel, the 'Desert Fox'.

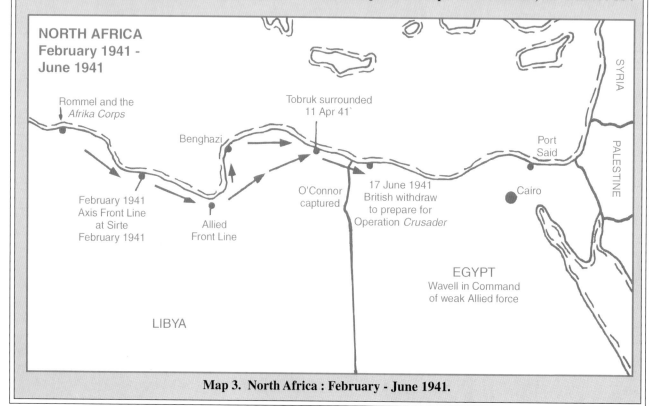

Map 3. North Africa : February - June 1941.

Montgomery spent some 10 weeks preparing his army for battle. Ten weeks spent reinforcing, training and planning. By mid-October he had at his disposal 195,000 men with over 1,000 tanks and many more in reserve - many of these latter were American Grants and Shermans. The Allied air force had almost complete control of the skies. Rommel had 100,000 men (half of them German), 540 tanks (half of them obsolete Italian machines) and 500 guns. His troops were short of ammunition, fuel and other supplies, much of which had to be brought some 1,200 miles from Tripoli.

On 23 October 450 guns began the devastating barrage which was to be the prelude to the Allied advance. Over the next two weeks, the British, South African, Australian and Free French troops took command of the battlefield and broke the German and Italian defences. Here at last was the victory the Allies had been waiting for. This was to be 'the great turning-point' - morale rose throughout Britain and the Commonwealth; at last we had something to show our Russian and American Allies. Germany had suffered her first major defeat of the war and for the first time in some two years, the church bells rang out in Britain.

Early November saw Rommel in full flight and when, on 8 November, Operation *Torch* - the Allied landings in Algiers - was mounted (see insert 11) the fate of the Germans and Italians was sealed. The 8th Army took Benghazi on 20 November and in early 1943, the vital port of Tripoli fell into Allied hands.

See - Clifford Altoft, Wilfred Codd, Gerald Hewitt, Leslie King, Noel Kitching,

Wilfred Pike and Roland Shephardson

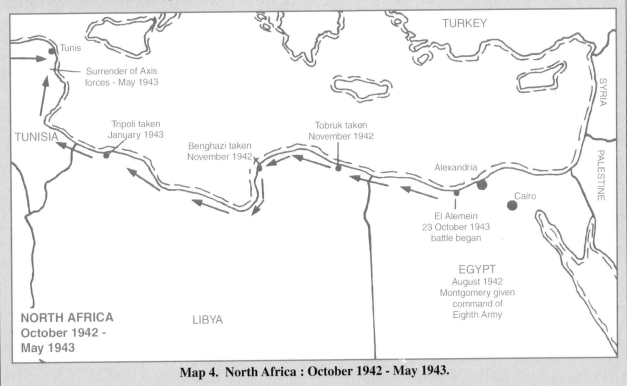

Map 4. North Africa : October 1942 - May 1943.

South American countries and then hide among the many West Indian islands waiting for vulnerable Allied merchant ships to be torpedoed.

In August 1942, the refuelled *Winkleigh* left Trinidad bound for New York in a convoy of some 21 ships. Only nine merchant ships completed that horrendous voyage which was constantly attacked by U-boats, usually at dawn and dusk. During this time Jim took a lot of 'pot-shots' at what he hoped were enemy submarines without much hope of damaging one.

The ship spent 10 days in New York and Jim enjoyed the good food and generous hospitality. Loaded with 40 tanks, quantities of army rations and ammunition

and with 16 aeroplanes on the deck, the *Winkleigh* left the USA in a convoy of 18 ships bound for the Caribbean. On this occasion no ships were lost to the enemy U-boats. Once again they topped up their coal bunkers in Trinidad and then Jim's ship left the convoy to sail alone to the Cape and on to Suez where it off-loaded its cargo.

The ship's next stop was Mauritius again where they picked up a cargo of sugar destined for the UK. The *Winkleigh* sailed round the Cape and joined a convoy of about 28 ships for the final part of the voyage across the Bay of Biscay. Although they had seven destroyers as escort, the ships were attacked at dawn and dusk for about a week and 14 of the merchantmen were sunk. Jim's ship finally docked at Greenwich in March 1943 and, as he had been away for 13 months, he was allowed a 12-day leave.

His leave over, he reported back to the Thames and was put aboard an 8,000 ton tanker, the *El Grillo*. She could carry some 10,000 tons of oil, had a crew of about 40 including 9 or 10 DEMS gunners and could manage about 10 knots at full speed. She was armed with a 12lb gun, four Oerlikons and four breach-loaders. As the 12lb gun needed about nine men to fire it, some of the merchant navy crewmen had to be trained to fire some of the other guns. When the ship was at sea in what were considered dangerous waters, the gunners worked in shifts of four hours on duty and four off. In less dangerous circumstances, they worked four hours on and eight hours off duty.

The *El Grillo*, bound for the east coast of America, joined a convoy of about 25 merchant ships escorted by a number of destroyers, corvettes and armed trawlers. On arrival in the USA, the ship was loaded with some 10,000 tons of diesel fuel at Bayonne in New Jersey and then sailed in convoy back to Southampton. The return voyage took about three weeks and two ships were lost to the U-boats. Jim and the *El Grillo* made two more trips to Bayonne. On the first voyage no ships were lost though the convoys were continually attacked by U-boats and Focke-Wulf Condor FW200 long-range bombers. These latter, the 'scourge of the Atlantic', had a range of some 2,206 miles and carried a 20mm cannon and 3,857 lbs of bombs. They had come into service in 1940 and quickly proved their effectiveness when engaged in bombing attacks on convoy attacks or as spotter planes for the U-boats. In their first year of operations they sank 11 ships and crippled the liner *Empress of Britain* which was later sunk by a U-boat. The Royal Navy's response to this new threat was to give the convoys an aircraft carrier escort and to put DEMS gunners like Jim onto the merchant ships. On Jim's second Atlantic crossing, they were less fortunate and five or six ships were lost on both the outward and inward voyages. After off-loading its cargo, the *El Grillo* was sent to a dry dock in Glasgow where the crew members watched apprehensively as the ship's heating system was improved. Here was a clear indication that they were bound for the Arctic.

Sure enough, Jim found himself aboard a fleet auxiliary vessel flying the blue ensign. The job was now to carry oil to be used to refuel Royal Navy vessels operating in the North Atlantic. In September 1943, they sailed from Loch Ewe in Scotland full of diesel oil and bound for Seydis Fiord in Iceland. There the ship remained for a number of months whilst naval warships tied up alongside and were topped up with fuel. Other tankers from England came to Iceland to fill up the *El Grillo's* tanks.

On 10 February 1944 the *El Grillo* had just been

'topped up' and was carrying an excessive cargo of some 11,000 tons of diesel fuel. The weight of this was bending the ship. At that moment five Focke-Wulf Condors were spotted flying high over the fiord. The *El Grillo's* guns were brought into action but to no avail as the enemy was well out of their range. The enemy planes proceeded to drop their bombs which did not hit the tanker but exploded in the sea quite close to the vessel. The ship's plates were blown in and she went down, bow first, broken in two, in about ten minutes. All of the crew managed to get into the ship's lifeboats and were soon picked up by a Norwegian cutter which took them back to Reykjavik. That evening 'Lord Haw-Haw' announced on German radio the sinking of the *El Grillo* - an action, he said, taken in retaliation for the recent sinking of the German battle-cruiser the *Scharnhorst*.

Jim now had to find his way back to England and chose to travel on a trawler bound for Hull. The boat was full of fish and Jim found the whole experience most uncomfortable. He was, of course, hoping that on landing he would be allowed some leave in Barton but in the event he was only to have one night in his own bed before being required to report back to Portsmouth for re-kitting and further training as a gunner.

Just before D-Day he reported to the captain of a coaster which carried coal from Cumberland (Silloth or Whitehaven) to Coleraine in Northern Ireland. He was the only gunner aboard a ship armed with a Lewis gun and two rifles. He stayed aboard this ship for about a year during which time he fired at nothing more than floating mines.

By VE-Day he had been moved back to Portsmouth and spent the night sleeping on the steps of the Guildhall there. After spending some time at the shore bases *HMS Series* and *HMS Blazer,* he was finally demobilised from *HMS Excellent* on Whale Island in April 1946.

Information from

Jim Clayton

Ron Clayton

**Corporal, 1040845
Royal Air Force Regiment
Ground Gunner**

Roland Clayton was born in 1921, the son of Mr Jack Wright and Mrs Elsie Eva Clayton of Humber Terrace, Barton-on-Humber. He attended St. Chad's School and church. On leaving school he was employed in the Handlebar Department of Hopper's Cycle Works. He was a member of Hopper's Club in Whitecross

Street and his hobby was woodwork.

In May 1941 he volunteered to join the Royal Air Force but found that he was unable to train as aircrew. As a result he reported for initial training as a ground gunner at Blackpool (one week) and Morecambe (six weeks). His next posting was to No 56 Operational Training Unit at the airfield at Sutton Bridge which was being used to train pilots. The ground gunners manned Vickers and Lewis guns which were sited in bunkers spread around the airfield perimeter. Their job was to engage any enemy aircraft which attempted to attack the base. At Sutton Bridge, where he was on a two hours on, four hours off day and night rota, Ron never fired his gun in anger.

In February 1942 Ron was sent back to Blackpool from where he came home on three weeks embarkation leave. On 23 March he sailed from Greenock on the *Cameronion* bound for Bombay. The voyage, which lasted for nine weeks, included stops at Sierra Leone, Cape Town, Durban, and Mombassa. From Bombay, a train journey took him to Orissa state where he was employed helping to establish a new airfield. Eventually it was completed and a squadron of Lockheed Hudson bombers arrived. These were employed bombing the Japanese troops in Burma and their ships on the high seas. Ron was again employed in the gun pits which surrounded the field but he did spend some time doing other tasks such as stacking bombs. During the 15 months he was there he never saw a Japanese aeroplane. He did get a few days leave in Calcutta and whilst in a cinema there the city was bombed!

His next move was to the depot at Secunderabad where he found that he was in the Royal Air Force Regiment. This arm of the RAF had been formed by Winston Churchill and with a strength of some 38,000 men became the biggest single unit in the whole of the British Forces. There he was trained in army techniques. He was placed in a new unit in which he was allowed to be with his friends and it was there that he teamed up with Pete Lidgett from Brigg and they stayed together for the rest of the war. On the completion of the training, Ron was posted to various airfields in India where he was usually engaged in patrol duties.

He eventually found himself in Madras from where he sailed to Chittagong in Bengal. From there he moved by lorry up the Dimapur Road to Imphal **(18)**. From there he was sent some 30 miles south to the airfield at Palelo - at that time the most forward field in Burma. It only had a short landing strip and Ron manned a twin-Browning gun in one of the pits which surrounded the field. The base was continually bombed and strafed by the Japanese. Ron was part of a 32-man unit of the RAF Regiment which consisted of a flight lieutenant, a sergeant, three corporals (including Ron) and 27 men. The main traffic at this base was B25 American bombers which landed for refuelling and Dakotas bringing in supplies for the army units at the

front some 12 to 14 miles to the south. Three men in Ron's unit were killed at Palelo when a Japanese shell landed in the gun pit. The Allies had 25lb guns on the airfield perimeter which were used to shell the Japanese front lines. The field also enjoyed periodic visits from Spitfire and Hurricane fighters which engaged any Japanese bombers flying in the vicinity. Usually no planes ever stayed the night at the Palelo field as it was far too dangerous. However, on one memorable night when some Spitfires did stay over, a force of Japanese sneaked onto the field and destroyed seven of the planes with 'Molotov cocktails'.

As the Allies advanced south through Burma, Ron was moved down with them. He found himself on various front-line airfields mounting guard duty on their perimeters. Finally he ended up in Rangoon just after it was liberated in May 1945. Here he caught malaria and was put into hospital. From there he was moved back to the Secunderabad depot in India and began training for the impending attack on southern Burma. However, before that could take place the war ended and having served for over three years in the east without break, Ron was sent to Poona for repatriation to the UK. His flight to England eventually landed at Huntingdon from where he was sent back to Barton for 101 days leave.

At the end of this he reported back to Belton Park for general duties and was then moved to Deanthorpe airfield outside Corby where he worked in the Orderly Room and as barman in the Officers' Mess. He was eventually demobbed from Cardington in July 1946.

Information from

Ron Clayton

Bernard Clipson

Leading Aircraftsman, 3200413
Royal Air Force
Aircraft Fitter

Bernard George Clipson was born in 1924, the son of Mr Samuel and Mrs Lily Clipson of Chemical Road, Barton-on-Humber (later 70 Garden Village). He attended the County School and subsequently worked for J.P. Maltby, chicken and fruit farmer on Tofts Road. His hobbies were football and cricket and he played for the Boys' Club.

In January 1940, he left Maltby's Farm and was employed full-time as a messenger boy at the ARP Report Centre in High Street (see *Barton Remembered, 1939-1945; Part Two, The Home Front*, pp 8-11). Some time later the authorities reduced the number of messenger boys at the centre and Bernard

Bernard Clipson.

left to take up employment with John Bramley, the farmer at Little Grange on Ferriby Road. At this time he became a fire watcher and also a founder member of the Barton Air Training Corps (see *Barton Remembered, 1939-1945; Part Two, The Home Front*, pp 24-25). In late 1941, he left the farm and was employed by his brother-in-law Sydney James who lived on Reed's Island and looked after some 250 sheep and 100 cattle which were fattened there and then transported by barge to Ferriby Sluice before being sent off to market. There was a house and a shooting lodge on the island. At weekends during the winter months, Bernard and Sydney sculled over to the sluice landing stage where they picked up parties of army and air force officers (with their batmen and provisions) who were taken over to the island to shoot the wild geese and ducks.

In late 1942 he volunteered to join as aircrew in the Royal Air Force and underwent initial training at St. John's Wood in London. During this period he failed the night vision test and so was unable to train as a pilot. Instead it was proposed to train him as a flight engineer but having no knowledge of engines, it was decided that he should be sent on a ground fitter's course at Cosford, near Wolverhampton.

Having completed that course, he was informed that there were no vacancies at that time on the flight engineers' courses so he was posted to No 567 Squadron, RAF Detling near Maidstone in Kent where he worked on Hurricanes, Martinets, Barracudas and Airspeed Oxfords. The work involved servicing the planes' engines. By now D-Day was imminent and all

postings and leaves were frozen so he was unable to go on a flight engineers' course. On the days immediately prior to D-Day (4-5 June 1944), Bernard spent his time painting black and white stripes on the wings and fuselages of all the Squadron's planes. This would allow them to be easily identified as Allied planes as they flew over the D-Day fleet armada and over the beaches. Ground crews were told that if casualties were high and airfields had been secured in France, they would be sent as immediate replacements. As it turned out they were not called upon.

In the early hours of the morning of 6 June, the Squadron's Commanding Officer announced over the station's tannoy that the landings were taking place. Bernard, along with two other fitters, was sent to 80 Squadron. A week after D-Day, German 'Doodlebugs' started coming over **(16)** and Bernard was fully employed servicing fighter aircraft which were sent up to shoot them down. Somewhat later, No 567 Squadron was moved to the Isle of Sheppey where a V2 rocket fell in a nearby field and damaged some of the aircraft. This was one of the earliest V2s to land in England and very soon after the explosion, 'top brass' and boffins arrived to inspect the site and pick up any pieces of the rocket which could be recovered. At the time Barnard was sitting in a Hurricane running up the engine. The explosion lifted the aircraft off the ground. Luckily it came to rest on its three wheels again but was damaged by flying debris.

In late 1944, the Squadron moved to RAF Hornchurch in East London where another V2 landed on the airfield runway - this time causing little damage. Whilst at Hornchurch, Bernard was posted to Libya where he was stationed at El Adam and from there to RAF Lydda in Palestine (which is now Ben Gurion Airport just outside Tel Aviv). These bases were called staging posts and they stretched from the UK through North Africa and Palestine and on to Iraq and India. Thousands of troops with their supplies and equipment were being flown out to India to take part in the Far East offensive against the Japanese. It was a non-stop, 24 hours a day operation with transport aircraft - Dakotas, Stirlings, Avro Yorks and Liberators - doing round trips, fully loaded on the way out and empty on the way back

Whilst at Lydda, Bernard witnessed the crash in which Kenneth Houghton died (see *Barton Remembered, 1939-1945; Lest We Forget*, pp 43-44).

After VJ Day, supplies stopped moving to the east and those former Japanese prisoners-of-war who were fit enough to travel by air moved through Lydda on their way back to the UK.

In February 1946 Barnard came back to England and he was demobilised in March of that year.

Information from

Bernard Clipson

Jack Clipson

Fusilier, 6981229
6th Battalion, Royal Inniskilling Fusiliers
Fusilier, Signaller, 'Regimental Barber'

John Hugh Clipson was born in 1917, the son of Mr Leonard and Mrs Ethel Clipson and lived with his parents at 5 Waterside Road, Barton-on-Humber. He attended the County School and was a member of St. Chad's church and the Constitutional Club. His hobbies were dancing and growing roses in his garden. On leaving school he worked in the family business as a hairdresser.

In March 1940 he received his enlistment notice which required him to report to the Royal Inniskilling Fusiliers at Fulwood Barracks in Preston, Lancashire. After being given tea - a boiled egg - he was put on the night ferry bound for Omagh in Northern Ireland for training. In August of that year he qualified as a signaller. He remained in the UK until November 1942 and on 15 January 1942, he married Gertrude Wilkinson and set up home at 28 Fleetgate in Barton.

Later in 1942, the Battalion moved to Scotland and in November, sailed from Greenock bound for Algiers **(11)**. He later saw service in North Africa, Algiers (November 1942-June 1943), Sicily (June 1943-September 1943) and Italy - including the battles at Salerno, Monte Cassino and Sangro River - from September 1943 until his demobilisation in February 1946 **(12)**. His wife did not see him from late 1942 until August 1945.

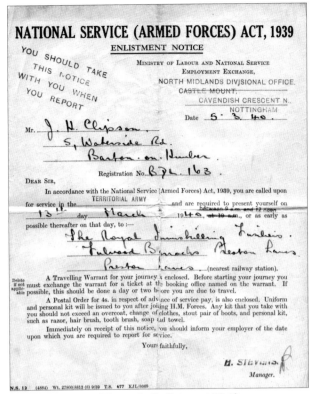

Jack Clipson's Enlistment Notice.

Although officially designated 'signaller', an undated newspaper cutting describes a meeting in Tunisia between Jack - the 'regimental barber' - and Fusilier Alf Porter of New Holland.

Information from

Gertrude Clipson (widow)

A full account of the actions of No 6 Battalion of the Royal Inniskilling Fusiliers in Sicily is deposited in Baysgarth Museum

Jack Clipson in Rome in 1945.

Jack Clipson's War Gratuity and Post War Credit.

John Clipson

Sergeant, 2089820
Lincolnshire Regiment
Royal Army Service Corps
Driver, Marine Engineer

John William Clipson was born in 1922, the son of Mr Samuel and Mrs Lily Clipson of Chemical Row, Barton-on-Humber. He was educated at the County School and subsequently worked at J.P. Maltby's poultry and fruit farm on Tofts Road (Appleyard Drive is built on the site of the farm). His hobby was playing tennis in Baysgarth Park.

He joined the Barton Territorials - No 8 Section of 383 Company, 46th Searchlight Regiment - when he was 17 and as a result was mobilised on 24 August 1939. The Section, under the command of Lieutenant Maw, moved to New Waltham and set up its searchlight awaiting the expected arrival of German bombers. (There were six searchlights in each section; four sections in a company; and four companies in a regiment. The six searchlights in No 8 Section were located at New Waltham, Pyewipe, Beelsby, Ashby-cum-Fenby, Humberston Fitties and Cleethorpes Bathing Pool. Each searchlight section was manned by 12 soldiers and was accompanied by its own petrol-driven generator. When not on duty, the men lived and slept in tents but later they were housed in timber huts. The No 8 (Barton) Section, which stayed together until 1944, initially consisted of Lieutenant Richard Maw (farmer), 2nd Lieutenant Riggall (farmer), Sergeant Mark Pickard (builder), Corporal John Bilton (from Barrow), Privates John Clipson, Sam Brook (from Brigg), Bob Blyth (worked at Pinchbeck's in George Street) and two other men from Gainsborough. The orders to turn on the searchlight came from Company

HQ at Westwood Ho! Barracks in Grimsby which had received a warning from RAF Digby.)

In April 1940, 46 Regiment was moved to Northumberland and the Barton Section was based at Longhirst, near Morpeth. The company HQ was in Longhirst Hall and was part of the defensive screen around Newcastle. John stayed at Longhirst for some 18-20 months before the Regiment was moved, half (including the Barton Section), to Dollar in Clackmannanshire, to become part of the defences of the Forth Estuary and half to Aberdeen. He remained at Dollar for about seven months before the Regiment was posted to the Orkney Islands. Here, based in Nissen huts just outside Kirkwall, they became part of the outer defences of the great naval base at Scapa Flow. Whilst there he was able to visit various warships. John visited the brand-new cruiser *HMS Jamaica* - the largest war vessel he had ever seen. He was amazed by the enormous size of the engine room. He also remembers seeing the arrival of the battleship *HMS Anson*. She was newly-built and still covered in red lead paint. Spare time was spent in Kirkwall and his other great memory is of the incredibly powerful winds which blew across the island. He also remembers the icy winter days which were spent in almost total darkness and the summer days when it hardly ever got dark.

At some time around Christmas 1943, the Regiment was moved by ship to Aberdeen and then on by train to Cornwall to become part of the Plymouth defences. Company HQ was at Saltash and John was based in a field near the small village of Tideforth. By mid-1944, the threat of German air raids was over and the whole Regiment was disbanded. John was posted to the RASC Waterbourne. Initially he spent several weeks in Manchester training as a marine engineer. From there he was posted to Rothesay on the Isle of Bute

---

8. Cape Matapan - the destruction of the Italian Fleet

In March 1941 information gleaned by British Intelligence from decoded enemy messages revealed that the Italian fleet had sailed into the eastern Mediterranean with the intention of attacking British convoys. Admiral Sir Andrew Cunnigham had three battleships - the *Warspite*, *Barham* and *Valiant* - in the area and he was determined to lure the Italian ships to their destruction.

Four Allied cruisers - *Ajax*, *Orion*, *Gloucester* and *Perth* - sailed from Piraeus in Greece as bait to be chased by the Italians onto the guns of the battleships as they sailed north-westwards from their base at Alexandria.

The Italians duly fell into the trap and their ships were attacked by torpedo carrying Swordfish aircraft from the carrier *HMS Formidable*, RAF bombers and the British fleet. The engagement took place off Cape Matapan at the southern end of Greece on 29 March 1941. Three Italian cruisers and two destroyers were sunk. The end for two of the cruisers was particularly swift as they were struck by 15 inch shells from point-blank range. A British admiral wrote: 'One saw whole turrets and masses of other debris whirling through the air and splashing into the sea. [The ships became] nothing but glowing torches and on fire from stem to stern.' Unfortunately, the brand new, 35,000 ton Italian battleship *Vittoria Veneto*, although damaged by the torpedo bombers, escaped to fight another day.

See - Clarke Dunn

for training on various types of boats. He continued training in Stranraer until he was posted as a sergeant to 935 Company, Waterbourne at Yarmouth, IOW. The Company's boats, once assembled, were to be used as ambulance launches in the Far East. They would have moved casualties from a beach to hospital ships anchored offshore. John was engineer on board AL (ambulance launch) *Benson*. It was fitted with two petrol-driven, 650 HP Hall Scot engines on lend-lease from the USA. Whilst this training was continuing, VJ Day was announced.

For some time afterwards, the launches were used to escort landing craft which were going to sea to dump unwanted ammunition off the Channel Isles. He also sailed to Cuxhaven in Germany and escorted a number of yachts back to England.

In May 1946 he was demobbed from York.

Information from

John Clipson

Haydn Cocking in Singapore in 1946.

Haydn Cocking

Private, 14960014
1st Battalion, Lincolnshire Regiment
Infantryman

Haydn Cocking was born in 1926, the son of Mr Herbert and Mrs Norah Cocking of 20 Marsh Lane, Barton-on-Humber. He was educated at the Church of England School in Queen Street and on leaving worked in the Office at Hopper's Cycle Works. He was a member of the Barton Boys' Club and took part in its concerts. He was also a member of the Barton Youth Choir conducted by Charles Southall (see *Barton Remembered 1939-1945; Part Two, The Home Front*, p 92). He attended the Primitive Methodist chapel in Queen Street.

On reaching the age of 17 in late 1944, he volunteered to join the army and underwent 16 weeks of initial training at the Sabroan Barracks on Burton Road in Lincoln. Along with a draft of some 100 other men, he sailed from Southampton to Bombay (via the Cape of Good Hope) on the *Empress of Canada*. From Bombay he travelled by train to Bangalore where he joined the 1st Battalion of the Lincolnshire Regiment which had been stationed in the East since 1922. At this time, the Battalion was badly under strength with only about 600 instead of its proper complement of 1,000 men. It formed part of the 26 Indian Infantry Division which was at that time employed in beach landings along the coast of Burma **(18)**. These complemented the main Allied thrust against the Japanese which was taking place down central Burma

with the aim of capturing Rangoon. When Haydn arrived, preparations were being made for a final seaborne attack on Rangoon - Operation *Dracula*.

In April 1945 the 1st Battalion was conveyed in troopships with a Royal Navy escort and was landed near to the city of Rangoon which was finally taken on 3 May. Naval guns and Hurricane fighter-bombers assisted the landing. Haydn was in the 1 Section of 3 Platoon of D Company. The Platoon was commanded by Lieutenant Bedford along with a sergeant. Each section should have had a corporal in charge, ten riflemen and one Bren-gunner. Because the Battalion was under strength, Haydn's section only had six riflemen at this time. Each infantryman carried a rifle and bayonet, 50 rounds of ammunition, two hand grenades, two Bren gun magazines, a ground sheet, blanket and an emergency pack of rations. These latter were only to be eaten if the usual food supply - American 'Compo' rations - were unavailable. 'Compo' rations included waxed packets of solid Spam, hard-tack biscuits and powdered egg. Tea was brewed as regularly as possible using a 'Tommy cooker' which used solid methylated spirit fuel.

Most of the Japanese, fearing that they would be caught between the 26 Division moving north and the 17 Indian Infantry Division advancing south, had fled to the east and after some 72 hours, Rangoon was taken. The arrival of Haydn's battalion in Rangoon was not, however, greeted with the enthusiasm awarded to the Allied liberating forces in France and the Low Countries. The Burmese assumed that the

9. The War against Japan - phase 1

During the period between the outbreak of war in September 1939 and the fall of France in 1940, the United States remained detached from events confident in their President's statement that his country would 'remain a neutral nation'. However, if Britain should fall into German hands, only the ocean would separate America's eastern seaboard from Hitler's mighty army, navy and air force.

Roosevelt quickly persuaded Congress to support a modernisation programme for the US Army and its Air Corps to help beleaguered Britain with supplies of arms, food and money. Even so, there was no mood in the nation for active participation in the conflict and that feeling persisted into 1941.

The Americans feared that their active participation in the war against Germany would provoke a Japanese attack, whilst by 1941 the last thing Hitler wanted was a war against the United States at the same time that he was busily engaged in his Russian campaign.

Meanwhile, on the other side of the Pacific Ocean the Japanese, though heavily engaged in a war in China, were seeking to benefit from the defeats sustained by the European colonial powers, France, Holland and Britain each of which held territories in the Far East. In September 1940 Japan, Italy and Germany signed a tripartite pact which guaranteed aid to the Japanese if they should become involved in a war with the United States and in April 1941 they signed a neutrality agreement with the Russians.

Although by now Japanese morale was sky high, two problems remained - the never-ending war in China and the economic war being waged against her, particularly by the Americans. In August 1941 the Americans tightened their economic sanctions and demanded that the Japanese stopped their aggressive actions against neighbouring countries or face 'any and all steps' which the Americans felt necessary to secure 'the safety and security of the United States'. Whilst talking continued the Japanese prepared for war and when, by the end of November, it was seen that further diplomatic activity was futile the stage was set for a pre-emptive strike against the Americans as a prelude to Japanese expansion to the south in search of oil and raw materials.

On Sunday 7 December 1941 the American Pacific Fleet was virtually destroyed as it lay at anchor in Pearl Harbor in Hawaii and what had previously been a largely European war now became one which encompassed the whole world with Britain, Russia and now the United States pitted against Germany, Italy and Japan. To Britain's great relief it was quickly agreed that aim number one was victory over Germany after which Italy would collapse and the Japanese would be defeated.

Initially every advantage lay with the Japanese because the British and Commonwealth forces were heavily engaged in the Atlantic and Mediterranean theatres in the war against Germany and Italy. The Japanese Army, Navy and Air Force quickly launched a great sweep into the south-west Pacific particularly aimed at the great British naval base at Singapore and the Philippines. The Japanese landed a force in northern Malaya with the intention of storming Singapore overland and when the only two British capital ships in the Pacific - the *Prince of Wales* and the *Repulse* - sought to counter this threat they were promptly sunk by a force of Japanese bombers.

The simultaneous Japanese attack on Hong Kong found the small garrison of British, Canadian and Indian troops hopelessly outnumbered and out-gunned and on 25 December their resistance ended.

During January 1942 the Japanese advanced down the Malayan peninsular towards Singapore and in early February stormed the city and port. On 15 February the British commander surrendered in what was described as the 'greatest defeat in the history of the British Empire' and some 130,000 British and Commonwealth troops became prisoners-of-war.

See - Alf Pike

arrival of the British would merely restore their prewar status as a British colony and they clearly would have preferred independence.

Following the meeting of the two Indian infantry divisions, Haydn's battalion was returned again to Bangalore where it prepared for the planned invasion of Malaya. The dropping of the atomic bombs and the surrender of Japan in August 1945 made this invasion unnecessary. Soon afterwards the 1st Lincolnshire Battalion joined the 26 Indian Infantry Division which was occupying Sumatra, one of the prewar Dutch East India colonies. Once again the Allied forces were greeted unenthusiastically by a local population intent on gaining its independence. Some bands of locals, armed and sometimes led by Japanese deserters, had to be disarmed before the occupation could be completed. Somewhat later, Hadyn's battalion was airlifted to the oilfields at Palembang in eastern Sumatra and again saw action fighting local insurgents who, in October 1945, had declared war on the Netherlands.

In October 1946, the regular soldiers in the 1st Battalion were sent back to the UK and Haydn found himself posted to the offices of ALFSEA (Allied Land Forces South-East Asia) in Singapore. Here, using the skills he learned at Hopper's, he performed office work for some six months. His next move was to do similar work in Hong Kong and it was from there in February 1947 that he was sent home by sea prior to his eventual demobilisation from York.

Information from

Haydn Cocking

Beatie Codd (later Cooper)

Petty Officer, 35002
Women's Royal Naval Service
Officer's Steward

Beatrice Sarah Codd was born in 1908, the daughter of George Henry Codd (a sloop's captain) and Alice Codd of 32 Far Ings Road, Barton-on-Humber. She had four brothers and one sister. She attended the Wesleyan School in Maltby Lane and later, when it

Beattie Codd.

opened, the County School in Castledyke. She left school aged 13 years and worked in domestic service in Barton. She volunteered to join the WRNS in 1942.

In May 1942, she was ordered to Rochester for training as an officer's steward and subsequently served in that capacity at *HMS Beaver* (the Royal Hotel in Grimsby), *HMS Wildfire* at Sheerness (where she was steward to the captain of the base), *HMS Beaver II* on Immingham Docks, and finally in 1945 at *HMS Demetrius* at Wetherby where she trained boys to be stewards. In 1945 she was promoted to the rank of petty officer. She left the WRNS on 11 May 1946 and it was recorded that she 'had carried out the duties of Petty Officer Wren Steward in the most capable manner. Is hardworking and possesses plenty of initiative, energy and common-sense. Takes charge well and has much moral courage.'

Before 1939 her life had been very much Barton-orientated so she is able to describe her years in the WRNS as a 'wonderful experience' which 'broadened the mind'. She particularly remembers guard duty at Rochester, standing in a hail of shrapnel from the hundreds of anti-aircraft guns in the dock area and also seeing a 'Doodlebug' (V1 flying bomb) flying inland over Immingham when she was stationed there.

Information from

Beattie Cooper (née Codd)

Wilfred Codd

Flight Sergeant, 538625
55 Bomber Squadron, Royal Air Force
General Duties

Wilfred Codd was born in 1918, the son of Mr John William and Mrs Mary Codd of Hull. The family moved back to Barton soon after Wilfred's birth. He attended the County School in Castledyke and afterwards first worked at the Ropery and subsequently with his father on a Humber sloop. His main hobby was walking.

Wanting to join the RAF Air-sea Rescue Branch, he travelled to London in March 1937 to sign on. However, when it was learned that he could not swim, he was told he could only enlist for general duties. If subsequently he learned to swim, he was to re-muster in the hope that he could join the Air-sea Rescue Branch.

He was sent to Uxbridge for three months initial training following which he moved to RAF Scampton where he performed general duties. In 1938 he was sent to No 55 Squadron, RAF Habbaniya in Iraq where he did a little bit of flying in Vincents - biplane bombers. These had a crew of three men: a pilot, an observer

Wilfred Codd in 1946.

and a rear gunner. Wilfred flew as rear gunner. A lot of time was spent on reconnaissance work over the Kurdish occupied part of northern Iraq and sometimes they were engaged in bombing raids.

He was in Iraq when the war broke out and soon afterwards, in late 1939, the Squadron was transferred to RAF Ismailia in Egypt. Here it was re-equipped with Blenheims. Wilfred's work was to maintain and rearm the planes whenever necessary. These planes were engaged in bombing missions against the Italian army in North Africa. Following the advance of the British army in 1940, the Squadron moved along the Egyptian coast using temporary runways in the desert **(7)**.

The German advance following the arrival of Rommel and the *Afrika Korps* caused the British to retreat into Egypt though 55 Squadron still used the desert strips. The Squadron helped the army at the Battle of El Alamein and, following this British victory, the planes were moved westwards to harass the retreating German army.

Following the German surrender in North Africa, the Squadron went to Greece but Wilfred was posted back to England. This involved him moving back to the Suez Canal to wait for a boat bound for England. Whilst there he was given charge of 12 German prisoners and when a boat did arrive, he travelled with them as far as Durban. There they were handed over and were sent to a British prisoner-of-war camp. Wilfred continued his journey home in some luxury on a former cruise liner. He volunteered to join the ship's gun crew and manned an Oerlikon on the upper deck.

10. The Convoy which saved Malta

Situated in the middle of the Mediterranean Sea, 1,000 miles from Gibraltar and 800 miles from Alexandria, is the tiny island of Malta which had been a British possession since 1814. During the period from 1940 to 1943 its 280,000 inhabitants were subjected to a constant aerial assault from the Axis powers which sought to dislodge the British from the island and thus become masters of the whole Mediterranean Sea from end to end. On many occasions its surrender seemed imminent but the indomitable spirit of the islanders and the valiant work of the minuscule British fighter and bomber force stationed there ensured that it was never taken and that it remained a constant thorn - *an unsinkable aircraft carrier* - in the side of the Italians and Germans as they sought to pursue their campaigns of conquest in North Africa.

Malta's worst sufferings came during 1942 when the enemy launched up to 10 bombing raids on the island every day. Food, fuel and ammunition supplies were in short supply and any convoys attempting to relieve the islanders' plight suffered severe losses from enemy air attacks. By the end of the year it has been calculated that the equivalent of some 100 tons of bombs had fallen on each square mile of the island, some 1,500 civilians had been killed and 24,000 buildings destroyed or damaged. On 15 April King George VI awarded the island the George Cross: 'To honour her brave people I award the George Cross to the island fortress of Malta, to bear witness to a heroism and devotion that will long be famous in history. George R. I.'

By mid 1942 the island's position was critical - supplies were practically exhausted and the population was becoming ever more hungry and exhausted. Unless a successful convoy could be organised it seemed more than likely that by mid-August the island would be forced to surrender. News of this once-and-for-all convoy - Operation *Pedestal* - could not be kept from the enemy who increased the numbers of submarines and aircraft in

On his arrival back in Liverpool in summer 1943 (he had by now been away some five years), he was sent to a small RAF station in the Romney Marshes in Kent. At this time the Allies were preparing for D-Day and Wilfred was in charge of a RAF support-group section whose role was to maintain aeroplanes and supply them with ammunition and other stores.

On D -Day + 3, his section was moved by boat from Newhaven to the Normandy coast where it was stationed at a temporary landing strip near Courseulles **(15)**. From here fighters flew to attack any German planes threatening the landings. The section, which now included many army personnel, moved eastwards following the advancing British army. It either laid down temporary airstrips or took over captured airfields. The temporary strips were formed with rolls of metal 'Somerfelt', six feet wide, which were laid in fields to provide a firm landing for the aircraft.

The section moved through France, Belgium, Holland and on into Germany. Wilfred was at Celle when the war ended and afterwards moved north into Denmark. He finally arrived in Copenhagen from where he was demobbed in late 1945.

Information form

Wilfred Codd

Betty Collingwood (later Cartledge)

ACW1, 439160
Women's Auxiliary Air Force
Balloon Operator, Flight Mechanic Airframe

Betty Collingwood was born in 1923, the daughter of Mr Sydney and Mrs Alice Collingwood of 5 East Acridge, Barton-on-Humber. She was educated at the County School and subsequently worked as a paint sprayer at Hopper's Cycle Works.

In December 1941, she volunteered to join the WAAFs and travelled to Lincoln where she signed on. From there she was sent to Bridgenorth in Shropshire where she did her initial training. She was next posted to Wythall near Birmingham where she did a nine month training course as a barrage balloon operator. This involved learning how to fly and maintain a balloon. Each balloon was filled with gas and tethered to a winch on the ground. Cable and ropes hung from the balloon and a small bomb was attached below the balloon. If an enemy aircraft hit the cables it would explode the bomb and thus be destroyed.

On completion of her training in 1942, she was moved to a balloon site at Attercliffe near Sheffield. Each site had one balloon looked after by some eight or nine WAAFs who lived in Nissen huts. They had to do their own cooking and washing. On receipt of a message warning of an imminent air raid, the balloons were launched.

By early 1944, the German air raids had ceased and the balloon crews were declared redundant. Betty was

---

the western Mediterranean. Eventually a force of 21 submarines, 784 enemy aircraft, 23 torpedo boats and what remained of the Italian fleet lay in wait for the Allied ships.

The Allies put together a convoy escort - Force Z - consummate with the importance of the venture. It was led by battleships *Nelson* and *Rodney* and also included an aircraft carrier squadron consisting of *Indomitable*, *Victorious* and *Eagle* (three carriers had never worked together before), three cruisers, a destroyer force of 14 ships, a close escort group designated Force X and other fleet oil tankers, submarines, corvettes and rescue tugs. The merchant ships in the convoy were among the fastest and most modern available. Most of them were British but two merchantmen and the tanker *Ohio* were American. They sailed from the Clyde and Scapa Flow on 2 August bound for the Mediterranean Sea which they entered on 10 August. The convoy was attacked repeatedly as it sailed towards Malta. It twisted and turned to avoid the enemy and its anti-aircraft gunners were continuously in action. The *Eagle* was soon sunk by a German U-boat, the *Indomitable*'s flight deck was hit, the heavy cruiser *Manchester* was crippled and eventually scuttled and nine of the merchantmen were sunk. A torpedo hit the vital tanker *Ohio* and for a while she lay stationary in the water and in danger of sinking. To save her she was lashed between two of the escorting destroyers, *Penn* and *Ledbury* and taken in tow by the minesweeper *Rye*.

Of the 14 merchant ships in the original convoy nine were sunk and only five damaged vessels reached the safety of the Grand Harbour. These latter included the *Ohio* which was finally nursed to safety, its decks awash but its vital fuel cargo intact. It seemed that every one on the island was present in Valetta to witness and applaud the arrival of their saviours. Twelve thousand tons of oil fuel, 3,600 tons of diesel and 32,000 tons of other supplies were quickly off-loaded. The islanders' rations were raised and hope for the future returned.

See - Ted Appleyard and Jack Austin

Betty Collingwood in 1941.

retrained as a flight mechanic - airframe at RAF Tern Hill in Shropshire. Following the six month training period, she remained at this camp looking after Harvards, Lancasters and Wellingtons.

In April 1946 she was demobbed from Bridgenorth.

Information from

Betty Cartledge

Ernie Coulam

Sergeant, 4807471
Lincolnshire Regiment
Instructor

Ernest Coulam was born in 1914, the son of Mr Charles Enzor Watkinson and Miss Florence Coulam of 33 Marsh Lane, Barton-on-Humber. He attended the Church School in Queen Street and after leaving worked variously at Hopper's Cycle Works, Major Sanderson's yard at Barrow Haven and Blyth's yard in Barton. He was a member of the Oddfellows' Friendly Society.

On 24 June 1940, along with a number of other Bartonians including John Dent and Arthur Gaddie, he was conscripted into the army and reported for initial training at the Grammar School in Spalding. The men lived in bell tents on the school playing field and did their 'square bashing' on the nearby main road. After six weeks, Ernie, John and Arthur were sent back to Barton as class B reservists to help produce the vast numbers of clay tiles which were needed to replace those blown off London buildings during the blitz **(6)**.

On 19 December 1941 he reported back to the Burton Road Barracks in Lincoln to carry on his army service. There he was placed in one of the infantry companies and underwent 10 weeks of further training. At the end of this period whilst John Dent and Arthur Gaddie went off to Africa, Ernie, promoted lance corporal, was chosen to stay behind in Lincoln and act as an instructor of new recruits.

At that time the Burton Road Barracks housed 4000-5000 recruits. Ernie became a lance corporal in 4 Recruit Company. Every Thursday, some 400 new recruits arrived at Burton Road and were put into one of six recruit companies for six weeks of initial training. Each of these companies had a sergeant, a corporal and two lance corporals in charge who were required to give the new recruits instruction in drill, the use of weapons and gas procedures. At the end of the six week period, the few really physically fit men in each company were transferred into one of the five infantry companies where they underwent a further ten weeks of training before being placed in one of the battalions of the Lincolnshire Regiment. The less fit recruits were transferred into another arm of the services - perhaps the Royal Artillery, REME, RASC or RAOC. The infantry companies did a lot of their field training at either Riseholme or on Greetwell Common.

Ernest Coulam.

Ernie stayed at Lincoln for the rest of the war constantly training new recruits, rising to the rank of sergeant. A few weeks after VE Day, he was given early demobilisation and sent back to Barton to help produce the thousands of roof tiles which would be needed in the building of new houses for the returning service men and women.

Information from

Ernest Coulam

Georges Coupland

Stoker First Class, LT/KX 126759
Royal Navy
Stoker First Class

Georges William Coupland was born in 1919, the son of Mr Henry Bedford and Mrs Florence Coupland of Victoria Terrace, Barton-on-Humber. He was educated at St. Chad's School and on leaving worked for six years as a brazier at Hopper's Cycle Works.

In March 1941, he volunteered to join the Royal Navy and after initial training at *HMS Royal Arthur* and *HMS*

Georges and Gladys Coupland on their wedding day in 1943.

Europa, spent the rest of the war on various ships escorting convoys of merchantmen **(6)**.

He was released from Lowestoft in March 1946.

Information from

Sandra Robinson (daughter)

Ken Cox

Corporal, 1952972
Royal Engineers

Kenneth Cox was born in 1922, the son of Mr Walter and Mrs Gertrude Cox (née Winship) of 46 Ramsden Avenue, Barton-on-Humber. He was educated at the Church School in Queen Street and subsequently worked as an excavator operator for Howard's of Lincoln and Bedford. He was a keen road cycle racer, member of Barton Wheelers and Barton Boys' Club. He attended St. Mary's church.

He joined the army at Aldershot on 15 January 1941 when he was aged 18 and there undertook his initial training. He was moved from there to No 1 METU (Mechanical Equipment Training Unit) at Newark. There he was promoted to corporal and was employed as an instructor on mechanical equipment - excavators, armoured bulldozers, cranes, derricks etc. Although he was assured that he would not be moved abroad, he was in fact posted to Sicily where he joined 135

Walt Cox (seated) and his brother Ken in Salonica in 1946.

Company ME, Royal Engineers and was employed rebuilding roads and bridges which had been destroyed and clearing debris from ports.

From Sicily he was moved to Taranto in Italy (12) where he was again employed repairing war-damaged roads, bridges and docks. His platoon slowly made its way northwards and finally ended up just to the north of Rome.

In early 1945, he was posted to Greece to help in the suppression of the communist uprising there. During this period he travelled into Albania from where some of the communists were infiltrating into Greece. His main job during this period was to maintain the heavy mechanical equipment being used by the Royal Engineers. A highlight of his years abroad occurred when he was based in Greece. He discovered that his brother Walter (qv) was stationed at Salonica, not too far away. His commanding officer sent him on a delivery there and they were able to spend a weekend together on Walt's 26th birthday.

Ken was demobbed from Aldershot on 2 February 1947.

Information from

Ken Cox

Irene Cox (wife)

Walt Cox

Fusilier, 158154
Royal Artillery/Durham Light Infantry
Gunner/Dispatch Rider

Walter Clarence Cox was born in 1920 the, son of Mr Walter and Mrs Gertrude Cox of 46 Ramsden Avenue, Barton-on-Humber. He attended the Church School in Queen Street and on leaving was employed by Howard's of Lincoln driving a steam roller. His hobby was pigeon racing.

He joined the army as part of the 1st Militia in 1939 and did his initial training in the Royal Artillery at Aldershot. He was trained on 25lb field guns.

He fought in the Middle East Campaign (7) and in Italy (12). He was also part of the force sent to Greece at the height of the civil war. Whilst there he met his brother with whom he celebrated his 26th birthday (see under Ken Cox, [qv]). Towards the end of the war he was transferred into the Durham Light Infantry as a dispatch rider and from there he was demobbed in 1945.

Information from

Ken and Irene Cox (brother and sister-in-law)

Herbert Dent

Gunner, Private, 1571071
Royal Artillery, West Yorkshire Regiment,
Northamptonshire Regiment
Gunner/Infantryman

Herbert Allman Dent was born in 1912, the son of Mr George and Mrs Martha Dent of Soutergate, Barton-on-Humber. He was educated at the Church School and on leaving was employed by Eastman's, later J.H. Dewhurst Ltd, the butchers' in High Street. He was a founder member of Barton Wheelers which at that time met in Hopper's Club in Whitecross Street. In January 1938, he married Beryl Bell at Holy Trinity church, Barrow and took up residence at Sunnybank, Barton.

On 15 July 1940, he was conscripted into the army and reported for initial training at Royal Artillery Depot at Catterick Camp before being transferred to Hartlepool where he joined a coastal defence battery of 6-inch naval guns pointing out to sea. He spent six weeks training there before being moved to Spital near Berwick-on-Tweed. There he became part of the permanent battery which manned two 6-inch guns defending the mouth of the River Tweed. There were four platoons of men in the battery - two platoons manned the guns whilst the other two were off-duty in the billets which were housed in a local schoolroom which had been taken over by the army. The guns

Herbert Dent.

Leaflet dropped by the Germans onto the Anzio beachhead in an attempt to provoke friction between the British and American troops and undermine the morale of the British forces.

were only fired 'in action' once when an unidentified ship approached the river and warning shots were fired at it. It proved to be 'friendly'. Herbert served at this battery until 1943 when a Home Guard unit came to take over. When these men had completed their training, they took the battery over and Herbert was moved into an infantry barracks at Berwick from where he was transferred into the West Yorkshire Regiment and underwent infantry training.

In early 1944, he was moved to Weybourne in Norfolk for more intensive infantry training. Following a short period of leave, he was moved by train to Liverpool where he boarded the troopship *Capetown Castle* - next stop Naples **(12)**!

From there he moved to a transit camp at San Martino where he was transferred into the 2nd Battalion of the Northamptonshire Regiment. His next move was again to Naples where he was shipped overnight to the Anzio beachhead **(13)**. The Allies were still not comfortably established here and the Germans were making every effort to push the Allies back into the sea. Herbert landed under shellfire and soon found himself digging in on a railway embankment not far inland. After a week there his B company was moved 'up the line' into an area called 'The Fortress'. Herbert describes this area as 'rough'. The company in front of his (C company) was captured and only spirited resistance by B company saved the day and the German advance was repulsed. After this engagement, Herbert remembers seeing a stretcher-bearer of the Northamptonshire Regiment standing on a ridge above the trenches talking to a German stretcher-bearer - they were telling each other where their casualties lay. It made him think - 'What was this war about?'

After about 10 days in 'The Fortress', B company was relieved and went to the railway embankment. Following a week's rest there, his company was moved to the coastal sector. By now the bridgehead was secure and the Allies were preparing to break out. The company advanced up the coast chasing the retreating German army.

Just before the Northamptonshires arrived at Rome, it was declared an 'open city' and the advance stopped. The Battalion was moved back for rest and regrouping and was sent from Taranto to Port Said in Egypt.

The Battalion was sent for a week's rest in the Gaza Strip. From there it was moved to Baalbeck in Syria and whilst there, Herbert spent his Christmas 1944 leave visiting Jerusalem and Bethlehem. He also spent a day in Beirut. During this time, another Bartonian, Lieutenant Geoffrey Brooks, son of Colonel Brooks, took command of Herbert's platoon.

In early 1945, his next move was back to Italy. By now the Allies had advanced into northern Italy and after a short spell there, the Battalion was moved to southern France. It landed at Marseilles from where it moved across France and into Belgium. From there he moved across the Rhine and into Germany and when the war ended, the Battalion was preparing to capture Lubeck docks.

Following VE Day, Herbert moved to nearby Schwerin. Whilst there, Herbert's Battalion was engaged as an occupation force. Part of its work was to prevent the many Poles in the town wreaking revenge on the German inhabitants. They also mounted guard on the frontier between the Allied and Russian zones to prevent 'East' Germans moving to the west. From there he got a week's leave. His next move was to Gottingen. From there he was sent home for demobilisation from York.

Information from

Herbert Dent

Jack Dimoline

Sergeant, 1513473
No 53 Searchlight Regiment Royal Artillery
attached to the Northumberland Fusiliers
Searchlight Operator

Jack Dimoline was born in 1919, the son of Mr Charles and Mrs Ethel Maude Dimoline of 34 Pasture Road, Barton-on-Humber. He was educated at the Church of England school and on leaving was employed in the Brakes and Handlebar Department at Hopper's Cycle Works. He was a member of the Hopper's Club in Whitecross Street.

In May 1939, he registered along with all Britain's other 20 year-olds in 'The First Militia' but was not called up until 16 October. He reported for three months of initial training at the Bradbury Lines Barracks at Hereford where he did his 'square-bashing' and was taught to man a searchlight.

His first posting was to Sedgefield Racecourse between Middlesbrough and Newcastle where he was a member of a searchlight unit attached to the 5th Battalion of the Northumberland Fusiliers. Its job was to pick out enemy aircraft which were intending to bomb vital industrial sites in the North-east, particularly the great chemical complex at Billingham. He became one of the eleven men (one sergeant, one lance corporal and nine privates) who operated a single searchlight. These had a 90 cm mirror (later they had a light with 150 cm mirror) in front of which there was a 75 volt, 150 amp light which gave out two million candle power. The heat given off by such a light would melt the snow off the roof of a house some distance away! For defensive purposes each searchlight unit was armed with a Lewis machine gun (later a .5" Browning) which would be used against enemy aircraft which attempted to destroy the light by flying down its beam and opening up with machine guns or cannons. The men worked a rota system in which each took a turn as cook. They were required to be on duty every night but had a day off every week. Attached to each group of searchlights was a sound locator which listened out for enemy aircraft and two spotters who, hopefully, made visual contact and identified the enemy planes. Each light had a RT (radio transmitter) set with which it maintained contact with the headquarters from where the order to 'stand to' was issued. During the height of the blitz in 1940, Jack was on duty and his searchlight was in action almost every night **(6)**.

In early 1941, Jack's unit moved to Ponteland near Newcastle and it set up its searchlight in a farmer's field. In mid 1942, a 'boffin' visited and fixed a new locational device to their searchlight. This proved to be an early radar set. From then on it was quite easy for Jack's light to find the enemy and lead onto the target all the other lights in the unit. In late 1942, he moved to RAF Ouston where they perfected the radar-guided searchlight system.

His next move was to RAF Scorton near Catterick where for about three months the searchlight was set up at the end of a runway used by a Canadian squadron of Beaufighter twin-engined planes. At this time the Germans were sending over small groups of bombers - three or four at a time - to keep the British defences on their toes but causing little actual damage.

In mid-1943, the unit moved to Alnwick which was on the path taken by enemy bombers making their way towards Glasgow. Whilst there, a new searchlight system was introduced. No longer were the lights to be scattered singly over an area of countryside but they were to be deployed in clusters of three lights at each location.

Later in 1943, Jack was moved to the Isle of Wight. The Allies had heard rumours that the Germans were about to launch a new, secret weapon against Britain and it was thought that the searchlight's radar would be particularly useful in locating and tracking these devices. Whilst waiting for something

Jack Dimoline (right) in Tromso, Norway, 1945.

to happen, Jack remembers standing on the north coast of the island looking over the Solent. Five great battleships dominated the scene and it was virtually impossible to see any of the Hampshire coast which was hidden behind an unbelievable mass of Allied shipping. When he went to look again on one morning in early June, all the ships had vanished as if by magic - Jack knew that the invasion of Europe was in hand.

The Germans' secret weapon - the V1 flying bomb or 'Doodlebug' - began to fall on England just after D-Day **(16)** and Jack (recently promoted corporal) particularly remembers seeing his first one. By now he was skilled in the recognition of enemy aircraft and at first the sight of this small flying object with a flame spurting from its tail had him completely baffled. He soon got to know them only too well. They flew too low for the heavy anti-aircraft guns to be effective and the searchlights were totally unnecessary as their flaming engines made them all too easy to see with the naked eye. Once sighted, every small and medium gun in the area opened up in an attempt to shoot them down. When their engines cut out, their progress was totally unpredictable and they could glide off in any direction.

Jack's next move was to Dovercourt near Harwich - 'Doodlebug Alley' as it was known. Here he was billeted in a house in Shingle Street in Orford Ness and, having left his by now useless searchlight on the Isle of Wight, he was employed for some three months moving anti-aircraft guns from inland sites to the coastline. Once sited on the seashore and firing out to sea, they were able to use the new proximity shells which exploded when they came close to their target.

By early 1945, the danger from these weapons was over and Jack was posted to the New Forest where he underwent retraining as an infantryman in 638 Regiment of the Northumberland Fusiliers. Training completed, his unit moved to Glasgow from where it was shipped to Tromso in Norway. Just before it arrived, the boat sailed past the upturned hull of the German battleship *Tirpitz* - an awesome sight. Jack landed in Norway two days after VE Day and was soon promoted sergeant. For the next six months he was employed all over Norway sorting out the defeated German garrison, sending some men home and detaining members of the SS for further interrogation.

On 7 December 1945, the Regiment's work done, it was disbanded and Jack found himself in the 630 Essex Regiment. He was posted to Bishop's Stortford where he helped the Commandant run the camp.

He was finally demobilised in February 1946.

Information from

Jack Dimoline

11. Operation *Torch*

On 8 November 1942 Allied troops, mainly Americans led by Dwight Eisenhower but including Free French and British forces, landed in the French territories of Morocco and Algeria. This action might answer the Russian pleadings for a second front which would relieve some of the pressure on their forces. For the first time it would bring American troops into the war against Germany and the use of their troops in the lead would hopefully avoid some of the political problems which may have arisen if the British (who had criticised the French after Dunkirk, attacked her fleet at Oran and sheltered de Gaulle) had been the major contributor to the campaign.

The initial landings faced some resistance from the Vichy-controlled *Armée d'Afrique* but by 11 November most of the French soldiers and sailors had joined the Allied side. The intention was next to move eastwards into Tunisia where no landings had taken place. Once again initial hesitation on the part of the Allied commanders allowed the Germans to organise their defences and Hitler, infuriated by what he saw as the perfidy of the Vichy government and its troops, ordered the occupation of the whole of France and the transfer of three more divisions to Tunisia. When the Allies did begin their advance they countered fierce resistance and this became even stronger when in January 1943 Rommel's retreating forces, weakened but still in good fighting order, also arrived in Tunisia. By February the German and Italian force totalled some 100,000 men. The opportunity for a quick victory had been lost and a bitter campaign ensued.

The 8th Army had to break the former French defences at the Mareth Line and then they and the troops from Algeria faced sharp counter-attacks further north. In mid February, a fierce battle was fought at the Kasserine Pass through which the Axis powers attempted to push and cut the Allied armies in two. That thrust was defeated and in late March Montgomery took the offensive and the 8th Army finally breached the Mareth Line. On 7 April, troops from Operation *Torch* striking from the east rendezvoused with elements of the Eighth Army from the west.

The Axis losses mounted, supplies dwindled and the RAF mounted ceaseless bombardments. Slowly but surely the enemy was squeezed into ever smaller enclaves around Tunisia and Bizerta with no hope of being reinforced or relieved. By early May, the Axis position was clearly hopeless. On the 7th the British 1st Army took Bizerta and on the same day Tunis, fell to the Americans. The 13th saw the complete surrender of the Axis forces.

Alf Drury

Private, 1807529
550 Company, Royal Army Service Corps
Army Catering Corps
Butcher-cook

Alfred Drury was born in 1921, the son of Mr Alonza and Mrs Fanny Drury of 22 West Acridge, Barton-on-Humber. He was educated at the County School and on leaving worked as a butcher-cutter first for Mrs Cox, butcher in High Street, and later for J.H. Dewhurst.

He attended St. Chad's church where he was a choir boy with his brother Harry and he was a long-time member of Barton Wheelers Cycle Club.

Alf was conscripted into the forces and joined the RASC. He was employed as a butcher-cook whilst in the forces. Alf saw service in North Africa **(7)** and Italy. Whilst in Italy **(12)** he was 'claimed' by his older brother, Harry Drury, and joined his unit. This move seems to have involved him transferring from the RASC into the Army Catering Corps.

His brother Cyril died on active service in 1940 (see *Barton Remembered 1939-1945; Part One, Lest We Forget*, p 29)

He was demobbed from Aldershot in September 1946.

Alf Drury.

Information from

Betty Drury (widow)

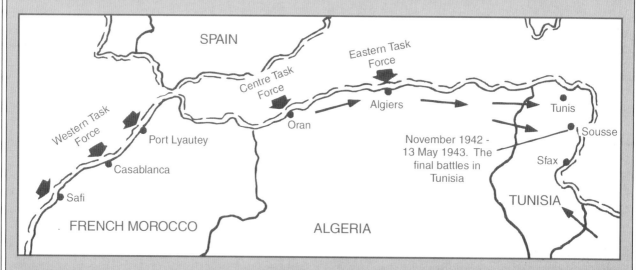

Some 250,000 Italians and Germans became prisoners-of-war in the greatest German disaster since Stalingrad. Africa was in Allied control, fear of Spanish intervention in the war was gone, the Suez canal was safe and Italy was clearly the next target - the 'springboard to Berlin!'

See - Ted Bones, Chris Braithwaite, Percy Chappell, Jack Clipson, Wilfred Eayres, Cecil Elwood, Hector and Stan Lawtey and Arthur Sobey

Map 5. Operation *Torch*, the landings in French North Africa on 8 November 1942, and the drive to Tunis. The Western Task Force under Patton sailed from the United States and landed at Safi, Casablanca and Port Lyautey; the Centre (American) and Eastern (British) Task Forces both sailed from Britain and landed at Oran and Algiers respectively.

Gerald Ducker

Radio Officer, British Merchant Navy
Radio Communications Officer

Gerald Vernon Ducker was born in 1919, the son of Mr Kenneth V. and Mrs Dorothy Maude Ducker of 8 Queen Street, Barton-on-Humber. He attended Barton Grammar School and Hull Technical College where he trained to be a radio officer in the Merchant Navy. He sang in the choir at St. Mary's Church.

He first went to sea in March 1940 and served continuously (on 17 different ships) until he resigned from the Merchant Navy in 1945. His wartime voyages, often in convoys, took him round the world and he served in the Atlantic **(6)**, Pacific and India-Burma theatres. He writes:

'Ships in convoy presented a magnificent sight at sea. The ships advanced on a broad front, lane after lane, as far as the eye could see. The escort ships were constantly patrolling on the outside, circling in from behind and on each side. They were mainly destroyers, frigates and corvettes, and very occasionally an Allied submarine, battleship or a small escort aircraft carrier. The speed of the convoy was the speed of the slowest ship which normally ranged from 5 to 10 knots. Air cover across the Atlantic was provided by long-range land-based planes from the UK, Iceland and Newfoundland. However, there was a large area in the middle of the North Atlantic which was not covered and consequently the U-boats concentrated on this area and made most of the sinkings. Occasionally the Germans sent out large four-engined bombers to track down a convoy's location and notify the U-boats as well as bombing and sinking some ships.'

As for cargoes, every ship was fully loaded with every kind of weapon, food, tanks, trucks, aeroplanes, ammunition of all kinds, gasoline, fuel oil, timber - even a large crate of Cuban cigars which every ship carried as a gift to Churchill from the people of Cuba. Needless to say the large crate was stowed in the captain's cabin!

Troop convoys were a big target for the Germans but they were always in fast convoys and had many more armed escorts.

Most British and Allied ships were armed defensively with a 4-inch gun on the stern and various anti-aircraft guns. The Royal Navy provided a number of sailors to man these guns in addition to some of the ship's crew.

His most vivid memory is of his ship - the *Empire Moonbeam* - being sunk by a German U-boat whilst part of a convoy travelling west to New York in 1942. The ship, in ballast, left Glasgow in late August 1942 and joined convoy ON127. The torpedo struck the engine room and killed most of the engine room staff. The ship caught fire and was later hit by a torpedo from another U-boat and subsequently sank. Fortunately, along with some 150 other survivors, he was picked from the sea by an escorting corvette, *HMCS Arvida* of the Royal Canadian Navy. He was landed safely at St. John's, Newfoundland where the local newspaper reported below a photograph the arrival of the survivors:

'Her decks jammed with survivors the H.M.C.S. Arvida reaches port. There were some stretcher cases but for the most part the men look healthy, despite their ordeal of more than three hours in the water. Three hours - it seemed like an eternity - when they watched their companions slip away ... They couldn't hang on any longer as the carley floats kept capsizing. They watched the ships of the convoy slip by, grey wraiths in the night, but the sea was infested with submarines and under these conditions, merchants ships must not stop. A sitting target is the U-boat's delight. So for hours the shouting of these men was lost in the night as they bobbed about in the water or clung to the rafts.'

Convoy ON127 lost seven ships and the escorting destroyer *HMCS Ottawa* whilst it sailed through that most dangerous area in mid-Atlantic. It was attacked ceaselessly for five days and nights.

Gerald travelled by train from St. John's to Vancouver where he joined a recently-built ship which sailed to England loaded with war supplies. On another

Gerald Ducker in 1945.

occasion his ship was attacked by German bombers in the entrance to the River Humber off Grimsby.

Information from

Gerald Ducker

Clarke Dunn MBE, DFC

Squadron Leader, 78455
Royal Air Force
Navigator

Arthur Clarke Dunn was the born in 1913, the son of Mr Arthur William and Mrs Anetia Dunn of Barrow Road, Barton-on-Humber. He was educated at the County School and Malet Lambert School in Hull. On leaving, he worked for Bladon's Department Store in Hull and later for W.H. Goodman's, an auctioneer and valuer. He married Winifred Friend at Cottingham church in the years before the war.

Clarke Dunn.

In early 1939, he joined the RAF Reserve and did initial training at Brough. In September 1939, he was called up into the RAF. His less than perfect eyesight prevented him becoming a pilot and he was trained as a navigator. Details of his service were recorded in the 50th Anniversary Booklet of RAF Patrington published in 1968:

'Squadron Leader Arthur Clarke Dunn, M.B.E., D.F.C., is now [1968] the chief Administrative Officer at R.A.F. Patrington. He joined the Royal Air Force right at the beginning of the War and, after a short period in France, he was sent to the Middle East taking part in operations in the Western Desert, Greece, Crete, Transjordan and Iraq. While he was in Greece, he was shot down over Valona, Albania, by an Italian plane and made his way back through enemy lines - part of the way on a donkey! He took part as a leading navigator in the Battle of Cape Matapan (8) and later held an administrative job in the Desert Air Force H.Q. On his return to England in 1943, he took part in intruder operations and flew in the famous low-level daylight attack of the Gestapo H.Q. in Denmark (19). Squadron Leader Clarke Dunn was made a member of the Order of the British Empire in 1944 and was awarded the Distinguished Flying Cross in 1945.

The citation awarding him the DFC reads:

'Flight Lieutenant Dunn has participated in many day and night sorties. He has served in Libya, Greece, Crete, Syria and Iraq, his most noteworthy action being in the Battle of Cape Matapan. During the Grecian campaign he was shot down over Bologna and had to walk back to his base. He also took part in the low level attack on the Gestapo Headquarters at Aarhus. Flight Lieutenant Dunn has proved himself to be a navigator of exceptional ability and his courage and devotion to duty have always been of the highest order.'

Information from

John William Dunn (brother)

Le Morrison, Historical Branch, RAF

Wilf Eayres

Driver Mechanic, 4810110
Lincolnshire Regiment/Royal Army Service
Corps
Driver

Wilfred Eayres was born in 1923, the son of Mr Wilfred and Mrs Ena Eayres of 3 Newport, Barton-on-Humber. He was educated at both the Church School and the County School. Both Wilf and his brother Raymond (see *Barton Remembered 1939-1945; Part One, Lest We Forget*, pp 31-32) attended the Methodist Sunday School and were asked to attend the Church of England Sunday School if they wished to continue attending the Church School in Queen Street. When they refused to do so, the Methodist minister made arrangements for them to transfer to the County

School.

On leaving school, he worked for Mr J.P. Maltby, a poultry farmer, on Tofts Road. He was later employed in the Machine Shop at Hopper's Cycle Works, at Leaning's farm and just before he went into the army on Elsham and Kirmington aerodromes helping to build the runways. He was a member of the local Boy Scouts' troop and the Barton Boys' Club. He was a member of the Sons of Temperance Friendly Society.

In June 1942, he was called up and reported for initial training at the Lincolnshire Regiment barracks at Burton Road in Lincoln. After about nine weeks, he volunteered to transfer into the RASC and was sent to Hadrian's Camp in Carlisle where he completed a driving course. His next move, in late 1942, was to 30 Motor Ambulance Corps at Kingussie near Aviemore in Scotland. There he joined the remnants of a RASC ambulance unit which had returned from Dunkirk. Wilf and his companions brought the unit back up to full strength. The unit had three platoons in each of which there were 28 ambulances, a few auxiliary vehicles (carrying water and other supplies) and some dispatch riders. One medical orderly accompanied every six vehicles. The ambulance which Wilf drove could carry four stretcher cases or twelve walking wounded. He spent Christmas there and had his first taste of haggis!

Wilfred Eayres.

In early 1943, the unit was moved to Shipley, near Bradford where it received refresher training which included driving and shooting. From there he travelled by train to Greenock where he boarded a troopship bound for Algiers **(11)**. He landed there at the end of February 1943.

From there the unit moved all over the battle area in North Africa taking casualties from field hospitals near to the front line to the main military hospitals in the rear. Sometimes, however, seriously wounded men would be put on trains, boats or aeroplanes for transfer to England.

At the end of the Africa Campaign, the unit was near Tunis where they remained until Sicily was invaded in June 1944. In July, Wilf's platoon was shipped in a tank landing craft to Syracuse from where it moved to its new base a seaside village some 20 miles to the north. Wilf's ambulance was loaned to a field ambulance unit and it was during this period that he served nearest to the front line bringing casualties from the battle zone back to the field hospital. On one occasion he had to pick up some casualties from a tank which was still burning when the ambulance arrived.

This was the period when units were being moved back to England in preparation for the Normandy landings. Wilf's unit was not among those chosen. Sicily **(12)** was soon conquered and Wilf's unit moved across into the 'toe' of Italy. Soon after landing on the Italian mainland, Wilf came across an elderly lady picking up driftwood on the beach. He enquired why she had not, like the rest of the local population, fled on the arrival of the Allied army. He was amazed to be told that she was English, had married an Italian before the war started, and had been born in Hull. She knew Barton very well!

The unit moved on to Taranto where they were able to see the wreckage of the Italian fleet which had been destroyed by Swordfish aircraft of the Royal Navy. From there Wilf moved up the Adriatic coast through Bari and Brindisi. Whilst he was at Bari, a lone German bomber attacked the tightly-packed Allied ships in the harbour and inflicted heavy damage and lots of casualties. It would appear that one of the bombs hit an ammunition ship which exploded with devastating results. Wilf was engaged moving casualties from the ships to the nearest military hospital.

He continued to serve throughout the Italian campaign and variously visited Naples, Rome, Florence, Venice and Milan. Following the end of the fighting in Italy, he had a short spell in Austria as part of the army of occupation. After VE Day, Wilf was moved to Monza near Milan and drove trucks taking English soldiers to Vilac in Austria on the first leg of their journey back to England. After doing this for about a month, the railway connection was restored and troops were thereafter

12. The Italian Campaign

By May 1943, the Allied victory in North Africa was complete and plans were put in hand to attack Sicily and Italy - the 'soft underbelly' of Europe. Having lost its best divisions, Italian morale was low and a speedy conquest of the peninsular seemed likely.

First, in early June, the islands of Pantelleria and Lampedusa which lay between Tunisia and Sicily were shelled and bombed into submission.

The landings on Sicily - Operation *Husky* - took place on 10 July. Ten Italian and three German divisions faced General Alexander's XV Army Group which consisted of Patton's 7th US Army and Montgomery's 8th Army.

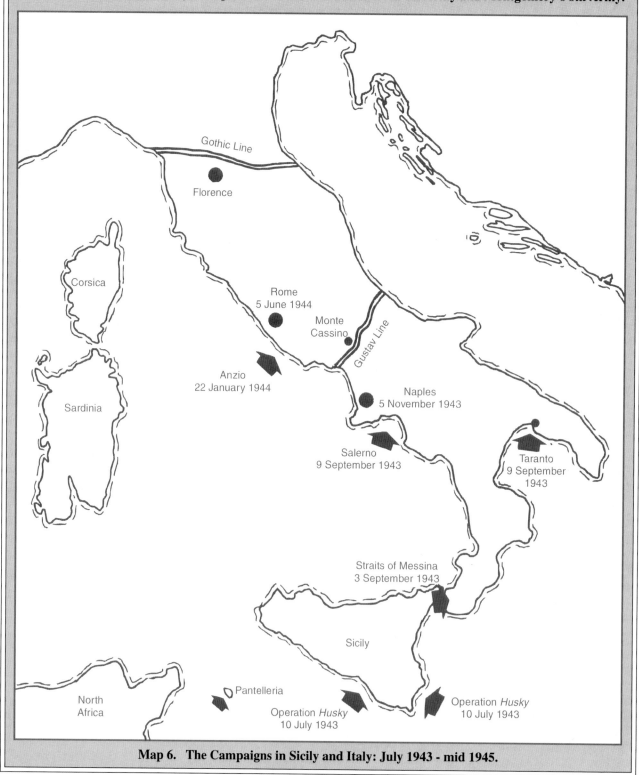

Map 6.   The Campaigns in Sicily and Italy: July 1943 - mid 1945.

In total, the force consisted of some 3,266 ships, 160,000 men, 1,008 guns, and 600 tanks. Within 38 days, resistance was ended and some 100,000 Axis prisoners-of-war were taken. Unfortunately, four enemy divisions, some 88,000 men, escaped to the Italian mainland, included among which was the crack German Herman Göering Panzer Division.

By early September, Italy's fascist leader of the previous 21 years, Benito Mussolini, had been deposed and executed and the new Italian leader, Marshal Pietro Badoglio, had signed an unconditional surrender and taken Italy out of the war. However, Hitler decided that German troops would carry on the fight in Italy with Field Marshal Kesselring in command.

On 3 September 1943, Montgomery's 8th Army crossed the Straits of Messina and landed on Italian soil. Meeting only light resistance it advanced speedily. On the 9th, the British 1st Airborne Division took the Italian naval base at Taranto and on the same day, the main Allied landings by Mark Clark's 5th Army - Operation *Avalanche* - took place at Salerno, south of Naples. The intention was that Montgomery should clear the peninsular south of Salerno whilst Clark was to push speedily on towards Naples. For some time, the Salerno landings were fiercely opposed by the main body of German troops and it was not until 15 September that the Allies were able to move north. On 5 September Naples was taken, unfortunately not before the Germans had undertaken an orgy of destruction which included the burning of some 200,000 priceless books and manuscripts held in the rooms of the city's Royal Society.

Further advance northwards was painfully slow in the face of fierce German opposition in rugged terrain and exceptionally wet weather. On 13 October, the 5th Army crossed the River Volturno but then came up against the German's Gustav Line of defences which stretched along the River Garigliano just south of Monte Cassino. Assaults during late 1943 and early 1944 failed to take the commanding hill on which the monastery stood and it was not until May that it finally fell into Allied hands.

Meanwhile, in January 1944, another Allied amphibious landing had taken place at Anzio, south of Rome. Once again initial success was followed by a period of stalemate and it was not until May that a break out from Anzio was possible and a general advance began. (See also p 77 for Anzio Beachhead).

On 5 June the Allies entered Rome, an event described by Churchill as 'memorable and glorious'.

Kesselring organised a good retreat and his troops fell back through various defensives lines and by mid-August had taken up positions on the Gothic Line north of Florence. In September 1944, this line was finally breached but the onset of the Italian winter again hindered further advances and it was not until April 1945, following the withdrawal of German troops to re-enforce the European and Russian fronts, that the Axis front in Italy finally collapsed totally.

It had taken 20 long, long months to clear the Italian peninsular - far, far longer than had ever been expected when the campaign began.

See - Clifford Altoft, Geoffrey Blakeborough, Ted Bones, Chris Braithwaite, Alan Bromfield, Jack Cartledge, Percy Chappell, Jack Clipson, Herbert Dent, Alfred Drury, Wilfred Eayres, Cecil Elwood, Noel Kitching, Hector Lawtey and Arthur Sobey

transported by rail. In September 1945, Wilf himself got a month's leave back in Barton during which time he was married to Emily Sleight at the Methodist church in Barrow-on-Humber.

On his return to Italy, he found that his unit had been disbanded and, after a short spell in a transit camp, he was moved as a driver to a Guards' unit at Pula in Yugoslavia (now Croatia). Here he was engaged on the 'mail-run' between Pula and Trieste - a distance of some 90 miles. During the drive up the coast he could view the wreck of the Italian liner *Rex* - a ship which had held the Blue Riband for the fastest crossing of the Atlantic.

In mid-1946, he was sent back to England and was demobilised at Woking in Surrey.

Information from

Wilf Eayres

Cecil Elwood

Lance Corporal, 2348066
Royal Corps of Signals
Teleprinter Operator

Cecil Elwood was born in Barton in August 1916. He attended Barton County School and Brigg Grammar School and subsequently worked as a sorting clerk and telegraphist at the Post Office in Barton. His hobbies were badminton and hockey, and he enjoyed singing with the Methodist chapel choirs in Barton and Goxhill.

He joined the Royal Corps of Signals at Prestatyn in North Wales in July 1940 and there received training to be a teleprinter operator. After finishing initial training, he moved to various places in Wales, England and Scotland. Whilst down at Bromley in December 1940, he became part of the 96 Telegraph Operating Section and he remained with that unit throughout the whole of the war.

In January 1941 the unit moved to Edinburgh and from there in March he was sent on detachment to Kinross where he joined the staff of the Signal Office at 4 Liaison HQ in the Polish Army. He remained there until December 1941 when he rejoined his company in Edinburgh.

In April 1942, he was posted from Edinburgh to Doncaster and his unit stayed there for some five months. From Doncaster he moved to Wimbledon

before, on 11 November 1942, being entrained to Greenock in Scotland. There he embarked on the *SS Duchess of York* and was landed in Algiers on 22 November **(11)**. From there he spent time at Setif and Souk Ahras working on the lines of communication between Algiers (HQ of combined 1st British Army and the American Forces in North Africa) and Tunis, the location of the fighting troops at the front.

In September 1944, following the invasion of Italy, he was moved to Naples **(12)**. Whilst there he visited the local NAAFI which was housed in the King's Palace, Pompeii and Sorrento. At Sorrento the was served with the most delicious cream buns he has ever eaten!

From Naples he moved to the transit camp at Leghorn from where, on a free afternoon, he visited Pisa. His next move, in April 1945, was to Marseilles where he joined a convoy which took him through recently liberated France to Belgium. From there he moved first to the small German village of Burgsteinfurt and then on to Munster. There he worked in the signals company office until he was demobilised in May 1946.

He has memories of meeting other Bartonians whilst he was abroad. In North Africa he bumped into George Oldridge, Alfred Griffiths and Roy Foster.

Information from

Cecil Elwood

Cecil Elwood at Prestatyn Training Camp in mid-1940.

Robert Fairbank

Private, 3965913
5th Battalion, Welsh Regiment,
Rifleman

Robert Fairbank was born on 8 May 1918, the son of Mr Robert and Mrs Mary Fairbank of 33 Ramsden Avenue, Barton-on-Humber. He was educated at St. Chad's School, Waterside and after leaving there worked as errand boy at Kirkby's Store (now the Old Mill). He subsequently worked in the Machine Shop at Hopper's Cycle Works before moving to South Ferriby to help build the cement works, (in which he went on to work for 43 years).

In January 1939, he was among those in the first call up ('The 21 Militia') and a group of Barton men (including Don Graves and Harold Fisher) set off from Barton Railway Station for Portland Bill where they joined the Welsh Regiment **(1)**. After his initial training, there he joined the Regiment's 5th Battalion.

From 1939 until 1944, he travelled around the UK acting as batman for one of the Battalion's officers who was employed in various battle schools teaching young officers. The Battalion also did a tour of duty at Kerr's

Barracks in Newry, Northern Ireland which included spells training in the Mountains of Mourne.

On D-Day + 3 he landed on Arromanches Beach in Normandy (15) and from there followed the invading Allied army across Northern Europe still acting as a batman to an officer in 'A' Echelon some miles behind the front line. He was near enough to the action to have sight of the bombing of Caen and the later paratroop landings at Arnhem.

Just before the end of the war, he moved with his officer to Brussels to run a centre in which soldiers, returning from the front, could spend a week's rest. It was there on his birthday, 8 May 1945, that he heard of the end of the war.

He returned to York for demobilisation.

Information from

Robert Fairbank

George Ferriby

Sergeant, T/188100
Royal Army Service Corps
Technical Clerk

George Albert Ferriby was born in 1915, the son of Mr Charles and Mrs Ethel Ferriby of Louth. He came to Barton in 1936 to work for the Dewey Brothers, Ironmongers in George Street, Barton-on-Humber.

In 1939-1940, he served in the Barton Auxiliary Fire Service (see *Barton Remembered 1939-1945; The Home Front*, p 14) before being conscripted into the army. In April 1940 he reported to Bulford Camp in Wiltshire for initial training as a clerk in the RASC.

Whilst on leave in June 1940, he married Marjorie Blyth at St. Peter's church, Barton.

He was subsequently posted to the No 1 Vehicle Collecting Centre at Aldershot where cars and lorries which had been impressed from their civilian owners were delivered, emptied of an amazing assortment of possessions which had been overlooked, camouflaged and issued to army units. During this time he also took possession of all the vehicles which had been brought over from France by the Free French forces before their country's capitulation. Colonel Charles de Gaulle (later to be President of France) handed the vehicles into George's care.

In 1942, his unit was disbanded as there were no vehicles left to impress and George was posted to 916 Transport Company at Wickham in Hampshire. Here he was promoted to sergeant and put in charge of all the 132 vehicles held by that unit. These were brand-new, American Studebaker, semi-articulated lorries. Other army units could phone to the local colonel RASC who instructed 916 Company to supply lorries for a wide variety of tasks such as delivering food, and NAAFI supplies, transporting personnel and

George and Marjorie Ferriby on their wedding day, 16 June 1940. They have a guard of honour formed by members of the Barton Auxiliary Fire Service in which George had previously served.

73

ammunition, or even delivering coal and coke.

In 1944 916 Company was amalgamated with 254 Transport Company and in August 1944 the new company sailed from Newhaven. It landed in the 'Mulberry' harbour at Arromanches in Normandy **(15)** This artificial harbour was constructed of massive steel and concrete caissons which were sunk in the sea to form an outer breakwater inside which floating roadways led to the beach. Ships anchored against the roadways could safely off-load the enormous quantities of supplies needed to sustain the Allied armies. The Americans built a similar harbour off their Omaha beach to the west. After landing, George's company soon found itself at Conti, near Amiens. Its task was to be continually available to carry army supplies to the front line troops as they advanced.

Gradually, the company moved forward through Holland, Belgium and into Germany and on Armistice Day, 4 May 1945, he was in Luneberg near to the site where Montgomery accepted Germany's unconditional surrender.

Following the end of hostilities, George was variously employed. First, he was put in charge of all the civilian petrol supplies in the Luneberg area. He also organised and controlled the tragic 'Eagle' convoys which transported displaced Polish civilians back to their homeland. They had been brought into Germany as slave labourers and were then being driven back in twice-weekly convoys with some 300 emaciated men and women in each convoy. He was also required to organise transport parties which were sent to the concentration camp at Belsen to clear up at that tragic site.

In January 1946 he was posted back to York for demobilization.

Information from

George Ferriby

Jack Foster

Sub Lieutenant (A) RNVR
No 815 Squadron, Fleet Air Arm
Pilot

John William Foster was born in 1923, the son of Mr John and Mrs Ethel Foster of Barrow Haven. He attended Barrow Church of England School and Hull Municipal Technical College. When he volunteered for war service, he was for the most part resident in Tofts Road, Barton-on-Humber.

In October 1942, he travelled to *HMS Daedalus* at Lea on Solent for initial training in the RNVR. From there

Jack Foster.

he was sent to *HMS St. Vincent* at Gosport where he underwent further training particularly in respect of aircraft and ships. After three months there, he went to Elmdon (now Birmingham Airport) where he learnt to fly in a Tiger Moth and was pleased to go solo after seven hours of dual flying.

In April 1943, he was shipped out to Canada from Liverpool on the former French liner *SS Pasteur* which had been converted into a troop carrier. He landed in New York and travelled by train to Kingston, Ontario where he learnt to fly Harvards. After 16 weeks very hard work, he was awarded his naval pilot 'Wings' and his Commission.

After being shipped back to England, he called in at *HMS Daedalus* where he was given a cheque for £65 with which to buy his full officer's outfits including two dress uniforms. He was then variously stationed in Shropshire, at Perth and finally at Crail (near Carnoustie) where he was taught to fly a Barracuda - a single-engined, torpedo bomber aircraft. Following this he moved to Easthaven (near Arbroath) where he began to learn how to land on an aircraft carrier. A strip of the airfield was marked out to resemble a carrier flight deck and every landing he made was marked until he was perfect.

His next move was to an aircraft carrier, *HMS Argus*, in the Clyde where, after four perfect landings he misjudged his fifth and crash-landed on the carrier's deck. He eventually passed the course and was sent home on leave awaiting an appointment.

During this leave he was married at Scunthorpe Registry Office to Hilda Robinson of Barton - the music teacher at the Convent School in Bardney Hall.

He was sent to Fearn in Scotland where he crewed up with a navigator and air gunner, and on 16 July 1944 he travelled from Barton to Liverpool to join a ship which sailed via the Mediterranean Sea and Suez Canal to Bombay. From Bombay another ship took him to Colombo in Ceylon where he was sent to an aircrew reception centre at Katukurunda.

From there he travelled by train to Trincomalee where his crew boarded *HMS Indomitable* and joined No 815 Squadron. (The *Indomitable* was a ship of some 30,000 tons with a crew of about 1,500. On board were four squadrons of aircraft - two of Barracudas and two of Corsair fighters - some 60 planes.)

First, the ship left the harbour to carry out a series of exercises flying aircraft off and back onto its deck. Sometime later, it sailed east towards the Japanese-occupied Nicobar Islands which lie between Ceylon and Malaya. Armed with dive bombs, Jack and his squadron flew to attack the harbour installations on Great Nicobar. The flight took place on a bright, cloudless morning and he particularly remembers thinking as he flew: 'JF, you are now going to war!' He was afterwards engaged in a number of anti-submarine patrols.

The ship returned to Trincomalee to fly off all the Barracudas which were to be replaced by American Grumman Avengers. No 815 squadron, having been in the Far East for over a year, was sent back to the UK. During the voyage home, Jack unfortunately contracted an ear infection which eventually resulted in his being prevented from flying again. After several operations he was discharged from the forces and returned to Barton in February 1946.

Information from

Jack Foster

Peter French

Flight Sergeant, 159376
Nos 160 and 230 Squadrons Coastal Command,
Royal Air Force
Air Gunner

Peter Godfrey Foord French was born in 1925, the son of Mr Reginald and Mrs Edith French of 17a Market Place, Barton-on-Humber. He was educated at the County and Barton Grammar Schools and on leaving became an agricultural student. He was a member of the Barton Boys' Club and played football for Barton Town.

In 1943 he volunteered to join the Royal Air Force and enlisted at St. John's Wood in London. He did his initial training at RAF Evanton in Scotland.

He subsequently served in Nos 160 and 230 Squadrons of Coastal Command flying in Liberators, and Sunderland flying boats. He saw service in Ceylon, Malaya and finally at Seletar in Singapore.

He was demobilised in mid-1946.

Information from

Peter French

Winston Garfoot

Signalman, 2360942
1st Corps, Royal Corps of Signals
Vehicle Mechanic Class 1

Winston Arthur Garfoot was born in 1918, the son of Joseph Robert William and Annie Elizabeth Garfoot of Bassingham. He was educated at South Witham and came to Barrow in 1932 and worked as a cycle erector at Elswick Hopper.

Winston Garfoot.

In 1934, the family moved to Barton and lived above Pinchbeck's shop in George Street. He played football for Barrow Haven and occasionally for Barton Town. He was a motor cyclist. In 1939 he married Frances Turgoose at St. Mary's church.

In June 1939, he registered for the 'First Militia' and went to Grimsby for a medical. He was one of the first of four Barton men - himself, George Gouldthorpe, Rowland Smith and Lesley Cressey (see *Barton Remembered 1939-1945; Part One, Lest We Forget*, pp 26-29) - who were conscripted into the forces. On 15 July, he went to Catterick Camp and began six months training as a vehicle mechanic in the Royal Corps of Signals.

Before the six months were up, he was sent to join the army in France **(2)** and served with the 1st Corps of Royal Signals, No 1 Wireless Section. His job was to drive the wireless truck, look after the batteries for the wirelesses and maintain his vehicle. He travelled widely in northern France and Belgium and was finally evacuated under machine-gun fire and bombs from the Dunkirk Beaches in May 1940. A tug brought him home **(4 - 5)**.

After landing at Ramsgate, he was sent to join his unit at Bakewell in Derbyshire. In 1942, he took part in Operation *Ironclad* - the invasion of Madagascar. This island was at that time occupied by French Vichy forces and the British had long seen that if it fell into enemy hands and became a submarine base, it would pose a grave threat to the shipping lanes from Europe to the Middle East and India via the Cape. The Operation was highly secret and was not even revealed to the Free French leader Charles de Gaulle. The landings began on 5 May 1942 but the final surrender of the Vichy forces did not take place until 5 November. The capture of Madagascar gave the Allies their first experience of a large-scale amphibious landing.

He was eventually transferred back to England via South Africa and was sent to York where he spent the last two years of the war as a vehicle mechanic in the workshop there. He was finally demobbed from Strensall on 3 February 1946.

Information from

Winston Garfoot

Ken Glover

AC1, 1651512
Royal Air Force
Armourer

Kenneth Glover is the son of Mr James William and Mrs Phyllis Mary' Glover of Queens Avenue, Barton-

on-Humber. He was educated at the Church of England School and on leaving worked at Greenwood's Brick and Tile Yard and at the Farmers' Company.

In 1942, he was conscripted into the Royal Air Force and after initial training at Padgate, served as an armourer at Skellingthorpe and Waddington airfields. There he loaded bombs and bullets into Lancaster bombers bound for Germany.

He was demobilised in 1946.

Information from

Ken Glover

Elsie Goodhand (later Hastings)

Corporal 2053120
Women's Auxiliary Air Force
Spark Plug Tester, Flight Mechanic and Fitter

Elsie Hastings was born in 1920, the daughter of Councillor and Mrs E. Goodhand of 3b Whitecross Street, Barton-on-Humber. She was educated at the County School and subsequently worked at Elswick Hopper and the Ropery.

In September 1941, she joined the WAAF at Bridgenorth and afterwards served at stations at

Elsie Goodhand.

13. The Landings at Anzio

Following the successful landings in Italy in early September 1943, the Allies met increasingly strong German resistance as they attempted to advance northwards. During the winter of 1943-1944, they attempted to breach the enemy's Gustav Line which ran between Minturno on the Mediterranean and Pescara on the Adriatic. The German resistance focused on Monte Cassino proved particularly hard to overcome.

In an attempt to speed up the advance, outflank the enemy on the Gustav Line and open up the road to Rome, four Allied Divisions landed at Anzio just south of the capital city on 22 January 1944.

Initial hesitation by the Allied commander allowed Kesselring, the German commander, to build up his defences and the troops on the beachhead were pinned down for some months by German guns, particularly the feared 88s, which overlooked all of the Allied positions. The British and American troops, cowering in their trenches, came in for some largely unfair criticism for their apparent inactivity and failure to advance. The final breakout came in May and coincided with the collapse of the Gustav Line after the fall of Monte Cassino on 18 May 1944. Rome was finally entered on 4 June.

Herbert Dent was at Anzio and there wrote down a poem - *The Song of Anzio* - which vividly describes the plight and feelings of the men trapped in that most hostile of battlefields.

Now we've travelled far since the day we left home
From the land of the East to the beachhead near Rome
We've seen many sights, some that we detest
And now we are quite certain that home is the best
So take my advice, and believe me it's sound
Get in the Home Guard, before call up comes round
And thank the good lord, you won't have to be
Where the Anzio beachhead sweeps down to the sea.

In the papers you've sent me from home I have read
The things that our critics (in armchairs) have said
They say that the campaign is going too slow
Then they ring for a car and go off to a show
If they can do better, they're welcome to try
The plans and white papers should make Hitler fly
But they would find it no game in a hole 4 by 3
Where the Anzio beachhead sweeps down to the sea.

There are workers at home who are striking I've read
They'd be better employed striking Jerry instead
This seems hardly the time to cause trouble and strife
When there's millions engaged in a struggle for life
I'll wager their folks wouldn't feel so grand
If they saw young Adolf goose step down the street
It wouldn't help much if we struck you'll agree
Where the Anzio beachhead sweeps down to the sea.

Now he's sent tanks against us without any crew
He's also sent leaflets to give us the blues
I've a horrible feeling that one day we'll see
His 88s shell us with Victory Vs
Now Kesselring got quite red in the face
He's scared, in case Hitler should send him to base
He's losing his punch for we've got him C.B. [confined to barracks]
Where the Anzio beachhead sweeps down to the sea.

I know there's controversy over their stars
They all want some ribbons and medals with bars
It seems to me that they're in a huff
In case folks should think they had not done their stuff
If you've done what you're asked does it matter a jot
Whether you have one or not
All the stars in the sky wouldn't help believe me
Where the Anzio beachhead sweeps down to the sea.

Now the question of troops going home does arise
The same inconsistent in most of our eyes
So don't be too hopeful when stating your case
You may be informed there's no shipping space
At least when you ask them that's what you're told
So now I've resigned to be here till I'm old
One favour I ask you send my pension to me
Where the Anzio beachhead sweeps down to the sea.

This song it is ending take heed what I say
From these words you may profit if you come this way
The first thing you need are a shovel and pick
For you must dig a hole and you must dig it quick
So if ever you land here first do as you're told
And don't let them kid you they're digging for gold
They're fighting and sweating for sweet victory
Where the Anzio beachhead sweeps down to the sea.

Hednesford (Staffordshire), Little Rissington, Topcliffe, Driffield, Halton (Buckinghamshire) and Manby. During her stay at Hednesford, she particularly remembers a young officer explaining to a hut full of new recruits the rules and regulations of life in the WAAFs. These included a reminder about the wartime shortage of paper and that as a result 'paper, toilet, for the use of' was in short supply. Everyone was expected to use 'only two papers per sitting, two sittings per day!'

Whilst with No 102 Squadron at Topcliffe in 1942, she spent her time testing hundreds of spark plugs from the engines of Lancaster bombers which were to take part in the 'Thousand Bomber' raids on Germany. She remembers Topcliffe being chosen for a royal visit which resulted in the whitewashing of stones outside the workshops, endless grass-cutting and the polishing of everything 'standing still'.

At Driffield she was promoted to corporal to be in charge of the spark plug testers and replaced a male colleague who was posted overseas. However, before he departed she was sent to the Officers' Mess to be in charge of the waitresses even though she didn't know the first thing about silver service. She was glad to get back to the workshops and during her time there she remembers a particular midday practice air raid warning. Being frequent occurrences, the WAAFs had got somewhat blasé about them and did not exactly rush to the shelters. On this day, however, a German bomber which chose to join the 'practice' promptly blew the roof off Elsie's hangar and living quarters!

On moving to Halton, she trained as a flight mechanic (engines). Later, at Manby, Elsie served with the Airborne Forces Experimental Establishment. There she flew as engineer with her CO, Group Captain Ubee. As Ubee had only one eye she flew on his blind side watching out for other planes, winding up the undercarriage and undertaking flight inspections and refuelling.

Her next move was back to Halton to undertake the 16 week course (it should have been three years) to become a fitter 2E. WAAFs were now needed to replace male fitters who were being sent overseas. A fitter was a higher grade of mechanic who serviced, prepared and inspected aircraft engines. Elsie was a fitter 2E and her work was involved with the servicing of all the engines in an aircraft. Such fitters were in the highest grade and received 5/10p (about 29p) per day.

In 1943 she married Kenneth Hastings, a Bevin Boy, at St. Peter's church.

In August 1945 she was demobbed at Beaulieu, Hampshire.

Information from

Elsie Hastings

Arthur Gouldthorpe DSM

Petty Officer, C/JX332988
Royal Navy
Coxswain

Arthur Mager Gouldthorpe was born in South Ferriby in 1908 and moved to Barton before the war. He was a captain on the sloop *Emily* sailing out of Hull. He was president of the Waterside Children's Sports Committee and a committee member of the Barton Football Club.

At the start of the war, he joined the Barton Civil Defence. In June 1942, he was one of the many local men working on the Humber who took up the offer of a six month's engagement in the Royal Navy to handle the small craft which were being prepared for the invasion of Europe. He reported for initial training to *HMS Pembroke* at Chatham and in 1943 was variously stationed at *HMS Dinosaur* at Troon and the Combined Operations' Pay and Drafting Office in Southend before he returned to *HMS Pembroke* in January 1944.

These experienced boat handlers found themselves engaged in assembling a fleet of mainly Thames lighters. The ships were given engines and some other minor modifications before being dispersed to avoid the prying eyes of German reconnaissance aircraft. Further training was undertaken to prepare their use

Arthur Gouldthorpe.

as beach supply vessels at the invasion. The petty officers who were to command these vessels were paid the princely sum of £5 per week - far more than the ordinary naval rating was paid.

At the invasion Arthur's ship - LBV (landing barge vehicle) 133 of the 13th LBV Flotilla - took part in the assault phase of Operation *Overlord* which itself was code-named Operation *Neptune*. The area Caen-Cherbourg became known as the 'Neptune Area'. LBV 133 sailed from Yarmouth to arrive on Gold Beach at H-Hour + 15 hours. H-Hour for Gold Beach was 0725 on 6 June 1944 **(15)**.

On 14 September 1944, he was recommended for an Immediate Operational Award 'for continuous devotion to duty throughout Operation *Neptune*, in that whilst acting as Coxswain on LBV 133 he kept his craft operational fit, and by his example of whole hearted cheerfulness and zeal helped maintain a high standard of morale throughout the flotilla under vary arduous conditions.' The citation was signed by the 13th LBV Flotilla Officer, Lieutenant H.G. Robins, and witnessed by the Divisional Officer, Sub Lieutenant W.R. Honey. On 27 December, the Commander-in-Chief Portsmouth signed: 'I agree with this recommendation' and Arthur was awarded the Distinguished Service Medal.

The award was posted in the *London Gazette* of 23 February 1945 under the heading: 'For courage, endurance and determination in transporting stores, vehicles and men in L.S.Ts. and L.T.Cs. and other vessels on the Normandy beaches.' The investiture took place at Buckingham Palace on 8 May 1945 and Arthur was accompanied by his wife and daughter.

He remained on naval duties and was posted to Burma where he assisted in the movement of released prisoners-of-war.

He was demobilised on 2 June 1946.

Information from

Nigel Smith (grandson)

Jarman, W.D., *Those Wallowing Beauties - the story of Landing Barges in World War II*, Lewes, Sussex 1997.

Donald Gouldthorpe.

Hopper's Cycle Works before he went on the Humber as mate on a barge. He played football for the Barton Boys' Club.

In June 1942, he was conscripted into the Royal Engineers and did his initial training at Preston. In November 1942, he was sent home on embarkation leave and later saw service in North Africa and Italy **(12)**. His pay book describes him throughout his service as a 'lighterman' and he seems to have been a crew member on a tug.

In November 1945, he was granted leave in the UK and was finally demobbed at Aldershot in November 1946.

Information from

Margaret Gouldthorpe (widow - née West - qv)

Donald Gouldthorpe

Sapper, 2162428
Royal Engineers
Lighterman

Donald Adamson Gouldthorpe was born in 1921, the son of Mr Charles and Mrs Maggie Gouldthorpe of Waterside Road, Barton-on-Humber. He attended the Church School and on leaving was employed at

George Greenwood

Guardsman, 2660634
Coldstream Guards
Guardsman

George Edward Greenwood was born in 1920, the son of Mr George Edward and Mrs Annie Greenwood of Brickyard Row, Maltkiln Road, Barton-on-Humber. He was educated at St. Chad's School and on leaving worked at Hopper's Cycle Works, and at both Hoe Hill and Greenwood's brick and tile works.

On 26 March 1940, he travelled to Grimsby and enlisted as a regular soldier in the Coldstream Guards. After initial training at Caterham, he joined the 4th Battalion of the Coldstream Guards and moved to London where he performed public duties at Buckingham Palace, St. James' Palace and Chequers. The Battalion became part of the Guards Armoured Brigade and George trained as a dispatch rider.

In January 1944, he went to Italy and became part of the Combined Mediterranean Forces. There he joined the 6th Battalion of the Coldstreams because that Battalion had suffered severe losses in the Italian campaign and required reinforcements (see *Barton Remembered 1939-1945; Part One, Lest We Forget,* p 22). He travelled from Liverpool to Italy on the *Highland Chieftain,* a former refrigerated boat which had plied between England and Argentina. He was landed in the docks at Naples and after taking part in the conquest of Italy **(12),** was part of the force which (in April-May 1945) made a dash for the important Italian port of Trieste which the Allies wished to secure before it fell into Tito's hands. Whilst stationed at a large barracks in Trieste, the Battalion took turns with

American units to guard the local docks and warehouses as well as taking part in patrols on the Italy-Yugoslavia border.

He was finally transferred back to England in June 1946 and demobilised into a country regrettably unable to house its returning soldiers. George arrived home to find his wife still living with her parents in Barrow Haven. For a time the two families continued to live in the one small house but, with little immediate hope of finding a place of their own, they took up residence in one of the empty Nissen huts at the former REME army camp situated alongside the road between Barrow Haven and New Holland. Within a short time, other couples, unable to get accommodation in proper houses, joined them and eventually water and electricity supplies were provided - all this in the dreadful winter of 1946-1947. After some time, George got a job in Major Sanderson's brickyard and was provided with a house in the yard. Such moving stories were repeated all over England - a similarly occupied Nissen hut site at the top of Sawcliffe Hill rejoiced in the name of Freedom Avenue - and it was to be many years before decent housing could be provided for everyone.

Information from

George Greenwood

George Greenwood, just after he joined the Guards.

Bob Griffiths

Sergeant, 2020104
Royal Engineers
Army Engineer

Harry Stanley Griffiths was born in 1920, the son of Mr William Henry and Mrs Nellie Griffiths of the Volunteer Arms, Whitecross Street, Barton-on-Humber. He was educated at Barton County School and on leaving was employed as a maintenance joiner at Hopper's. He subsequently worked for Richmond's of Retford. He was a member of the RAOB, Barton Wheelers and the Cycle Works Club. He attended St. Peter's and St. Mary's churches.

He enlisted into the Royal Engineers in June 1940 and was sent to the 4th Training Battalion at Colchester. After four months of initial training, he was posted to 249th Field Company at Ashington in Northumberland. The main work there was the installation of anti-personnel mines and the building of pill-boxes on the beaches of the north-east coast from Whitley Bay down to a point north of Sunderland. These were intended to hamper the expected German invasion.

This work lasted until early 1942 when Bob was moved to Combined Operations under Lord Louis

Bob Griffiths at Bideford in 1942.

Mountbatten at Bideford in North Devon. The main job there was preparation work for the invasion of Europe **(15)**, in particular the problems associated with moving all types of vehicles off landing craft, through the water, and onto a beach. The joints on a Sherman tank would be sealed with balloon fabric and Bostik adhesive. Under this would be laid cordite strips so the when the tank reached land the driver could blow off the sealing fabric and be ready for action. They also laid a pipeline across the Bristol Channel from Swansea to Ilfracombe, an experiment which would eventually lead to the laying of the PLUTO pipeline to the Normandy beaches. The Bristol pipe used the type of under-sea telegraph cable which crossed the Atlantic, though here the telephone lines were not inserted and the petrol travelled down the hollow core of the tube. This pipeline was used throughout the rest of the war to supply fuel landed at Milford Haven for transfer to South-west England.

Shortly after the D-Day landings, Bob had an accident which put him in hospital which resulted in him missing the excitement of the invasion. It was intended that he should accompany a crane which would have crossed to France.

On his recovery, he moved back to Bideford and continued his experimental work for the forces - particularly that associated with the campaign in the Far East. He particularly remembers working on the bridge which was to have been built across a river into which ran very high tides.

When the war ended, he was seconded to the Education Corps where he acted as an instructor in carpentry and joinery for troops who were about to be demobbed. He himself was demobilised in mid-1946 from York.

Information from

Bob Griffiths

Betsy Grimbleby (later Needham)

Private, W168443
Auxiliary Territorial Service
No 590 Mixed Heavy Anti-Aircraft Battery RA
Radar Operator

Betsy Ellen Grimbleby was born in 1923, the daughter of Mr Charles Henry and Mrs Gladys Grimbleby of 47 Ings Lane (now Far Ings Road), Barton-on-Humber. She attended the County School and on leaving was employed in the Spinning Mill at the Ropeworks. She attended Miss Furniss' 'keep fit' classes at the County School and went dancing and to the cinema.

On 31 July 1942, she volunteered to join the ATS and reported for initial training at Queen Ethelberga's School at Harrogate where she was paid 9/6d per week. From there she moved to Oswestry in Shropshire where she did six weeks training on radar. This involved learning how to work a radar set and identify enemy aircraft. An IFF (identification, friend or foe) secondary radar signal was emitted by friendly aircraft to ensure that they were not shot at. At this station, men in the RA and women in the ATS were formed into batteries which included women 'predictors' (visual targeting of an enemy plane); 'spotters' (who plotted enemy aircraft movements on a large board); 'height finders', plus the men who manned the actual

Betsy Grimbleby, March 1946.

anti-aircraft guns.

Betsy was put into 590 Mixed (men and women - some Batteries were men-only) Heavy Anti-Aircraft (commonly referred to as 'ack-ack') Battery, Royal Artillery which was sent to Anglesey for further practice as a full battery. A full battery consisted of eight guns but when on active service it was deployed on two separate gun sites - four guns on the headquarters' site under the command of a major (who commanded the whole battery) and four on the 'off-site' some distance away, under the command of a captain.

After a period of leave, the Battery formed up in November 1942 on a platform at King's Cross Station and from there was sent to Lippitt's Hill on the edge of Epping Forest where it waited the completion of the guns sites which it was to occupy. Betsy's 'off-site' section went to East Bedfont in Middlesex where four guns, radar equipment and Nissen hut accommodation were waiting. Eighteen ATS members worked the radar installation in continuous eight-hour shifts. Initially Betsy, as well as working her radar shifts, was required to do guard duty, work in the cookhouse and perform other tasks. Eventually she passed her trade test and became a qualified radar operative which meant that she had to perform no other extra duties and received a slightly higher rate of pay! Enemy aircraft were still attempting to bomb London during the night **(6)** and the Battery was called into action.

In 1943 the Battery moved to Essex for a month's firing practice. A spotter plane trailing a long 'sleeve' flew over the sea and the Battery, using live rounds, took aim at the 'sleeve' in the hope of hitting it.

Betsy does not remember a single raid during daylight hours at this time but, before she left, the Germans began to send over their new weapon the V1 flying bomb which the British quickly christened 'Doodlebugs' or 'Buzz-bombs' **(16)**. During the first days of this assault the government, fearing mass panic in the country if news of this awesome weapon became widely known, decreed that Betsy (and everyone else in the South-east) was not even to mention the V1 in letters home.

In early 1944, the Battery was moved to Enfield in Middlesex. Later in 1944 it moved to Iwade, a little village in Kent just off the Isle of Sheppey. The Battery was stationed there when VE Day was celebrated and at about this time, the army began to disband its mixed heavy anti-aircraft batteries and the members were put into different regiments. Betsy was put into the Royal Army Ordnance Corps at Burscough in Lancashire where she worked as a clerk. She was there on VJ Day and was demobbed form there in May 1946.

Information from

Betsy Needham

Brian Grimbleby

Private, 14655218
2nd Battalion, Lincolnshire Regiment
Infantryman

Brian Grimbleby was born in 1925, the son of Mr Charles Henry and Mrs Gladys Grimbleby of 47 Ings Lane (later Far Ings Road), Barton-on-Humber. He attended the County School. On leaving he worked as a general hand at Hall's Ropeworks. He was a member of Toc H.

In July 1943, he was conscripted into the army and did his initial six weeks of training at Carlisle. From there he was transferred to the Burton Road Barracks in Lincoln and joined the Lincolnshire Regiment. After ten weeks further training at Lincoln, he was posted to Stobs Camp near Hawick where he joined B Company of the Regiment's 2nd Battalion.

Field training continued there and near Inverness where the Battalion practised assault landings onto a beach. In 1944 the Battalion was moved to camps in Suffolk and Hampshire. Just before D-Day his camp was 'sealed'.

On 5 June the Battalion marched to the quay at

Brian Grimbleby, Belgium 1944.

Southsea, near Portsmouth and boarded the many LCIs (landing craft infantry) which were to take them to Normandy. Each LCI had about three Royal Navy men aboard as crew and held a platoon of infantrymen (about 30) - Brian's was commanded by a Lieutenant. His ship sailed at dusk and the men rested on hammocks below deck before being called up at daybreak when they still were not in sight of land. Just before they landed in France, a minister on Brian's craft gave a short address and the platoon prayed together. The 2nd Battalion, part of the 9th Infantry Brigade of the 3rd British Division, landed on Sword Beach at about 7.30 am on 6 June **(15)**.

The further actions of the 2nd Battalion of the Lincolnshire Regiment are recorded in the biography of Ren Jickells (qv).

Information from

Brian Grimbleby

John Grimbleby

AC2C (Aircraftsman 2 Cadet), 3040644
Royal Air Force
Pilot Training

John Edward Grimbleby was born in 1925, the son of Mr Frank and Mrs Mary Grimbleby of Butts Road, Barton-on-Humber. He was educated at the Council and Barton Grammar Schools. On leaving he began training as under-manager at Hall's Ropeworks. He was a member of the Barton Boys' Club and the local troop of the Boy Scouts. He was also a member of the Barton Air Training Corps in which he had been promoted to the rank of flight sergeant (see *Barton Remembered 1939-1945; Part Two, The Home Front*, pp 24-25).

On reaching the age of 18, and wishing to ensure that he joined the RAF and if at all possible get a commission, he volunteered to enter through the University Air Squadron Scheme. For six months, from October 1943 to April 1944, he was a student at St. Andrew's University in Fife studying mathematics and French to inter-BSc standard. Students were taken on flights from the nearby airfield at Leuchars and his studies included RAF subjects such as basic navigational techniques, armaments and signalling in Morse code.

In April 1944, he was posted to the ITW (initial training wing) in the Grand Hotel at Scarborough where he spent the next four or five weeks. John was housed on the 6th floor and was required to run up and down the stairs without fail! There he underwent various aptitude and medical tests to see which aircrew

position he was best fitted for. At the end of his stay in Scarborough he was posted to RAF Elmdon (now Birmingham Airport) for training as a pilot.

The initial training was in a Tiger Moth, a two-seater, single-engined biplane with dual controls. His aptitude as a pilot confirmed, his next move should have been overseas for further training. However, there were so many pilots being trained at that time that there was a bottleneck in the system and John was sent to RAF Weeton, near Blackpool where he wiled away his time learning to drive all kinds of vehicles from private cars up to articulated lorries.

Having passed his driving course, he was posted to RAF Culm Head near Taunton where he spent the next 10 months driving various vehicles on such jobs as aircraft retrieval and the conveyance of petrol.

In early 1945, he was at last able to proceed with his pilot training and was sent to Rhodesia. He sailed on the ex-liner, then troopship, the *Caernarvon Castle* via the Mediterranean and Suez Canal and landed at Mombassa. From there he went on to Durban and from there by train to Bulawayo in Southern Rhodesia (now Zimbabwe). For the first month, the training concentrated on classroom work on the theory of flying. He was then posted to 28 EFTS (Elementary Flying Training School) at Mount Hampden near Salisbury (now Harare) where he received his pilot training flying single-engined Cornells (see photograph). After 80+ hours of experience, which included aerobatics, cross-country flights and night flying, his training was

John Grimbleby during flying training.

A Canadian-built Fleet-Fairchild Cornell training aircraft of 28 EFTS at Mount Hampton, Southern Rhodesia.

terminated when, in August 1945, the Japanese surrendered and the war was over.

At this point, John was given the option of signing on for a further three years service or returning to 'civvy-street'. John chose the latter and slowly made his way home. He arrived back in England in late 1945 and, after spending long periods employed as a driver, he was finally demobbed in May 1947.

Information from

John Grimbleby

Norman Grimbleby

Stoker First Class, PKX743709
HMS Belfast, Royal Navy
Stoker

Norman Grimbleby was born in 1926, the son of Mr Charles Henry (an army sergeant in WW1) and Mrs Mabel Grimbleby on 12 Dam Road, Barton. He was educated at St. Chad's School and on leaving worked for two years in the Press Shop at Hopper's Cycle Works. He was interested in football and running and was a member of the Sons of Temperance Friendly Society.

In April 1944, he volunteered to join the Royal Navy and was sent for initial training to *HMS Royal Arthur* - formerly the Butlin's holiday camp at Skegness. From there he moved initially to *HMS Duke* at Malvern and

then on to Portsmouth for his final training as a stoker working on coal-fired boilers and turbines.

On finishing his training in late 1944, he was posted as Stoker 2nd Class to the light-cruiser *HMS Belfast* at Portsmouth. (The *Belfast* is the last surviving, large naval vessel which took part in WW2. Since 1971, she has been moored in the Thames at London as a visitor attraction. Her keel was laid on 10 December 1936 and she was launched by Mrs Neville Chamberlain (the Prime Minister's wife) from Harland and Wolff's Belfast yard on 17 March 1938. She weighed some 10,553 tons and had a crew of 850 officers and men. Her armament consisted of 12 6-inch guns in four turrets, twelve 4-inch dual-purpose guns, 16 anti-aircraft pom-poms and eight anti-aircraft machine guns. She also carried three aircraft. Her armour plating was meant to withstand up to 8-inch shells which meant that she should have been able to give battle to any German ship except the biggest battle-cruisers and battleships. At full speed she could sail at over 32 knots, equivalent to 37 mph on land. She was finally commissioned on 5 August 1939, less than a month before Britain declared war on Germany. Late in 1939, she survived a hit from a magnetic mine off Rosyth in Scotland and in late 1943, played a major role in the sinking of the German battle-cruiser *Scharnhorst* in the Battle of the North Cape. D-Day found *HMS Belfast* off the Normandy beaches shelling shore positions and she continued to perform this role for some time. However, in mid-July she was recalled to England to be re-equipped for service in the Far East. It was at this point that Norman Grimbleby joined the crew.)

HMS Belfast left for the Far East in the summer of

Norman Grimbleby (right) in Columbo, Ceylon.

1945 to become part of the BPF (British Pacific Fleet). She sailed through the Suez Canal and, after stopping at Colombo in Ceylon, she arrived at Sydney in Australia in August 1945 - about the time when the Japanese finally surrendered.

Norman's various jobs aboard involved boiler cleaning and engine room and boiler room watch-keeping duties. However, he was eventually given to job of 'tanky' - the man who looked after all the ship's fresh water supplies.

From Australia, *HMS Belfast* sailed to Shanghai to aid some 5,000 Britons who had been imprisoned by the Japanese. She also sailed to Japan and whilst there Norman was able to make short visits to both Hiroshima and Nagasaki soon after they had been devastated by atomic bombs. As Norman says, 'Two hours ashore was enough. There was nothing there, just a load of matchwood.'

On a visit to China, one of the ship's crew caught smallpox and as a result the ship was put into isolation. She was anchored offshore at Hong Kong for three weeks with only a single launch providing contact with the mainland and bringing over supplies. He vividly remembers that each sailor was allowed one can of beer per day during this period. Luckily, no other sailor caught the disease.

HMS Belfast eventually arrived back in England on 15 October 1947 and soon afterwards Norman was demobbed.

Information from

Norman Grimbleby

Ralph Grimbleby

**Able Seaman, C/JX 710800
Royal Navy
Radar Operator and Plotter**

Ralph Grimbleby was born in 1926, the son of Mr Charles Henry and Mrs Gladys Grimbleby of 47 Ings Lane (now Far Ings Road), Barton-on-Humber. He attended the County School and on leaving was employed first by Mr A. Osgerby and later as a joiner's mate at the Farmers' Company. He was a member of the Barton Boys' Club and played in their football team. He attended the Wesleyan Chapel in Waterside.

In June 1944, he volunteered to join the Royal Navy

Ralph Grimbleby.

The destroyer *HMS Rocket* in which Ralph Grimbleby served.

and reported for initial training at *HMS Royal Arthur* at Skegness. From there he was transferred for further training to *HMS Ganges* at Ipswich and *HMS Valkyrie* on the Isle of Man. At the latter, he trained as a radar set operator. When his training was complete he moved to *HMS Collingwood* at Fareham near Portsmouth to train in aircraft plotting.

In March 1945, he joined *HMS Begum* at Greenock in Scotland. From there they sailed to Belfast where the ship was loaded with aircraft and bombs to be delivered in Sydney, Australia. (The *Begum* was a lend-lease aircraft carrier which had originally been a merchant ship but had had its superstructure removed and replaced with a small flight deck. The only way to get aircraft airborne from this short deck was with the use of a catapult. The ship had a crew of some 160.)

The unescorted voyage took six weeks during which Ralph was employed as radar operator. This ship was equipped with the latest American radar systems - one which could detect aircraft flying within some 14 miles of the ship and the other which could detect ships at a distance of some 15 miles. The operators, like the rest of the crew, worked the normal ship's watch rota, using two watches - Port and Starboard, each of these divided into two parts, ie First Port Watch and Second Port Watch. Every member of a ship's crew was in one of these watches. A typical three-day watch rota for a radar operator at sea would involve being on duty from 0000-0400 (the Middle Watch); 1600-1800 (the 1st Dog Watch, a two-hour watch which changed the shift pattern around); and on the second day from

0400-0800 (the Morning Watch) and 1800-2000 (the 2nd Dog Watch); and on the third day from 0800-1200 (the Forenoon Watch) and 2000-2400 (the Night Watch). The other watch was known as the Afternoon Watch from 1200-1600.

On arrival at Sydney, they discharged the aircraft and sailed on to deliver the bombs to the US base at Manus Island, one of the Admiralty Islands off the north-eastern coast of New Guinea. Unable to get close to the island owing to the shallow sea, the bombs were off-loaded into US landing barges and taken ashore. His great memory of his short visit to this island was consuming American cold beer and ice cream, a delight unavailable to British seamen. Unloading completed, the ship sailed to Trincomalee in Ceylon (now Sri Lanka) where it was loaded with more aircraft and set sail as part of a fleet including battleships and other aircraft carriers which were to go into combat down the Malayan coast. On leaving the harbour, his ship struck a reef and had to sail to the dry dock at Bombay for repairs. A skeleton crew was left on board and Ralph was moved to the barracks in Bombay where he stayed for some six months before he was returned on an LCC (landing craft carrier) to *HMS Pembroke* at Chatham. In July 1946, he joined the destroyer *HMS Rocket* which escorted the aircraft carrier *HMS Implacable* out to Malta where she was engaged in deck-landing trials - training pilots to land their aircraft on a carrier at night. The *Rocket's* job was to pick up any pilots who missed the ship! Ralph's job was again as radar operator making sure that there were no other ships or planes in the area. After six weeks, the *Rocket* returned to Rosyth in Scotland. (Ralph served on the eighth and last *HMS Rocket* which was built in 1942 as part of the Emergency War Programme. She displaced 1,705 tons and carried four single 4.7 inch guns, a pom-pom, six Oerlikon guns and eight 21-inch torpedo tubes. She had a crew of 175 men and could sail at 36¾ knots.)

In late December 1947, Ralph left Rosyth and travelled back by rail to *HMS Pembroke* at Chatham from where he was demobilised.

His brother Clarence died on active service, see *Barton Remembered 1939-1945; Part One, Lest We Forget*, pp 41-42.

Information from

Ralph Grimbleby

Bob Harrison

Sergeant, 14708582
Royal Artillery
Wireless Operator, Driver, Unit Clerk

Robert Terrence Harrison was born in 1926, the son of Mr Robert and Mrs Frances Mary Harrison of 14 Hungate, Barton-on-Humber. He was educated at the Church School and was a cadet in the local St. John's Ambulance Corps. He attended St. Mary's and St. Peter's churches. On leaving school, he moved immediately to Bath where he was employed in a solicitor's house as a valet. In April 1942, the house was destroyed by fire and bombing in one of the German air force's *Baedeker* raids. These were reprisal raids following an RAF attack on Lubeck and Rostock - German towns with a significant number of historic buildings. Apparently, the *Luftwaffe*, using available *Baedeker* Guides (tourist books), sought out similar targets in England and consequently mounted raids on Bath, Canterbury, York, Norwich and Exeter. Bath was raided on two consecutive nights and it was late on the second that Bob's house was destroyed. Following these dramatic events Bob moved into the solicitor's office where he began training as a clerk, in which post he remained until he got his call-up papers in January 1944.

He reported for initial training at Goojaret Barracks in Colchester. From there he was posted to Sunnyvale Camp (a former holiday camp) at Rhyl in North Wales. Here he became a member of the Royal Artillery and underwent further training as a driver/wireless operator. He next moved for field training to Cromer where he was billeted in a seafront hotel. Here he was attached to a medium artillery regiment which each day practised 'action in the field of battle'. Bob's job was to man the wireless set and maintain contact between the observation posts and the gun emplacements. On finding that he was underage to proceed into an active unit, he was required to repeat the Cromer course!

His next move was to Berwick-on-Tweed from where, after a short stay, he travelled by train to Glasgow and in January 1945 boarded a former P & O liner - the *SS Ormonde* bound for India. The ship joined a convoy

Bob Harrison standing in the 60 feet wide, 18 feet deep crater left after a German high explosive bomb dropped in Bath during a *Baedeker* Raid in 1942.

14. The Bevin Boys

During 1943, coal production in Britain had fallen to below 2,000,000 tons and even though conscripted men could opt to become miners rather than enter the armed services, few chose to do so and the number of miners fell from 766,000 in 1939 to 700,000 in 1943. The war effort demanded that more men should dig more coal.

As a result on 2 December 1943, the Minister of Labour, Ernest Bevin, informed the House of Commons that this 'urgent national necessity' required that in future one in every ten men conscripted into the armed services would be chosen by ballot to serve as coal miners. He estimated that by April 1944, some 30,000 men would have undergone a period of training and, suitably supervised by experienced miners, would be available for work underground.

The first batch of 'Bevin Boys', most of them only 17 years old, were chosen by ballot on 14 December 1943 and began their training on 18 January 1944. They were paid a weekly wage of £2/10/6d but after deductions for lodgings, meals, laundry, transport to the pit and insurance they were left with only 3/6d (17½p) spending money. Only about a third of the 'Boys' proved suitable for work at the coal face and most were engaged in haulage or maintenance work underground.

Whilst many 'Bevin Boys' worked satisfactorily, others felt themselves insulted at having to perform this badly paid, highly disciplined, labouring work when they had perhaps looked forward to becoming fighter aces. Their bad behaviour, poor attitude and frequent absenteeism set a poor example to the other young miners. It was reported that in the Midlands coalfield 'The miners regarded them [the Bevin Boys] with good-natured aloofness, the volunteers [those men who had freely chosen to enter the mines] with lofty amusement. The miners were lofty but non-committal, and watched them with a half-humorous, half-bitter smile. Here they were, conscripting people for the pits, said the miners, after all these years throwing colliers on the scrap heap and leaving them to rot!... It would do the Bevin Boys no harm to see what the pits were like, but as for increasing production - a fat lot of difference they would make. Why, it would be more trouble to teach them than to do the work yourself.

See - Keith Burman

at Greenock heading for Bombay. During the voyage, stops were made at Gibraltar (where the *Ormonde* left the convoy and proceeded on its own), Port Said and Aden. Bob's job on the ship was to man one of the rocket guns mounted on the boat deck. He fired these in practice, never in anger.

From Bombay he moved by train first to Kalyan and then on to Deolali (properly Devali) outside Bombay. Here whilst on parade, he was given the choice of either joining a new parachute regiment which was to be dropped in the Burmese jungle or proceed to join the 14th Army in Burma. Bob chose to join the 14th.

Following a five-day train journey across India and a trip on a paddle steamer, he landed at Comilla in Eastern India. There he was delayed whilst the Allies secured the landing strip at Meiktila in central Burma which had changed hands frequently during the preceding weeks **(18)**. In March 1945, he was flown in on a Dakota and quickly transferred into 7th Battery, 4th Field Regiment, Royal Artillery manning 25-pounder field guns. Soon the Battery was moved forward with the 5th Indian Division passing through Yamethin, Pyinmana and down to Toungoo. He eventually reached Pegu in south Burma. The guns were constantly in action, firing at the retreating Japanese army and Bob was engaged alongside the guns communicating to them information supplied from forward observation posts. Such information would

Bob Harrison.

include ranges, angles of sight and the strength of charge to be used.

At Pegu, the Regiment was transferred from the 5th Indian Division to the 17th 'Black Cat' Indian Division. It moved north-eastwards into the Shan States (still in Burma and north-east of Mandalay) and was stationed at Taungyi. Again the guns were constantly in action firing at the Japanese retreating into south-western China. During this period, Bob learned that the Germans had surrendered and the war in Europe was over.

From Taungyi, the Regiment moved south again to Thaton at the very southern tip of Burma. There it was to be re-grouped prior to the Allied drive into Malaya. At this time the atomic bombs fell on Japan and the war in the East ended.

Following the end of the war, Bob's regiment was moved back to Taungyi and was engaged in peacekeeping duties. Here he became a unit clerk responsible to the battery commander, a major, for the administration of the unit. He was promoted to the rank of sergeant. During this period Bob's name came out of the hat in a ballot to decide who should go on a LIAP (Leave in Advance of Python). This involved him sailing back to England for a six-week leave on the *Monarch of Bermuda* - a former luxury cruise liner. On the return voyage on the *SS Worcestershire,* the ship was full of Italian prisoners-of-war who were landed at Naples. Bob acted as guard commander to these men. Following his return to the

Regiment, it was moved to Rangoon and from there onto a troopship - the coal-burning *SS Rajuli* - which sailed in January 1946 to Singapore. The unit moved from there over the causeway to Johor Baharu.

The Regiment was posted to Tampin in the middle of a rubber plantation in central Malaya. Whilst there, Bob was informed that his cousin, Gordon Newbitt, was the NAAFI manager at Taiping (also in Malaya). They eventually met at Georgetown on Penang Island. Gordon had been a Bevin Boy but because of problems with his health, he had left the mines and immediately joined the NAAFI. It was from Tampin that Bob was sent home aboard SS *The Empress of Scotland* (formerly *The Empress of Japan*) for demobilisation from York. He finally returned to Barton in October 1947.

Information from

Bob Harrison

Arthur Hedley

Private, 7615637
5th Battalion, East Kent Regiment (The Buffs)
Infantryman

Arthur Waterlow Hedley was born in 1919, the son of Charles and Elizabeth Hedley of Ings Lane, Barton-on-Humber. He was educated at the County School and subsequently worked at the Ropery and as an axle maker in the Machine Shop at Hopper's Cycle Works.

On 15 November 1939, he was conscripted into the army and, hoping to make use of his skill as a machinist, he was sent into the Royal Army Ordnance Corps. He did his initial training at the Woolwich Arsenal but on its completion he was transferred into the Buffs and underwent infantry training at its depot in Canterbury. On Boxing Day 1939, he married Margaret (Peggy) Burfoot at St. Peter's church in Barton.

On rejoining the 5th Battalion of the Buffs, the unit was quickly shipped to the Continent aboard the troopship *Lady of Man* and joined the British Expeditionary Force **(2)**. He was armed with a rifle (minus bayonet) and was issued with five rounds of ammunition.

When the Germans eventually launched their assault into Western Europe, Arthur's battalion was quickly overrun and the men were ordered to disband, throw away the bolts of their rifles and make their way to the coast as best they could. Having no maps or compasses, Arthur and his companion used the sun as a guide in his attempt to walk to safety. At first they

CARD FOR GOOD SERVICE

14708582

To:- *Bdr Robert Terence Harrison.*
Royal Artillery.

Your DEVOTION TO DUTY has resulted in your name being brought to my notice. I wish to thank you for your valuable services and to express my appreciation for the fine example you have set.

Will Slopford

acting SUPREME ALLIED COMMANDER
SOUTH EAST ASIA COMMAND

Date: *9 Sep '46*

The CARD FOR GOOD SERVICE which Bob Harrison received in 1946.

saw no German soldiers but hid where they could when enemy tanks thundered past. Eventually they stumbled into a German camp where they were accosted by an officer armed with a revolver. All the time expecting to be shot, his papers were examined and he was forced to hand over his watch. Then, somewhat to their amazement, they were ordered to walk off. Thinking that they might now be shot in the back they decided to make a dive for the nearest ditch if danger loomed. To their amazement nothing happened and they walked away.

It quickly became clear that they would never reach the coast and they were again picked up by another German unit. This time they were not released but marched away to the rear of the German lines. Eventually they were loaded into railway wagons and began a long journey eastwards across Central Europe. Their eventual destination proved to be Poland where Arthur was placed in a POW camp somewhere near Posen as prisoner number 2429.

The prisoners were housed in large wooden huts which had a central corridor off which were smaller rooms each housing some 20 prisoners. In the centre of each room there was a wood-burning stove and the men slept on bunks with straw-filled palliasses. They were moved between winter and summer camps and spent their time variously doing jobs such as filling in shell holes in the nearby countryside, digging up tree roots or off-loading railway wagons full of briquettes.

The guards, who treated the prisoners reasonably, appeared to be young and old men who were unfit for military service. The food was generally poor with watery cabbage soup and boiled, unpeeled potatoes for the evening meal and a fifth of a rye bread loaf and some cheese for other meals. They were given *ersatz* coffee to drink. Things improved somewhat when Red Cross parcels began to arrive with their supplies of tinned meat and fruit, tea, sugar, powdered milk and chocolate. Arthur was also very pleased to receive occasional supplies of *555* cigarettes from his Barton friend Fred Ashton. He was allowed to correspond regularly with his wife and could receive photographs. Obviously the letters were censored.

There were no British officers in the camp which was run by the sergeants. There was a roll call every morning and evening but everyone was always there as there was no incentive to try to escape. Clearly, they were so far from England that any attempt to get home would have been hopeless. During the five years that Arthur was a prisoner, they got no news about the events happening in the war - they were unaware of the London blitz or even D-Day and lived in the continual hope that the war would be over soon.

In late 1944, with the end of the war in sight, the prisoners were led south out of the camp and into Upper Silesia. During one stay in a camp there they were strafed by a Russian fighter plane - an event which they did not enjoy but did at least show the prisoners that the Allies were not too far away. They trudged on throughout the winter months of 1945 in freezing conditions. Along the roadside they passed frozen corpses at regular intervals. They had no idea where they were going and slept at night in any building which was found to be available. After some weeks the weather began to improve and Arthur vividly remembers that the column was approaching a bridge when suddenly the guards vanished! They soon found that they were in Germany and were welcomed into an American army camp. There they were fed splendidly and slept for some nights in feather beds - what luxury. On finding that Arthur could speak some German, he became batman to an English officer who seemed to have been attached to the American unit to look after the British prisoners.

Soon afterwards, along with a number of other POWs, he was put aboard a Lancaster bomber and flown back to England. He was transferred out of the Buffs and into the RAOC so that he could be stationed in Barton to work in the sheds beside the railway station where large numbers of American motor bicycles, jeeps and lorries were stored and maintained. Here he learnt to ride a motor cycle and passed his test.

Arthur was one of the men who attended the dinner for ex-POWs given by the Barton UDC at the Swan Inn (see photograph on the back cover) in late 1945 (see *Barton Remembered 1939-1945; Part Two, The Home Front*, pp 102-3). He was finally demobbed in 1946.

Information from

Arthur Hedley

Gerald Hewitt

Private 1141047
Royal Artillery, Surrey-Sussex Yeomanry, Royal Army Service Corps
Driver

Gerald Sydney Hewitt was born in 1921, the son of Mr Sidney and Mrs Florence Mary Hewitt of Ings Lane, Barton-on-Humber. He was brought up with his two sisters at 3 Westfield Brickyard, Barton-on-Humber. He attended St. Chad's School and left at 14 to work for a short time at Hopper's. He later worked for Kirkby the grocer as a delivery boy and carrier to nearby villages for a wage of 10/6d per week. He next moved to Dickinson's selling goods on commission from a three-wheeled tricycle. This paid 12/6d per week. Finally, he worked as mate on the Humber Keel *Kathleen* for Barraclough's of Grimsby. Just before the war started, he got work at Greenwood's Brick and Tile Works where his father worked as a master builder. Then in mid-1941, he moved back onto the river, sailing again on the *Kathleen*. His hobbies were fishing, shooting, swimming and boating on the brickyard ponds.

He twice tried to join the RAF but was turned down as both working on the river and in the brickyards were reserved occupations. He was eventually dismissed from the brickyards as he refused to work excessively long hours. After working three weeks at the chemical works, his call-up papers arrived and on 19 February 1942, he reported to Bulford Barracks and became a member of 12 Field Training Regiment, Royal Artillery. He was subsequently transferred to Aberystwyth to complete his training and then to Dovercourt, Harwich. He was only at Dovercourt for one week but whilst there he mounted guard on an anti-aircraft gun armed only with a bayonet strapped to a broom handle!

He was next sent home on embarkation leave after which he reported to Wellington Barracks in London. From there he travelled by train to the Clyde where he boarded a troopship which sailed as part of a convoy on the way to Durban. There were only 28 gunners on the ship and they were housed in pleasant quarters above deck aft of the wheelhouse. Gerald acted as batman for three officers for which he received extra pay! The ship first put in for refuelling at Freetown where no one was allowed on shore. However, the soldiers were amused to watch local boys diving for pennies which they threw into the water. For the next part of the voyage, Gerald slept on deck to get some relief from the heat. The convoy then split. Gerald's half went to Durban, the others to Cape Town. On landing at Durban, their first sight was a lady in white standing on a wooden box singing *Land of Hope and Glory*. Gerald's unit, 30 Royal Artillery Regiment, was sent to Clairwood Camp some 10 miles inland. From there the Regiment was allowed to have passes into Durban from noon until midnight. Two weeks later, the gunners were sent by train to Pietermaritzburg to act as guards at a large German prisoner-of-war camp. The fairly long journey took them through 'The Valley of a Thousand Hills' in Zulu country. Whilst at this camp, Gerald was befriended by the Thornto-Dibb family who later, when he was stationed in Egypt, sent him parcels of tinned fruit.

After a few weeks in Durban, he boarded a French troop ship the *Felix Russell* and in mid-1942 he was landed just south of Suez. From there a railway journey took his unit to Heliopolis near Cairo. The following months were spent as a driver supplying petrol and ammunition to units fighting in the Desert Campaign (7) and also on tank transporters recovering damaged tanks from the battlefields. In November 1942, he spent his 21st birthday on guard duty at an ammunition dump. And he spent Christmas 1942 in the Sinai Desert feasting on bully beef stew and biscuits!

Gerald and Kathleen Hewitt on their wedding day.

In December 1942 he was transferred into the 144 Surrey-Sussex Yeomanry which had just retired from the Desert Campaign.

In mid-1942, various Allied campaigns in the Middle East had secured the area and ensured that oil supplies were safe for the rest of the war.

The Surrey-Sussex Yeomanry was posted first to Sinai and later to Sidon where it undertook policing duties connected with the vital Allied occupation of the area. Later the unit moved to Damascus where the 9th Army undertook manoeuvres in the nearby mountains. From there he was posted into northern Iraq and camped in the desert some 12 miles from Mosul. Here Gerald drove a five-ton truck to get rations for his unit and he was also sent down to the River Euphrates to fill five-gallon petrol cans with river water which was used for washing. On his return from the river, he put one or two of the cans outside each of the tents. Near to the camp, there was a small village in which lived the families of workers in the oil fields. Here there was a lovely swimming pool which the soldiers were allowed to use on occasions. It was at this camp that Gerald caught sandfly fever and became gravely ill. For nearly a week his body was packed in ice to keep his temperature down and he was only allowed to eat one banana a day. Following his recovery, he went on a week's holiday to the Rowandas Gorge where he visited a sheik's home through the middle of which ran a mountain stream. On another occasion he went out hunting small deer. Having failed to see any, he

15. Operation *Overlord*

By early 1944, Hitler's army was being pushed back in both Italy and on the Eastern Front. The Allies were demanding his 'Unconditional Surrender' and the creation of a third front with landings in north-western Europe would surely seal the fate of the German Reich.

For some time -

• the Russians had been demanding speedy action from America and Britain to take some of the pressure off their forces,

• the Americans had been critical of the apparent lack of urgency shown by their British ally in opening 'The Second Front',

• and the British, having learnt some painful lessons during the abortive raid on Dieppe in 1942, were reluctant to mount an invasion which was not meticulously prepared, with complete co-operation between the various armies, navies and air forces.

Preparations for the greatest-ever seaborne invasion began in earnest in early 1944. It was to be led by a supreme commander, the American General Dwight Eisenhower, and would involve the deployment of some 3,500,000 service personnel in 1,600 merchant ships, 4,000 landing craft, 1,200 warships, 3,500 gliders and 12,000 aircraft. Every conceivable obstacle was considered and catered for: two artificial 'Mulberry' harbours were to be towed across the Channel; a pipeline, 'PLUTO' (Pipeline Under The Ocean), was to be laid on the seabed to ensure that the troops received a constant supply of fuel; tanks called 'Crabs' were developed to clear minefields; others would float in the water on their way to land; yet more would destroy concrete emplacements, and AVREs (armoured vehicle royal engineers) laid their own metal carpets to move or carry their own bridges for crossing dykes. As far as was humanly possible, nothing was to be left to chance. The landscape of much of southern England was transformed as it became a giant barracks, naval base and airfield all forming an integrated fighting force. As Eisenhower wittily remarked, 'Only the great number of barrage balloons floating constantly in the British skies kept the islands from sinking under the waves.'

The Dieppe raid had shown the need to create a massively strong bridgehead in the minimum of time, and so the plan was to land some 156,000 men on the first day and that within two months more than 2,000,000 would have arrived along with some 500,000 vehicles. The organisation of such a force presented awesome problems which were gradually overcome - often with a mixture of 'prayer and swear'!

But where should the invading force be landed? Two obvious sites presented themselves - the shorter crossing to the Pas de Calais or the longer one to Normandy. The latter, with its good, open beaches and the major port

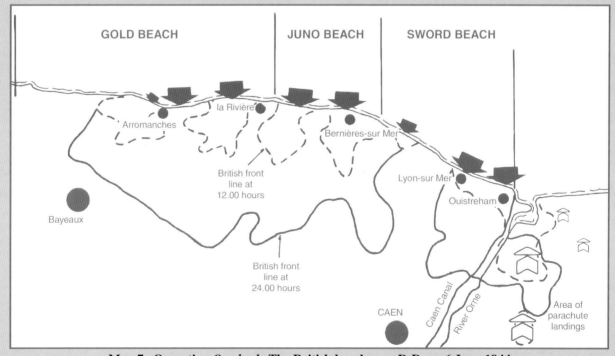

Map 7. Operation *Overlord*. The British beaches on D-Day - 6 June 1944.

of Cherbourg to hand, was eventually chosen, but at the same time elaborate measures were to be taken to convince the enemy that they should expect the landings in the area just across the Channel from England. All along the coast the Germans had been busy building their 'Atlantic Wall' defences whose apparent strength allowed Rommel to declare, 'We can face coming events with the greatest confidence.'

The invasion force - 21st Army Group, with Montgomery in overall command of all the ground troops - consisted of two elements, the US 1st Army under Bradley and the British 2nd Army under Dempsey. The Americans were to land in two waves - the VII Corps on 'Utah' Beach on the Cherbourg peninsular would form the western flank of the *Overlord* assault and quickly move to capture Cherbourg whilst to its east, V Corps would assault 'Omaha' Beach between Port-en-Bessin and Isigny. Dempsey's force (which included Canadian troops and numerous men from Barton-on-Humber) was again deployed in two Corps - XXX Corps (which included the 7th Armoured Division) would land on 'Gold Beach' at Arromanches and 1 Corps would assault 'Juno' (the Canadian beach) and 'Sword' beaches to the east. Across the River Orne to the east of Sword Beach, the 6th British Airborne Division was to land by parachute and glider and set out to secure the bridges over the Caen Canal and the River Orne.

It had been decided that the landings should begin on 5 June, but a storm in the Channel caused Eisenhower to delay for a day and so the first Allied troops did not go ashore until the 6th. In its 9 am broadcast that day, the BBC informed the British people of the momentous and long-awaited news: 'Under the command of General Eisenhower, Allied naval forces supported by strong air forces began landing Allied armies this morning on the coast of France.'

During that first day - 'The Longest Day' as it has since become known - the assault troops had the constant support of naval barrages and air force sorties by bombers and fighters. By 9 pm that evening, Allied planes had flown 25,000 sorties - the once vaunted *Luftwaffe* managed only 319! The German reaction to the invasion was confused. Rommel, the overall commander, was away celebrating his wife's birthday. Von Rundstedt was convinced the Normandy landings were a diversion and that the 'real' landings would come later in the Pas de Calais, and Hitler vacillated and would not order panzer reinforcements to move to counter the threat. By the time the Germans had realised their mistakes, the bridgehead was more or less secure and more troops poured ashore in preparation for the eventual breakout which came some eight weeks later. This followed a titanic struggle to take Caen and weeks of fierce fighting through the *bocage* countryside of Normandy where the sunken roads, thick hedgerows, stone walls and high banks were of very great advantage to the defenders.

The Germans concentrated their panzer divisions against Montgomery's troops on the Allied left flank and this allowed the Americans to the west to launch their Operation *Cobra* which swept into the heartland of France from the area around Avranches. One prong of this attack eventually swung east and north and the German Army B was caught in a pincer movement between the American force and the British and Canadian troops moving down from the north. 10,000 Germans were killed, 50,000 taken prisoner and vast amounts of equipment fell into Allied hands. The German troops who escaped to the Seine in some disarray had little left with which to fight. On 25 August, Paris was liberated by US General Patton who reached Verdun by the end of the month. To the north Montgomery advanced along the Channel coast and on 31 August, Amiens fell to the US 1st Army. A victorious end to the Second World War was now guaranteed.

See - Charles Atkinson, Jack Broddley, Jack Bromfield, Harold Burton, Jack Clapson, Wilfred Codd, Robert Fairbank, George Ferriby, Arthur Gouldthorpe, Bob Griffiths, Brian Grimbleby, Walter Horne, Ren Jickells, Frank Kitching, Arthur Knight, Charles Newton, Wilf Pike, Walter Readhead, Fred Sobey, Harold Welch, George Wright.

prepared to travel back to camp when he met an armed convoy which was escorting the Regent of Iraq. The Regent offered Gerald a bottle of beer and the two enjoyed a chat whilst it was being drunk.

Gerald's next move was to a camp not far from Beirut in Lebanon but after staying there for some time he was moved, just before Christmas 1944, to Sidon.

In early 1945, he was transferred into the Royal Army Service Corps at Alexandria. Here he was billeted some 50 yards from King Farouk's palace with its lavish garages housing all his 'flash' cars. On learning that he had some experience with boats, he was for a time seconded to the motor boat section where he became coxswain of a ship manned by an Arab crew. They covered the embarkation of troops and took orders out to the various vessels in the harbour. From Alexandria he was sent to Port Said where he took over the embarkation officer's launch which used to go out to meet vessels flying the quarantine flag because of some disease on board. The medical officer would ring Gerald when a ship was due and needed to be visited.

In late 1945, he sailed from Suez to Toulon and then travelled by train to Dieppe from where he sailed to Newhaven. From Newhaven he was sent to Oulton Park camp near Leicester where he continued working as a driver. Whilst based at Leicester he had a bad accident at Syston airfield which resulted in his spending nine weeks in the hospital at Newark and a later spell convalescing in Halifax. He was subsequently demobilised on a class B release.

Information from

Gerald Hewitt

Walter Horne

Corporal, 1511261
Royal Artillery, Royal Electrical and Mechanical
Engineers
Gunner, Unit Armourer

Walter Horne was born in 1918, the son of Mr Walter and Mrs Jenny Horne of 117 Waterside Road, Barton-on-Humber. He attended St. Chad's School and on leaving worked in the Press Shop at Hopper's Cycle Works. His hobbies were fishing and he attended both St. Chad's and St. Mary's churches.

On 10 October 1939 he was called up in the First Militia and travelled first to Sheffield for enrolment before moving to Kinmel Park near Rhyl in North Wales where he was trained as a Royal Artillery anti-aircraft gunner.

He was posted to the 43 Middlesex Anti-Aircraft Regiment and his unit was based at St. Mary's Cray in Kent. During the London blitz **(6)** in late 1940, he was continually on duty manning a 4.5 inch anti-aircraft gun attempting to shoot down the German bombers and fighters. The 4.5s were the biggest guns used against enemy aircraft. Each had a crew of 5 men - one on the elevation control, one on the turntable, one on the firing platform, one loader and one man (usually a lance-bombardier) in charge. A skilled crew could fire one shell about every 30 seconds and a stock of some 50 shells was piled up around each gun. A separate team nearby worked the range and directional finding equipment and their instructions were relayed by field telephone to the guns which were aimed accordingly.

Following the end of the London blitz, his unit was moved to Birmingham for a similar purpose. Whilst there he thinks that his gun (one of eight on the site) shot down one enemy bomber but certainly the crew suffered from a rain of enemy incendiary bombs. Wherever possible, the bombs were picked up in steel helmets and thrown into the nearby lake.

When the blitz on Birmingham came to an end, his unit was transferred by rail and ship from Edinburgh to Scapa Flow. They did not take their guns but found a battery of 4.5s waiting for them. During his whole stay there - just over 12 months - he never fired a shot in anger.

Walt's next move involved a trip to Ballykinley in Northern Ireland where he formed a new battery which fired rockets rather than shells. This was a new experimental anti-aircraft weapon and consisted of two rockets fired from rails. There were 64 of these pairs arranged in a square so that when firing took place, some 128 rockets shot into the air and should have formed an area of explosions which would have downed any enemy aircraft nearby. Unfortunately, many of the rockets failed to travel on the trajectory required and shot off in all directions!

When training was completed, the Battery moved to Coventry. The blitz on Coventry had already taken place and the rockets were only fired once in anger, still in an experimental role and once again the effect was not all that successful. It was only later that these rocket systems were perfected and similar systems were used as field artillery on D-Day.

In May 1943 he was transferred into the REME at Preston to be trained as an armourer. On completion of his training, he was moved to the army workshops at Hastings. By now the invasion of Europe was imminent and he joined a services re-enforcement unit of 30 men. This unit had among its members soldiers from REME, RASC, RE, RAOC plus two tank crew

Walter Horne.

with a corporal in charge. They were to sail to France and join any units which had suffered casualties.

Just before D-Day, the unit was moved from Hastings to Canning Town in London where it embarked on a troopship. After five days on board - much of it spent anchored out at sea off the south coast - he was landed in an assault craft on Gold Beach at about midday on 6 June **(15)**. Somewhat surprisingly, the unit found out on landing that it was not due to arrive in France until D + 6 so, being told to look after themselves for some days, they set up a 'private' camp about a mile inland.

He eventually joined 30 Corps workshop where armaments (from a pistol to a field gun) were repaired, inspected and/or modified. Somewhat later he was promoted to the rank of Corporal in 30 Corps HQ. With these units he followed the advancing Allied army as it moved through France, Belgium, Holland and Germany. On VE day he was in Nuremberg and from there he was demobbed in February 1946.

Information from

Walter Horne

William Horne.

William (Bill) Horne

Sergeant, 1592584
No 44 (Rhodesia) Squadron, Royal Air Force
Mid-upper Gunner

John William Horne was born in 1925, the son of Mr Walter and Mrs Jenny Horne of 117 Waterside Road, Barton-on-Humber. He attended St. Chad's School and on leaving worked in the handlebar department at Elswick Hopper and then in Greenwood's Brickyard. Just before he volunteered for the forces in 1942, he was working with his father on a Humber barge.

He enrolled at the Air Crew Receiving Centre at St. John's Wood in London. From there he was sent to Whitely Bay for training as an air gunner. Following this he went to numerous other centres to continue his training. Finally, he 'crewed up' at Bitteswell, an operational training unit, near Leicester. From there he flew in Wellingtons on 'Nickel Raids' over the coast of north-western Europe. 'Nickels' was the code word for propaganda leaflets that were dropped by aircraft of both the RAF and the USAAF with the hope of demoralising those who found them. Subsequently, in mid-1944, he joined No 44 (Rhodesia) Squadron at Dunholme Lodge which moved to Spilsby later that year. King George VI had honoured No 44 Squadron with the '(Rhodesia)' suffix because of the Squadron's high proportion of Rhodesian aircrew.

No 44 (Rhodesia) Squadron, flying four-engined Lancaster bombers, took part in numerous night raids over Germany and Czechoslovakia. Daytime raids were made on the Erf dams in the Rhine Valley and the Dortmund-Ems Canal.

A Lancaster bomber had a crew of seven men - a pilot, a navigator, a flight engineer, a bomb aimer (who doubled as front gunner when necessary), a wireless operator, a mid-upper gunner and a rear gunner. Whilst raiding an oil refinery near Bohlen south of Leipzig in early 1945, his plane was shot down by a Junkers Ju88 and a Messerschmitt Me410. Following an initial attack from the rear by the Me410 the Lancaster took the usual evasive action and dropped some 1,000 feet. However, waiting at the bottom of this descent was a cleverly-positioned Ju88 which shot the Lancaster to pieces as it began to level out. With the bomb load still intact, the pilot ordered the crew to bale out and all seven airmen parachuted 10,000 feet safely to the ground. It was later discovered that this successful landing of a whole crew from such a height was probably an all-time record.

Bill landed in the target area at Bohlen and, realising that a massive bombing operation was about to take place in this very area, he ran as quickly as he could across the snow-covered countryside. Clearly, his footsteps would give him away and there was little or no chance of an escape. Six or seven hours after landing, he was captured by some German soldiers. They took him back to their anti-aircraft camp and then

95

next day he was handed over to the *Luftwaffe* who took him to a SS interrogation centre (a *Dulag Luft*) near Frankfurt-am-Main. Here he met two other members of his crew - the pilot and the wireless operator. They were put into solitary confinement ('sweat boxes') and after three days underwent a fortnight's interrogation. The Germans wished to know details of squadrons, bomb loads and targets. The crew members were threatened that they would be shot as saboteurs. They revealed nothing and were marched off to an American-run transit camp at Luneburg. Here they were kitted out with a blanket, a greatcoat and a good meal. They were only there for some 16 hours before the camp was evacuated in the face an imminent attack by the American army to the west.

In about February 1945, the Allied inhabitants of the whole camp, guarded by a number of German soldiers and dogs, marched down towards Bavaria. After about a fortnight on the road a halt was called at *Stalag Luft 3* - a camp occupied by some 5,000 Allied servicemen. They stopped there for about 10 days and then, accompanied by the occupants of the *Stalag*, (by now the column was some six miles long) they set off again. On one occasion they marched for almost 24 hours on the promise of a long-awaited meal. This proved to be a bowl of pea soup. The intention was to take the party through the Brenner Pass into Italy but when they were nearly there, it was discovered that the British were advancing northwards towards the Pass and so the march continued on into Bavaria. Things were in a very bad state in Germany with SS troops roaming the countryside looking for deserters or escaped prisoners-of-war. News also came through that Hitler had threatened to exterminate all Allied prisoners before the end of the war so quite a few of them took any opportunity presented to flee the column and attempt to escape. Such actions were pretty fruitless and most of them were recaptured.

The march continued to *Stalag 7A* at Moosburg (a few kilometres south-east of Riedlingen) in Bavaria which was reached in May 1945. This was quite a large camp occupied partly by Russian prisoners-of-war and partly by the Allies. After a few days, the prisoners could hear Allied gunfire which proved to be coming from American tanks under the command of General Patton. Eventually, the camp was taken. The prisoners were informed that they were probably safer in the camp than free in a countryside over-running with unreliable Russian soldiers. So they stayed put until the Americans consolidated their hold on the area and were able to bring up trucks to evacuate the camp.

Bill was taken to an airfield from where he was flown in a Dakota to Reims in France. There the RAF took over and flew him to RAF Cosford. Following a period of recovery in hospital he was released on leave.

Information from

Bill Horne

Ren Jickells

Private, 4808813
2nd Battalion, Lincolnshire Regiment
Infantryman

Renold Jickells was born in July 1920, the son of Mr J.W.A. and Mrs Blanche Jickells of 77 West Acridge, Barton-on-Humber. He attended the Church School in Queen Street, worshipped at St. Chad's church in Waterside and was a member of the Barton Boys' Club. His main interests were football and cricket. Before the war he worked in the brickyards during the summer and in the Handlebar Department at Hopper's Cycle Works in the winter.

Soon after the outbreak of war, he joined the Local Defence Volunteers - later to become the Home Guard and he also used to keep the ARP warden company in his post at Providence House.

In November 1940, he joined the 2nd Battalion of the Lincolnshire Regiment at Burton Road Barracks in Lincoln. His four brothers, Jim, George, Eric and John, and his sister Zena all served in the armed forces. After his initial training at Lincoln, he left to join D Company of the 2nd Battalion, then stationed at Sherbourne in Dorset. Here, and at Invarary in

Ren Jickells.

Scotland, early 'commando-style' training took place for a 'special mission', but eventually the Lincolnshires were stood down and the task - the invasion of Sicily - went to the 1st Canadian Division. During 1943, Renold was first at Loch Fyne practising beach landings, speed marches and exercises with tanks, and later at Hawick and in south-western Scotland. May 1944 found him at Camp A12, Creech Wall Wood and on the 26th of that month the camp was 'sealed' and nobody was allowed in or out. On 5 June 1944, the unit moved to a camp at Southsea near Portsmouth and from the pier there they embarked on landing craft for the 'great adventure' - D-Day.

On 6 June 1944, he landed at Hermanville-sur-Mer as part of the 8th Infantry Brigade of the 3rd British Division of the 2nd British Army.

Renold's hazy memories of the D-Day landing are interesting - 'Actually I cannot remember much about the landing: lots of shells flying about, our warships shelling the German positions. It was off the beach at a gallop to our rendezvous point, besides I was soaking wet having lost my footing and fallen into the water, losing three tins of self-heating soup into the bargain.' The loss of the soup was something of a disaster for Renold. During the Battalion's period in 'sealed camp' prior to D-Day, he had been allowed out, under escort, to visit a dentist. Unfortunately, his false teeth could only be delivered some six weeks later and as a result he landed in France minus teeth and very dependent on liquid food. Somewhat remarkably, the 2nd Lincolnshires suffered no casualties on the beaches.

Renold's division landed on Sword Beach - the most eastern of the landing zones - and its immediate task was the capture of Caen **(15)**. This they almost accomplished, but late on the first day a counterattack by the German 21st Panzer Division halted progress. By nightfall, 2nd Army was some six miles inland - only about half the distance originally planned.

Little progress was made until early July when Caen was eventually taken after a massive aerial bombardment. The 2nd Lincolnshires was not part of the force which entered the city but had played a major role in its capture by holding the Division's left flank near Herouville on the River Orne against strong German pressure. During this period, the Battalion suffered heavy casualties losing 10 officers (including the Commanding Officer) and 200 other ranks either killed or wounded. Five weeks after landing, the Battalion retired to Lion-sur-Mer for five days of well-earned rest.

In mid-July, the plan was to break out of the bridgehead and the 3rd British Infantry Division was to attack from positions east of the Orne and take Troarn. Even though the town was mercilessly bombed and shelled whilst the infantry waited for two whole days in their slit trenches, the enemy was well dug in and the strong German defences prevented its immediate capture.

The Battalion lost a considerable number of men, dead or injured, battling to capture Troarn and on 22 July it retired west of the Orne to regroup.

That rest lasted only two days after which the whole 3rd Infantry Division was moved from the left flank of the invasion over to the right flank where the Americans had broken out from Avranches. The Battalion was in action in the area around Vire before making camp for about a month, first at the village of Landisacq - midway between Tinchebray and Flers - and later south of Flers. Training in river crossing and a visit to the theatre at Flers to enjoy a show with Flanagan and Allen of the Crazy Gang were the highlights of this period which followed some 10 weeks of almost continuous action.

On 29 August, the Battalion moved and finally stopped at the village of Vatismenil, 40 kilometres SE of Rouen, still a long way behind the Allied front line. Another move forward took place on 14 September when the Battalion crossed the WWI battlefields and halted near Lille St. Herbert, once again within earshot of the battlefield ahead. It was given the task of crossing the Escaut Canal and establishing a bridgehead on the further bank. This task proved easier than some of the previous actions and, although some men were killed or wounded, Renold's D Company came out of it in good shape.

Renold spent Christmas Day 1944 out of the front line at Maastricht in Holland. As usual, the officers served the dinner but soon afterwards the Battalion was put on standby due to the Germans launching their counteroffensive in the Ardennes - 'The Battle of the Bulge'.

On 24 February 1945, the 2nd Lincolnshires entered Germany to take part in Operation *Veritable* to clear the Germans from the area between the rivers Maas and Rhine. Twelve hours after capturing the town of Kerkenheim - 'not a lot of bother' - it was required to attack the village of Winnekendonk which was defended by a detachment of German parachutists. Here things proved much more difficult. The tanks supporting the Battalion were knocked out in the first 10 minutes with still about a mile of open ground to cross before reaching the town. Hand-to-hand fighting resulted in many deaths and Renold lost his best friend there. The Germans lost some 140 men, killed or wounded, and the remaining 80 surrendered.

On 28 March 1945, the Battalion crossed the Rhine.

On 18 April, Renold took part in a mopping-up operation to take Stuhr. Renold remembers firing about a dozen mortar shells at a German position following which about 20 of the enemy came out and surrendered. For his part in this action, he received a Commendation Card signed by the 3rd British Infantry Division Commanding Officer, Major General L.G. Whistler which reads - 1 congratulate you on your exemplary courage and leadership in the battle of Stuhr on 18th April 1945'. A very proud moment indeed.

The Battalion's final action, on 26 April, involved the capture of the German town of Bremen. On VE Day, 8 May, the Battalion was in Lengerich, a German village near Osnabruck. Renold had fought in every battle across northern Europe. He was never injured and after the Battalion had a spell in Israel and Egypt from July 1945 to July 1946 - 'Just out there long enough to get a nice tan' - Renold was finally demobbed in July 1946.

Six members of his family served in the forces (see list) and all returned home at the end of the war.

Information from

Renold Jickells

The History of the Second Battalion The Lincolnshire Regiment in North-West Europe; June 1944 - May 1945. No author or other details given

Tom Kerridge

Lance Bombardier, 1596237
Royal Artillery
Gunner

Tom Kerridge.

George Thomas Kerridge was born in 1910, the son of Mr Thomas and Mrs Ruth Kerridge of Ings Road, Barton-on-Humber. He was educated at St. Chad's School and on leaving was employed as a bricklayer's mate at Hopper's Cycle Works. He was a member of Barton Toc H and 1st Barton Scout Troop attached to St. Mary's church.

In July 1940, he was conscripted into the forces and joined the Royal Artillery in which he was trained as an anti-aircraft gunner. He was posted to RAF stations at Scampton, Binbrook, Hemswell and Aberystwyth where he manned anti-aircraft guns which were positioned on the top of towers which surrounded the airfields.

Later he boarded ship to travel to Singapore but on the voyage the convoy was attacked by the Japanese and was diverted to India. From there Tom travelled through Assam and Burma and fought in the campaign to prevent the Japanese invading India **(18)**. His return from India was delayed as it was decided that those injured should be moved first.

He was demobbed in January 1946.

His brother Herbert died on *HMS Hood* (see *Barton Remembered 1939-1945; Part One, Lest We Forget*, pp 45-46).

Information from

Ethel Kerridge (widow)

Eddie Kerridge (son)

Les King

Gunner, 893423
Royal Artillery
Gunner

Leslie King was born in 1919, the son of Mr Thomas and Mrs Annie King of 18 Pasture Road, Barton-on-Humber. He attended the County School and his main hobby was bicycle riding. On leaving school he worked for a short while in the Front Forks Department at Hopper's Cycle Works before taking up employment as a joiner with Gill and Hill of Winterton at a wage of 19/11d (99½p) per week. One job he particularly remembers was helping to build the houses in Ramsden Avenue in 1937-1938.

In May 1938, he travelled to Woolwich and joined the Royal Artillery. Following completion of his initial training, he was sent to Fargo Camp on Salisbury Plain where he trained to become part of the crew on a 6-inch howitzer. On Christmas Eve 1939, he was part of a detachment which was sent to Ipswich where it joined the local Territorial unit to form the 67 Medium

Les King worked for the Schneider family as a joiner whilst he was a prisoner near Dresden.

Artillery Battery. About the time of Dunkirk, the Battery and its 16 howitzers was moved to Royston in Cambridgeshire to guard the local airfield which it was feared might be used by the Germans in the expected invasion of England.

In late 1941, the Battery travelled to Avonmouth near Bristol and boarded the *Rangatiki*. The ship sailed down the west coast of Africa and stopped at Durban where the soldiers were allowed to go ashore. In early 1941, the ship berthed at Port Said and the Battery moved west to take part in the fighting in North Africa **(7)**.

In November 1941, British and Commonwealth troops launched Operation *Crusader*, a new offensive aimed at recapturing Cyrenaica (eastern Libya) and relieving the encircled port of Tobruk. The German commander, Rommel, was initially caught unawares (he was planning the capture of Tobruk) but soon rallied his forces and thwarted the Allies headlong advance. However, in mid-December, Rommel pulled his *Afrika Corps* back to await reinforcements and the Allies, similarly weakened after the month-long campaign, were unable to make good their advantage. By 6 January 1942, the Allies reached El Agheila and there their advance stalled. On 21 January Rommel, mounted a counteroffensive and soon the Allies were in headlong retreat once again. By 29 January they

had retaken Benghazi and in mid-1942 a new, apparently unstoppable enemy thrust, threatened Egypt itself and completed the encirclement of Tobruk. The retreat of the 8th Army continued apace and by late June, Rommel was approaching El Alamein, only about 100 miles from Alexandria.

On 21 June 1942, Les was among the 35,000 Allied servicemen who were taken prisoner at the fall of Tobruk. This was Britain's greatest military defeat since the fall of Singapore.

Les was shipped from Benghazi to Brindisi in Italy and for some three to four months was held captive in various Italian prisoner-of-war camps. In late 1942, he was sent on a 17-day rail journey (50 prisoners in every cattle truck) and ended up as POW 253916 in the German prisoner-of-war camp, Stalag IVB, near Dresden. Prisoners in this large camp were held at various locations and Les found himself with some 60 other Britons in an old schoolroom surrounded with barbed wire and guarded by members of the German army. Les found the older German guards 'OK', the younger ones 'Horrible'. Usually, he was made to work on the 'heavy gang', off-loading coal from railway wagons or moving timber. In late 1944, he began to be employed by a Dresden joiner, Herr Schneider, making chairs and desks for offices - this work was tolerable and he was well-treated by his German employer who gave him some of his family's food, although at that period the Germans were chronically short of food themselves. Les was now receiving Red Cross parcels and he treated the Schneiders' daughter to pieces of his chocolate.

On the night of 13/14 February 1945, a massive raid by over 750 Lancasters of RAF Bomber Command devastated Dresden, a city previously rarely bombed. On the following day, 450 American bombers attacked in a follow-up raid. This action was part of Operation *Thunderclap* - a scheme designed to precipitate the German surrender by destroying the country's rail network. Dresden contained a major marshalling yard through which troops and supplies were being moved to the Eastern Front. In all, some 1,478 tons of high-explosive and 1,182 tons of incendiary bombs were dropped, a fire-storm was created. The 'officially notified dead' totalled nearly 40,000 and at least another 20,000 were killed.

Les watched these awesome raids from his camp on a hill overlooking the city. Later the prisoners were taken into the ruins and were made to collect up those bodies which could be found and burn them on great pyres.

As the war came to an end, Les and his fellow prisoners were marched out of the camp and, after walking through Czechoslovakia and Poland, were eventually freed by the Russians. American lorries soon arrived to pick them all up and after a short stop at Nuremberg, where they were fed properly for the first time in three years, a captured Junkers 88 flew them to Reims in France. There they were deloused and reclothed before being flown in a Lancaster bomber to an air base in Oxfordshire. After a period of leave in Barton, he was sent first to the Military Hospital at Colchester and then to Newcastle for demobilization.

Information from

Les King

Fred Kirk

Sergeant, 4800438
Royal Artillery
Gunner

Fred Kirk was born in 1914, the son of Mr Tom (killed in 1917 when his ship struck a mine in WW1) and Mrs Nellie Kirk of Goxhill. The family moved to Chemical Row in Barton soon after Fred was born. He attended St. Chad's School where he enjoyed drawing and painting. He left school one dinner time and started work in Greenwood's Brickyard in the afternoon. He subsequently went on to work in the Crankshop at

Fred Kirk in Calcutta.

Hopper's Cycle Works. He was a member of the Barton Oddfellows' Friendly Society.

In 1932, he travelled to Woolwich and signed on for six years service in the Royal Artillery. There he did his initial training and did some work on horse-drawn 18 lb field guns. Later in the year he was transferred to the 2nd Battery of the 1st Anti-Aircraft Brigade at Blackdown, Hants. This mechanised (not horse-drawn) battery was equipped with four 3-inch anti-aircraft guns which could be used against tanks. (These guns had a crew of about 11 men - two laying the gun on the target, one at the breech, one loader, two men handing up the shells, two or three setting fuses, one manning the open sights, one 'togger' who pulled the rounds into the breech, and one sergeant in charge of firing.)

After some time at Blackdown, he was put on garrison duties which involved looking to the welfare of the soldiers' wives.

In 1934 Fred's name appeared on a 'draft' for India and he spent his nineteenth birthday on the steam-driven, *HMT Lancashire* which sailed from Southampton, stopped for a time at Suez and, after three weeks at sea, finally came into port at Karachi. From there a troop train took Fred on to Peshawar where he joined the 8th Anti-aircraft Battery. Most of the time here was spent training as there was no fighting in the area. He was paid in rupees by the Indian Government but his most vivid memories are of the incredible heat and the ever-hungry mosquitoes.

Fred's next move involved a journey to the Himalayan - Afghan frontier where one of the local tribes - the Mohmands - was causing trouble. Whilst there he was taken very ill with malaria and had to be taken back to the military hospital at Peshawar where he spent some six weeks in bed. After his recovery, he moved back to his battery and army life continued. Fred was awarded the Indian General Services Medal for his part in the campaign against the Mohmands.

In 1936, the Italians attacked Abyssinia and the British, fearing that their interests in the Arabian Peninsular were threatened, moved troops into Aden. Fred's battery was amongst those chosen to re-enforce the garrison there and, now on a war footing, was given eight guns. During this period in Aden, King George V died, an English fleet of warships came to the port and Fred spent his time in routine drills and training. Eventually, it was decided that the Italian threat had passed and the Battery was moved back to India to complete its tour of duty.

Very soon after arriving back in Peshawar, Fred fell ill again and in 1937 it was decided to send him back to England for a change of climate. A medical board graded him C1 - 'Unfit for Service Overseas' - and he boarded the troopship *SS Nevasa* for the journey home. He arrived back in England in February 1937 and was immediately transferred to the military hospital

16. 'Doodlebugs' and 'Flying Gas Mains'

In April 1943, British intelligence sources reported to the government that the Germans were developing weapons of mass destruction in the form of pilotless planes and rockets. Mass panic throughout the population was feared and defence precautions were put into operation.

Six days after D-Day on the night of 12/13 June 1944, the first pilotless planes (V1s) crashed into south-eastern England. On the 16th June, the government announced to the British people that this new weapon had been unleashed and though the cabinet ruled that they should be called 'flying bombs' most people referred to them as either 'doodlebugs' or 'buzz bombs'. Every day for about a fortnight after the initial strike, 100 V1s were launched against England. Of every 100, about 40 were shot down by planes or ground artillery but over half reached their target - Greater London - particularly areas to the east and south of the city. The fiery emission of the plane's pulse-jet engine was clearly visible in the sky at night; its buzzing noise grew louder as it ran out of fuel, spluttered and finally died. This was the moment those below dreaded as they waited for the inevitable crash and the violent explosion of the 1875lb warhead - hopefully not too near themselves or their own house. Blast was the greatest threat after the explosion which shot arrows of glass over an area of a square quarter mile. The V1 which most people remember was the one which struck the Guards' Chapel in West London on 18 June. A service was in progress attended by many distinguished officers and 119 people were killed and 102 seriously injured.

Once again, evacuation procedures were put into operation and some one and a half million mothers, babies and schoolchildren left London and its suburbs.

In mid July, it was decided to redeploy all available anti-aircraft guns on the coast facing north-west Europe. Their fire was to be guided by radar and they were to use proximity shells which exploded near to their targets. This strategy proved highly effective for, in the next seven weeks, well over half of all the V1s launched were shot down - on one day the gunners scored 90 hits out of 97 V1s spotted. Gradually the threat receded; people began filtering back; the beer supply to the worst affective areas was increased and things began to get back to normal. In late August, Montgomery's 2nd Army advanced swiftly from the Seine to Antwerp and in doing so captured all the V1 launch sites in the Pas de Calais and largely ended this particular threat to England's civilian population. Some V1s continued to be launched either from piloted planes or from sites further east. Although the majority were still aimed at London some fell further north and on Christmas Eve 1944, a salvo was aimed at Manchester. The final V1 attack recorded was on 29 March 1945 - from then onwards Britain's air raid sirens were obsolete.

It seems that in total, some 10,500 V1s were launched of which nearly 3,500 were destroyed in flight by fighters, gunners or barrage balloons. A recorded 2,420 reached the London area killing 5,475 people and severely injuring some 16,000 more and 2,448 hit Antwerp after it had been liberated by the Allies. At the height of the barrage, 20,000 homes were being destroyed or damaged each day.

Unfortunately, the virtual ending of the V1 threat in autumn 1944 was not the end of this particular story. On 8 September 1944, the first of a series of mysterious, shattering explosions rocked the Chiswick area of London. Once again, tight security was decreed in an attempt to prevent panic and early explosions were blamed on gas leaks. Eventually on 10 November, Prime Minister Churchill had to announce that the Germans were now attacking with a new weapon - the fearsome V2 rocket - talked about as 'flying gas mains'. Forty-five feet long and weighing some fourteen tons, each of them cost twenty times as much as a V1. They were however far more destructive with a range of 200-220 miles, carrying a one ton warhead. It arrived unheralded and at great speed and the first anyone knew of a V2 rocket was when it landed.

In total some 1,115 V2s were launched. These were mainly aimed at London where some 518 landed. 2,754 people were killed and over 6,000 badly injured. The last V2 rocket fell in Kent on 27 March 1945.

See - Bernard Clipson, Jack Dimoline, Betsy Grimbleby and Eunice Marsh

at Netley in Hampshire. The authorities there decided that his C1 grading was correct and that, although he was fit to finish his army service, he was not to be sent overseas.

Following a period of home leave, he was told to report to a Royal Artillery battery at Lichfield. This proved to be the 1st Brigade Anti-Aircraft Battery which he had served in earlier at Blackdown, so he was back with some old friends. His six years of service were now coming to an end and, in preparation for his return to 'Civvy Street' he was sent on a fitter's course at Hounslow Heath in Middlesex (now the site of Heathrow Airport). This he passed with flying colours but rather than accept the good job he was offered in London, he chose to return back to Barton. Here work was hard to find and after short spells making 'slop' bricks in Frank's Yard at South Ferriby and at Blyth's Yard in Barton he finally found employment in the Packing Department at Ferriby Cement Works. During the nine months he spent as a civilian he married his childhood sweetheart, Phyllis Blood at the Trinity Wesleyan chapel.

On Friday 1 September 1939, Fred received notification that 'All reservists will report to their respective depots immediately.' He duly reported to a tented camp on Sandown Racecourse in Surrey **(1)** and on the following Sunday morning, whilst having a break in a tearoom in nearby Esher, heard Neville Chamberlain's announcement that our country was at war.

He was soon moved to Bulford Camp on Salisbury Plain and after spells in Leeds, Lichfield - he was there when the British soldiers returned from Dunkirk - and Anglesey he joined the Leeds Rifles Heavy Anti-aircraft Regiment based at Wentworth Park, near Barnsley. His unit was equipped with four 4.5-inch anti-aircraft guns and was part of the defence ring around Sheffield. They fired some shells at German bombers but never, as far as Fred knows, hit anything. By now he had been medically regraded B1 and began to fear that he might be sent overseas once again.

His fear proved well grounded for, towards the end on 1942, the unit was ordered to Greenock where it boarded a troopship bound for India via the Cape of Good Hope. After some three months at sea - much of the time spent avoiding enemy submarines - Fred's ship arrived at Bombay where the unit was transferred to the former liner *Mauritania* which took it on to Calcutta. After spending some time there, the Regiment was moved to Assam from where it began its journey into Burma and through its jungles. Fred had become part of what became known as 'The Forgotten Army'.

The Japanese army had advanced through Burma during early 1942, threatening India and cutting lines of communication along which the Allies were able to supply the Chinese army.

In 1944, Fred found himself in the area of Imphal, just inside Assam **(18)**. The siege of that town began on 30 March and lasted for three months. On 19 November, following weeks of airborne drops to the British troops, Operation *Extended Capital* was launched. The Japanese, unable to maintain supplies to their army, were finally defeated, losing some 13,000 soldiers. The tide was turned - and the Allies could begin to advance back into Burma. At one time during this period, Fred's battery found itself surrounded and was told to stand fast, fight to the last man and, if necessary, destroy its guns. Miraculously, this was not necessary.

Soon after this, Fred's malaria returned and he was sent back to India. On recovery, he was posted back to Burma and spent some time in a holding unit before being posted to the base ordnance depot where he was promoted to the rank of corporal, placed in charge of a vehicle park and was waited on by a native servant! Other duties included transporting ammunition through the jungle to forward units.

News arrived that the unit was to prepare itself for the invasion of Singapore but at this time news came through that A-bombs had been dropped on Hiroshima and Nagasaki and the plan was abandoned. The Japanese surrendered soon afterwards and Fred waited his turn in the 'Python' system. This was a procedure which calculated a man's turn for demobilisation. Eventually, Fred's name was posted and he travelled home finally to be give his civilian clothes at York and sent on his way back to Barton.

Information from

Fred Kirk

Frank Kitching

Signalman, 2597731
Royal Corps of Signals
Wireless Operator

Frank Kitching was born in 1921, the son of Mr John and Mrs Hannah Kitching of Shildon, County Durham. His father was Headmaster of St. Chad's School, Waterside (see *Barton Remembered 1939-1944; Part Two, The Home Front*, pp 113-114) and had served in the 8th Battalion of the Durham Light Infantry on the Somme in WW1. Frank attended St. Chad's School in Waterside and Barton Grammar School. He attended St. Chad's church and both St. Mary's and St. Peter's churches. He was a keen sportsman and played cricket for Barton. On leaving school in 1939 he joined Barclay's Bank in Trinity House Lane, Hull.

In early 1941 aged 20, and realising that he would soon be receiving his call-up papers, he walked into the recruiting office off Paragon Street in Hull and volunteered to join the RAF as a fighter pilot. However, he soon found that only university graduates or men with Higher School Certificates would be accepted as trainee pilots so, like his brother Noel (qv), he volunteered to join the Royal Corps of Signals. He received his joining instructions in March 1941 and travelled to Ossett where he undertook his initial training - 'square bashing' - and was billeted in a disused textile mill.

Following his initial training, Frank was posted to Huddersfield for signal training. During this period, he was billeted in a house in Fitzwilliam Street, Huddersfield. Initially the men slept on straw palliasses

Frank Kitching.

on the floor but, on a visit to Harrogate, Frank bought himself a sleeping bag and a Lilo and thereafter slept more comfortably. The training involved learning the Morse code and the operation of different receiving and transmitting sets. In his limited periods of spare time, Frank enjoyed himself playing for the Signals Training Brigade Cricket Team.

Later in 1941 Frank, was posted first to Staindrop in County Durham and somewhat later to Barnard Castle. During this period he was lucky to be granted regular leaves and he travelled first by bus to Richmond or Darlington and then by train to Barton.

In 1942 he was attached to the Border Tank Regiment stationed at Hawes in Wensleydale. The Regiment had Churchill tanks and on one occasion they were all put on a train and transported to Castle Martin in Pembrokeshire for tank range firing.

At the end of April 1943, Frank was posted to the East Riding Yeomanry at Rendlesham in Suffolk. Here he found life pleasant with regular exercises touring the lovely Suffolk villages practising radio communications. In February 1944, the Regiment moved up to Forres on the Moray Firth near Inverness. Here the East Yorkshire Yeomanry with the 13/18 Hussars and the 4/7 Dragoon Guards formed the 17th Armoured Brigade. He was billeted in the Forres Hydro Hotel and at a meeting in the great ballroom there the commander, Brigadier Prior-Palmer, told the men of the plans for the forthcoming invasion of Europe. 27th

Armoured Brigade was to act independently and to be equipped with DD (duplex drive) Sherman tanks which had been water-proofed and could travel through water six feet deep. They were to land on D-Day as part of the 3rd British Infantry Division.

In April, the Brigade moved south and by the 18th arrived at its new home at Pitworth Camp in Sussex. New signals vehicles were delivered and Frank got one of his own. In this he travelled across northern Europe as wireless operator to Major Edward Morley-Fletcher in command of 'B' echelon. The task was to maintain supplies of petrol and ammunition to the companies of the Regiment. During the stay at Pitworth, the Brigade was inspected by King George VI. Eventually it moved to a 'sealed' camp near Portsmouth to await embarkation.

At 4.30 pm on 5 June 1944, the assault tanks set sail for Europe. Frank sailed on an LCT (landing craft tanks) at about 2 pm on 6 June. It carried some Sherman tanks, other vehicles and a 15 cwt truck which Frank was to ride in. His wireless vehicle travelled separately. During the rough crossing most of the men were badly seasick and the sympathetic naval crew offered them some relief in the form of dry toast.

Early on the morning of 7 June - D-Day + 1 - Frank arrived off Sword Beach **(15)** near Ouistreham.

'I do not think anyone could fail to realise that history was being made and that he was taking part in the greatest armada of all time. The sea off France was full of craft of all kinds from LCTs to troop carriers, destroyers, cruisers and battleships. An unending stream of aircraft, fighters and bombers, passed overhead either as our protective escort or on other missions of destruction.'

Frank's LCT was unable to get to shore during that morning and drifted westward with the tide to finally land its cargo on Juno beach near Bernières-sur-Mer. They were separated from the rest of the Regiment which had landed on Sword Beach near Lion-sur-Mer and they spent the next two or three days trying to join up with their comrades.

Between 17 and 28 June Frank's regiment was encamped at Hermanville-sur-Mer, a small village north of Caen mounting probing attacks to test the enemy's defences. At this point, the British 2nd Army faced a considerable German force and the Allies had to build up their strength before they could mount a real break-out from their beachhead. On 2 July, the East Riding Yeomanry was pulled back to Luc-sur-Mer for three days respite from the constant shelling. On the afternoon of 8 July, Frank witnessed the armada of some 2000 Allied bombers which passed overhead on the way to bomb Caen - 'It was an awesome sight and we could smell the gunpowder miles away.'

On 15 July, the Regiment crossed the Orne and passed

the hundreds of gliders which had carried the airborne troops who had landed on 5 June. They established camp near Troarn and whilst there one, of their 3 ton trucks, full of ammunition, was hit by a German bomb and exploded. Frank describes conditions here as the worst he experienced - the land had been flooded by the Germans. As it was very hot and sultry the area was an ideal breeding ground for millions of insects including mosquitoes. As soon as trenches were dug, they filled with water and life resembled something like that suffered by the men in the First World War.

By mid-August, the German retreat out of northern France began in earnest and by September, Frank's unit was on the move every day. On 2 September, he passed through Rouen where cheering French crowds lined the streets. Later the Regiment was involved in the capture of the port of Le Havre and soon afterwards it crossed the Seine on a Bailey bridge.

Frank's letter home dated 21 October recorded: 'We went straight through Belgium. Our truck was not running well and we were on our own the whole way. We had no rations and were getting hungry. Having passed through Amiens, Arras and Lille we decided to stop near Douai. My French managed to get us some supper in a pub. In spite of the fact that they had so little we had a good meal of French soup, potatoes and an egg. They put two nice mattresses down for us in the kitchen. In the morning they gave us coffee and cognac and we were on our way.'

On 31 October, Frank reported home that the port of Antwerp had been taken and that he was hoping to have 48 hours leave in Brussels. His pay had just been raised by one shilling a day to six shillings and nine pence (34p). By late November, the Regiment was in northern Holland at a place called Oudenbosch. There they were accommodated in a monastic school run by a number of brothers. 'On arrival, the advance parties were asked by the Head Brother how many men we had. To the reply of over 800 he said, "But we could not possibly do with that number, we have only 500 beds." To soldiers who had slept outdoors nearly every night since well before 6 June and been thankful for a roof as shelter, the very idea of a bed seemed almost unbelievable.'

On 19 December, the Brigade was ordered to move again. The German counteroffensive through the Ardennes had taken the Allies completely by surprise and after a journey of some 120 miles, the Regiment found itself in an area south of Louvain. The weather was bitterly cold with sleet and occasional snow. Frank was lucky to be allowed a 48 hour leave in Brussels for Christmas.

All too soon this break was over and Frank found himself back in the very cold Ardennes. Here he found himself billeted with Auguste and Evelyn in the village of Hotton. Evelyn had been an active member of the Belgian resistance movement collecting arms which

had been parachuted into the country. (Frank visited them for two weeks in 1947.)

On 17 January, the Brigade was told that it would be equipped with Buffaloes for the crossing of the Rhine, and in early April Frank found himself in Germany and soon the war in Europe was over.

On 18 June, he wrote home from Laboe near the Keil Canal. He had travelled through Bremen and Hamburg and had been amazed by the destruction wrought by the Allied bombers. In mid-July he was sent into Denmark and was based in a barracks in the town of Haderslev where he waited for his transfer back to England.

Following a period of leave at home in Barton, he returned to Tunbridge Wells where he learned that he was about to be posted to the Middle East. On 4 December 1945, he began his journey first from Newhaven to Dieppe and from there by train to Toulon. There, on 10 December, he boarded the liner *Celicia* and eventually landed at Port Said in Egypt. From there he travelled by train to Cairo and started life in the Almaza camp. Whilst in Egypt, he visited many of the famous historical sites and museums. His visit to the Cairo Museum allowed him to view the Treasures of Tutankhamun.

In early 1946, he boarded a train for the journey to Jerusalem where he was stationed at the famous Allenby Barracks. There he worked nights as a clerk in the Casualty Office organising the transfer of personal in and out of the station. Once again this posting allowed him to enjoy the sites of this ancient city as well as Bethlehem and the Dead Sea.

At this time Palestine was still a British Mandated Territory in which for many decades Jewish immigrants had settled among the local Arab population. Before 1939, but increasingly after 1945, the Jews wished to establish an independent homeland in Palestine and be allowed to bring into the country any and all possible Jewish immigrants. Various Jewish terrorist organisations (Haganah, Irgun and the Stern Gang), at this time working together in the Jewish resistance movement, were hoping to promote these causes and Frank was in the Allenby Barracks when he heard the great explosion - the work of Irgun - which blew up part of the King David Hotel in Jerusalem. Ninety-one people died in the blast - Britons (including 20 soldiers), Arabs and Jews.

At this time, Frank was eagerly awaiting his release from the forces and was toying with the idea of taking a qualification in French with a view to entering the teaching profession. He was given permission to join a course at the Army Formation College which was housed on the summit of Mount Carmel. After one month's tuition led by a French Jewess (who said she had never been to France!), Frank was awarded a certificate which stated that he would be 'eminently suitable as a Frenceh master'!

Soon Frank was on his way back to England by sea across the Mediterranean and by train across France. On 14 August 1946 he was demobilised form the depot at Knaphill near Woking where he received his civilian clothes and £32/10/0 War Gratuity (10/- [50p] for each month which he served). He later received his Post War Credits of £41/1/0.

Information from

Frank Kitching

Noel (later John) Kitching

Lance Corporal, 2591755
Royal Corps of Signals
Signal Office Operator

John Noel Kitching was born in 1919, the son of Mr John and Mrs Hannah Kitching of Shildon, County Durham. His family moved to Barton in 1930 when his father, John Kitching, became Headmaster of St. Chad's School in Waterside (see *Barton Remembered 1939-1945 Part Two; The Home Front*, p 113-114). He attended both St. Chad's and St. Mary's churches and his hobbies were sports (football, cricket, hockey and ice-skating), stamp collecting and photography. He was one of the first pupils at Barton Grammar School

Noel (later John) Kitching in Cairo in 1941.

when it opened in 1931 and left in 1936 to work in the Midland Bank at Harrogate.

On 3 April 1940, he travelled to Enfield and joined the Royal Corps of Signals. From there (and just after the evacuation from Dunkirk) he was posted first to 18 Division Signals in Norfolk and later to Scotland. In March 1941 he moved to join 'O' Signals Division at Knutsford in Cheshire. (This was a fortuitous move for Noel. Soon after he left it 18 Division sailed to the Far East. It was landed at Singapore and when that base fell to the Japanese on 15 February 1942, the whole Division was taken prisoner. In total 130,000 British troops fell into Japanese hands - the greatest single defeat in British history. Noel could well have been one of those taken.)

In April 1941 on board the *Reina del Pacifico,* he sailed from the Clyde on a convoy - escorted by *HMS Repulse*, and *HMS Renown* - which travelled to the Middle East via Freetown and the Cape of Good Hope. A severe storm in the Cape region caused the ship's cargo to move in the hold and as a result the ship took on a severe list. It was necessary to put into Durban for repairs and John spent six weeks there waiting for the next convoy to Suez to arrive. He eventually boarded the *New Amsterdam,* and in May 1941 finally disembarked in the Suez Canal area. After a period of training at Atmena near Cairo, he joined 70 Division Signals for active service in Palestine, Lebanon and Syria guarding the oil pipeline from Iraq to the Mediterranean ports.

In October 1941, he returned to Alexandria and sailed in the destroyer *HMS Jaguar* to Tobruk where he was part of the force which relieved the Australian 9th Division which had held that vital port during the famous 'Siege of Tobruk'. He stayed at Tobruk **(7)**, still under siege, for two months until the port was finally relieved in late November 1941. From November 1941 until June 1942 he stayed in Tobruk and the El Adem area with 4 Line of Communications Signals during the 8th Army's battles with Rommel's *Afrika* Corps.

On 20/21 June 1942, he was in the Signal Office in the harbour area of Tobruk when the town fell. The fall of Tobruk, with the loss of 70 tanks and 35,000 soldiers captured was the biggest blow to Allied morale since the fall of Singapore. Noel Kitching was among the few - about 30 soldiers and crew - who, on the evening of 20 June escaped aboard a motor torpedo boat. The next day he was landed at Mersa Matruh where he entrained for Alexandria. From there he was sent back to the signals base camp near Cairo and allowed a week's leave.

On his return in early July, he was posted to 28 Operating Section of the 8th Army Signals in General Montgomery's tactical headquarters some 10 miles behind the lines at El Alamein. His work involved passing coded messages to the divisional headquarters of the 9th Division and also SBO work.

After the successful counterattack at El Alamein in October-November 1942, the German and Italian armies were in full retreat and Noel entered Tripoli in December. He was there when Winston Churchill visited the 8th Army and spoke to the troops at army HQ.

The continuing advance drove the Axis forces back into Tunisia until they finally surrendered in May and some 250,000 enemy soldiers were captured.

Later in May, Noel sailed from Tripoli to Malta and he was there for six weeks working in the underground Allied War Headquarters at Valetta. The work here involved planning for the invasion of Sicily. Two days after the Allied landings at Syracuse on 10 July, he landed on Sicily with 8th Army Headquarters and was on the island throughout the whole campaign which resulted in its complete capture.

When the 8th Army crossed to the Italian mainland, he remained with HQ Signal Office during the whole of the advance up the peninsular and followed the German withdrawal into Austria. He celebrated VE Day (8 May 1945) in Venice.

After some 4½ years abroad, he was repatriated from Naples to RAF Wittering in the bomb-bay of a RAF Lancaster. He remained in the Royal Corps of Signals until August 1946 when he was demobilised. He was in Barton on VJ Day - 15 August 1945.

Information from

John Kitching

Arthur Knight

Sapper, 2155650
Corps of Royal Engineers
Lines of Communication/Port Repairs

Arthur James Knight was born in 1921, the son of Mr Jim and Mrs Edith Knight of Victoria Terrace ('Rabbit-pie Row'), Barton-on-Humber. He attended the County School and on leaving, took an apprenticeship as a bricklayer with the builders Stamp and Sons which had premises in Brigg Road. A lot of his apprenticeship was spent on the building of the Catholic church in Whitecross Street. In the early years of the war, Arthur moved to work at Killingholme, building walls around the oil storage tanks there. After that job was completed, he went to Purfleet in Essex to complete similar work there. On returning home he worked on Elsham and Wickenby airfields. He was a member of the football team at the Barton Boys' Club.

In March 1942, he was called up to join the army and reported for training to the 3rd Training Battalion, Royal

Arthur Knight.

Engineers at Bowbridge Road, Newark. On completion of his training, he was posted to Aldershot where he joined a demonstration platoon to show other soldiers how to lay mines, build bridges, and use explosives and camouflage. After this work, he was sent to the Port Maintenance Section at Faslane in Scotland where the army was making the port operational by building deep water berths with railway sidings. Whilst here he was also employed maintaining a decoy station on the nearby hills. Here were burnt masses of straw bales mixed with wax. The flames were intended to lure German bombers to drop their loads onto these flames in the mistaken assumption that they were bombing the industrial sites in Glasgow and along the banks of the Clyde. After completion, the docks at Faslane were used by 'Liberty Ships' bringing servicemen and essential war supplies over from America. (After the war Faslane became a base for UK nuclear-powered submarines.)

Just before the invasion of Europe, a new unit - 1052 Maintenance Company - was formed in preparation for D-Day. In this company there were all manner of craftsmen including joiners, drivers, sign-writers, bricklayers, and platelayers. Following a spell in Kent, the Company was landed on D-Day + 1 on Juno Beach in Normandy **(15)**. Here his job was to maintain the beachhead and ensure that stores and equipment moved freely to the troops further inland. Afterwards he moved forwards, first to Ostend, where he helped to make the port operational again. Many sunken boats blocked the harbour and the roads, cranes and lighting had all been destroyed. Thereafter he followed the advancing army through France, Belgium and Germany. His final job was in Hamburg where again much work had to be done to make the port operational. It was here that he heard he was to be posted to the Far East but he had only reached Bruges when news was received of the dropping of the atomic bombs and the war was over.

He was now 'companyless' and the army appeared unable to decide what to do with him. He was eventually sent on indefinite leave before he received orders to move to Egypt on what became known as a 'Cook's Tour' of duty. There the army camps became overcrowded with men waiting for demobilisation. Soon Arthur and many others were again sent home on indefinite leave. After some seven weeks at home his turn came and he was told to report first to Halifax and from there to York from where he was finally demobilised.

Information from

Arthur Knight

Hector Lawtey.

Hector Lawtey

Corporal, 4803999
6th Battalion, Lincolnshire Regiment
Signaller/Radio Operator

Hector Lawtey was brought up by his two aunts, Ethel and Eidie Lawtey, who ran a sweet shop at 43 High Street, Barton-on-Humber. He was educated at the Church School in Queen Street and attended both St. Peter's and St. Mary's churches. He worked as a shop assistant at Tuthill's Grocery Shop in the Market Place and was Scoutmaster for the 2nd Barton-on-Humber Scout Troop. He enjoyed playing billiards at the Church Institute (now the Assembly Rooms) in Queen Street.

He was conscripted into the army on 15 September 1939 at the Burton Road Barracks in Lincoln. After signal training (Morse and semaphore) at Stores Park he was posted to the HQ Company of the 6th Battalion of the Lincolnshire Regiment. In 1940, the Battalion moved to Southampton from where it sailed to Cherbourg. After staying some time at Rennes, it moved on to join the BEF **(2)** in the front at Douai. As a support Battalion, it did not see much action and lost only a few men. Eventually, the British were forced to retreat, the Battalion was split up and Hector was evacuated from Dunkirk **(4 - 5)** after spending a day and a half on the beach and some 12 hours in the water - all the time under constant aerial bombardment. He was finally picked up by *HMS Venomous* and landed at Dover.

After regrouping at Aldershot, the Battalion moved to various locations in the UK for training. In late 1943 he sailed in a Polish ship from Glasgow as part of the Eastern Task Force of Operation *Torch* **(11)** which was to attack French North Africa using many of the American troops newly arrived in the UK. The 6th Lincolnshires landed at Algiers and joined the 1st Army campaigns in North Africa. This Army drove eastwards towards Tunis and by May 1943, the Axis forces in Africa surrendered.

The 6th Lincolnshires did not take part in the Sicily campaign or the initial invasion of Italy, but on 9 September 1943 the Battalion was part of Operation *Avalanche* in which the Anglo-American 5th Army under General Mark Clark landed at Salerno, just south of Naples **(12)**. After initial heavy fighting, it joined up with Montgomery's 8th Army and proceeded to advance up Italy. By now the Italians had surrendered and were fighting with the Allies.

The German army continued to fiercely resist the Allied advance up Italy. In January 1944, determined to reach Rome, the 5th Army launched the attack on Monte Cassino and faced a determined German garrison. The 6th Lincolnshires took part in some of the fiercest fighting of the war here and it was not until 18 May that Polish troops entered the empty monastery. Hector was wounded here and was out of the action for about a month.

Some time after the battle, Hector's battalion travelled to Cairo for a period of rest before being sent back to Italy - this time as part of the force moving up the east

17. Operation *Market Garden*

Following the fall of Paris in late August 1944, the Allied armies advanced to liberate most of France and Belgium. By then there were over 2,000,000 Allied troops on the European mainland - three-fifths of them Americans. On 1 September, Eisenhower took over command of all of the ground forces from Montgomery who was not best pleased at what he saw as his demotion. Soon afterwards, a major disagreement regarding the strategy of the campaign further soured the relationship between these two men. Montgomery favoured a single thrust into Germany using troops under his command; Eisenhower, all too aware that such a move would down-grade the efforts of US General Patton, favoured an advance on a broad front.

In any case, September proved to be a month of few successes for the Allies. Whilst their lines of communication back to the Normandy beaches were very long (German garrisons still held Le Havre, Boulogne, Calais and Dunkirk), the German lines were now very short. To add to the supply problems Montgomery, though he had captured Antwerp, failed to open the port to Allied ships.

At that juncture, and somewhat surprisingly for a soldier renowned for the very careful preparation of any scheme he undertook , Montgomery came up with a bold new plan to outflank the Germans' main line of defence - the Siegfried Line - and attack Germany by the 'back door' through Holland. US and British airborne divisions would be dropped behind enemy lines, seize three strategically important bridges, and thus facilitate a quick advance of Allied armour onto the North German Plain. Even reliable reports from the codebreakers at Bletchley Park, who warned of the presence of large numbers of German panzer troops in the Arnhem area, failed to stop Montgomery going ahead.

Operation *Market Garden*, as the plan was codenamed, was hastily launched on 17 September. The first part of the plan - *Market* - went quite smoothly and the US 82nd and 101st Airborne Divisions duly took the bridges at Eindhoven and Nijmegen. However, further to the north the British 1st Airborne Division, whose goal was the capture of the bridges at Arnhem, was (as a result of an air plan imposed by the RAF) dropped some eight miles away from its target and then met severe resistance from the 9th and 10th SS Panzer Divisions which were regrouping in the area. Following days of vicious house-to-house fighting in Arnhem itself, and an attempt by the Guards Armoured Division to relieve the paratroopers by moving overland from the south, the British were overwhelmed and on 27 September were forced to surrender.

Of the British 10,000 paratroopers who landed, 1,200 were killed, 6,642 were either taken prisoner, injured or reported missing and 2,163 made it safely back to Allied lines. If the daring plan had succeeded, the popular cry 'end the war in 44' might have become a reality. Unfortunately, Arnhem did indeed prove to be 'a bridge too far' and indicted that Montgomery was fallible after all.

See - Gordon Linley and Arthur Sobey

coast of the peninsular.

From there, in late 1944, he was moved to Greece. The Germans had recently withdrawn and the Allies feared a communist take-over similar to that which had taken place in Yugoslavia and Albania to the north. The British were rapidly reinforced in Greece - not knowing that Stalin had already decided that Greece was not to be the target of a communist take-over.

Following the German surrender in 1945, he was moved to Austria on peace monitoring duties before eventually being discharged from the forces in Vienna.

His overwhelming memories of the war are of the friendships which were forged during that time and the destruction which he witnessed, particularly at Monte Casino.

Information from

Hector Lawtey

Stan Lawtey MM

Private, 4807011
6th Battalion, Lincolnshire Regiment
Infantryman/Stretcher Bearer

Stanley Lawtey (see front cover) was born in 1913, the son of Mr Edwin and Mrs Alice Lawtey of Newport, Barton-on-Humber. He attended the Church School in Queen Street and afterwards worked at the Appleby Frodingham Steel Works in Scunthorpe. He was a keen gardener.

He joined the army in late 1939 (or was it 1940 or even 1941?) and was enlisted into the 6th Battalion of the Lincolnshire Regiment. He saw service in North Africa and Italy. (See the biographies of Ted Bones and Hector Lawtey [both qv] for the story of the 6th Battalion of the Lincolnshire Regiment.

During the battle at Sedjenane in Algeria **(11)** on 3-4 March 1943, Stan did sterling work as a stretcher bearer. It was, however, in a battle some seven weeks later that Stan won his Military Medal (see front cover). The Allied advance on to the Goubellat Plain was being held up at a feature known as Arghoub Hamra. The crack Herman Goering Division was holding this position and was causing great problems. The commanding officers of the Lincolns and the King's Own Yorkshire Light Infantry along with an artillery officer met to discuss the problem when a shell hit their position and killed them all. This delayed proceedings but eventually an attack was mounted. It was during this battle that Stan won his award. The citation reads -

'The Award of The Military Medal To 4807011 Private Stanley Lawtey

'In the attack on Arghoub Hamra ... at dawn on 22nd April 1943, Private Lawtey was Stretcher Bearer for his Company. In the final assault on a fortified farm the company suffered eight casualties most of whom it was impossible to evacuate, until the capture of the final objective.

'These wounded men, lying in the open, were being subjected to mortar and shell fire. Private Lawtey, without hesitation, took charge of the situation, and getting men to assist him, carried the wounded to a gully which provided some protection, crossing an area where two men had been wounded by anti-personnel mines. In spite of an enemy M.G. [machine gun] which opened fire on the Company from an adjoining farm, Private Lawtey gathered all the wounded and provided shade for them from the increasing heat.

'Finally Private Lawtey was himself wounded by an enemy shell. During the whole action this soldier's persistence in his difficult duty, and his constant cheerfulness, even after being wounded and in pain, was a magnificent example.'

Information from

David Lawtey (son)

Ted Bones

Gordon Linley

Flight Lieutenant, 164560
No 299 Squadron, Royal Air Force
Navigator

Gordon Henderson Linley was born in 1923, the son of Mr Herbert and Mrs Florence Linley of 22 Priestgate, Barton-on-Humber. He was educated at the County School and after leaving first worked as a lorry driver for W.J. Davies, General Hauliers of Whitecross Street. His hobby was playing cricket and he was also a member of the local Air Training Corps which met at the Grammar School (see *Barton Remembered 1939-1945; Part Two, The Home Front*, pp 24-25) and the Boy Scouts. As a young boy he sang in the choir at St. Peter's and St. Mary's churches.

He volunteered to join the RAF in late 1941 and, after reporting to Lord's Cricket Ground, was transferred to the Initial Training Wing at Babbacombe in Devon. Here he was trained in navigation and gunnery as well as general air force duties.

From there, in 1942, he went to Rivers in Manitoba, Canada for 30 weeks of navigation flying training in Avro Ansons. After returning to England in early 1943, he was 'crewed up' at Slape in Shropshire on twin-engined Wellington bombers. He was soon converted to four-engined Sterling bombers and in mid-1943 he joined No 299 Squadron at Wethersfield in Essex where he undertook further training flights. A Sterling bomber had a crew of six - a pilot, a navigator (Gordon's

Short Stirling P for Peter of 299 Squadron. Note the glider-towing mechanism under the rear fuselage.

Gordon and Bette Linley about to leave on their honeymoon in 1946.

Eunice Marsh (later Whiteley)

Petty Officer
Women's Royal Naval Service
Officer's Steward/Hall Porter

Eunice Miriam Marsh was born in Waterville, County Kerry, Ireland, the daughter of William Edwin and Mabel Maude Marsh. Her father was a customs officer and the family moved to the Shetland Islands before coming to Barton in the early 1930s. Eunice lived variously in Dam Road, Queens Avenue and Butts Road. She attended the County School in Castledyke for two years before moving to complete her education at the Convent School in Bardney Hall. Whilst at school she was chosen to be the Carnival Queen of Barton. On leaving school, she was employed as an usherette at the Oxford Cinema in Newport and there met her future husband.

In 1940, without telling her parents, she travelled to Grimsby and volunteered to join the WRNS. She was required to report to Chatham and there found herself employed as an officer's steward though she also did some book-keeping work in the Wardroom. Later she was employed as the hall porter with a staff of her own.

She has memories of marching on parade in front of the Royal Family and was in London close to the location where the first 'Doodlebug' landed **(16)**. On VE Day, she took the night train up to London and was in the crowd outside Buckingham Palace when

job), a bomb aimer (who acted as second pilot), a wireless operator, a rear gunner and an engineer. From there the Squadron moved to Shepherd's Grove in Suffolk where it was involved in the towing of Horsa gliders carrying airborne troops on the landings at Arnhem and the Rhine crossing. These gliders would carry about 24 soldiers or a jeep and a small gun. Gordon flew to Arnhem **(17)** and dropped containers with supplies for the troops on the ground. He also flew about a dozen sorties dropping supplies to the French Resistance fighters. On these flights, the Sterlings operated at 1,000 feet or below and carried the containers in the converted bomb-bay. On release, a parachute was opened and the container dropped safely to the ground. In total he flew over 1,000 hours including training.

Following VE Day, his crew was split up and he was posted to Istres in Southern France (about 20 miles form Marseilles) where he was employed as a briefing officer handling the transport aircraft which were flying out to India and the Middle East.

He was finally demobbed in November 1946 from Weeton near Blackpool in Lancashire.

Information from

Gordon Linley

Eunice Marsh.

the Royal Family made its memorable appearance on the balcony. She returned to Chatham next morning and being somewhat AWOL (absent without leave), she had to climb back into the barracks through a downstairs window!

In late September 1946, she was granted 14 days leave and on the 27th she was married to Cecil Whiteley, the owner of Barton's two cinemas (see *Barton Remembered 1939-1945; Part Two, The Home Front*, pp 75-78) at the priory church in Bridlington where her parents were living at the time. Her new husband promptly whisked her off to Manchester Airport where they flew first to Paris and then on to Geneva for their honeymoon. One of Eunice's clearest memories was being served bananas for the sweet course at dinner - a fruit very rarely seen in England during the war years! Whilst she was in Geneva, she received a worried phone call from her mother informing her that the naval authorities had no record of her leave (the officer who had granted it had been demobbed) and that she was considered to be a deserter. The couple left Geneva on 11 October and were back in Barton on the 12th. Eunice reported back to Chatham on the 14th, the misunderstanding was cleared up, and she was duly demobbed on the 16 October 1946.

Information from

Eunice Whiteley

Wilfrid Marshall-Ducker at No 5 BFTS in Florida, summer 1945.

Wilfrid Marshall-Ducker

AC2C, 3041150
Royal Air Force Voluntary Reserve
Aircrew Training

Kenneth Wilfrid Marshall-Ducker was born in 1926, the son of Mr Kenneth V and Mrs DM Ducker of 8 Queen Street, Barton-on-Humber. He attended the County School and Barton Grammar School where he was twice Victor Ludorum and helped to build the School's air raid shelters at the beginning of the war. His hobbies were building Meccano models, constructing flying models and experimenting with radio design and circuit construction. In 1941 he was one of the first Barton youths to join the town's newly-formed Air Training Corps and gained air-experience in Wellingtons, Lancasters and Oxfords, mainly with No 103 Squadron based at Elsham. He was selected for instruction in solo glider flying which involved him staying weekends at Lincoln.

When in May 1943 he reached the necessary age of seventeen years and three months, he volunteered to join the Royal Air Force and was selected for pilot/navigator training. This involved him undertaking six

months of academic study with Durham University Air Squadron. During this period he lived in the Castle at Durham and flew Oxfords from Ouston, near Newcastle. Further flying training took place at Carlisle - flying solo in Tiger Moths and at the BFTS (British Flying Training School) at Clewiston, Florida, USA . During this time the war ended, flying courses were abandoned and he was demobbed in 1947.

Information from

Wilfrid Marshall-Ducker

Beula Mellors (later Hammond)

Leading Aircraftswoman, 2039575
Women's Auxiliary Air Force
Clerk

Beula Mellors was born in 1923, the daughter of Mr Percy and Mrs Bertha Mellors of 24 Queens Avenue, Barton. She was educated at the County School in

18. The War Against Japan - phase 2

By the middle of 1942, the Japanese had achieved most of their wartime objectives. The occupation of Malaya, Burma and the Philippines provided the necessary raw materials for war and the seizure of the oilfields in the Dutch East Indies satisfied the Imperial Navy's thirst for fuel. These victories had been quite easily achieved against weak and unprepared enemies. Japan's two greatest opponents, Britain and, in particular, the United States might have been bruised but defeated they certainly were not. It was decided that once the war in Europe was successfully completed, all Allied attention would be focused on the final victory over Japan.

Between 1942 and 1945, the Japanese army was required to occupy large areas of south-east Asia as well as the Chinese mainland. Fighting continued unabated in China and against British and Commonwealth troops in northern Burma. Meanwhile growing United States sea power was threatening the navy which had achieved such a stunning victory at Pearl Harbour and, in the naval engagement at Midway Island in June 1942, a stunning American victory 'spelled the ultimate doom of Japan.'

In December 1942, an offensive into upper Burma was begun by the 14th Indian Division. This aimed to drive down along the coast and take the airfield at Akyab from where Rangoon could be attacked. Although initially successful, the advance soon ran into stiff Japanese resistance on the Arakan peninsular and by May 1943 had been driven back to its starting line. Meanwhile, in February 1943, Orde Wingate led the first of his 'Chindit' guerrilla expeditions behind Japanese lines. These were to be supplied by air and would hope to cut the supply lines to the enemy's forward troops. In both campaigns the roadless mountains and jungles on the India-Burma border proved formidable obstacles to progress.

The Japanese advance through Burma had cut off the Chinese from the outside world. By 1944 the Americans had gained full control of the Pacific Ocean and saw that their next task was to defeat the Japanese army on land. It was therefore essential that the Burma Road be reopened in order that Chiang Kai-shek's Chinese army, which had launched an offensive to take Myitkyina airfield in October 1943, be kept supplied with arms. The Japanese, also appreciating the importance of this route and its continued closure, chose to strike first. Their pre-emptive strike in February 1944 started with a diversionary raid in the Arakan to draw away Allied troops. This move was followed in early March by a major thrust into Assam (north-east India) where it was intended that Operation *U-Go* would capture the key British communications and supply base at Imphal before an advance on towards the rail centre at Kohima and then possibly even Delhi itself! General Slim, the British Commander, forewarned of the Japanese plan and by now having a superiority of manpower and firepower, was able to pull back troops from other nearby areas and withstand the ferocious assault on the Imphal plain and at Kohima where, for a while, Allied forces were completely surrounded. Unwilling to accept defeat, the Japanese fought a series of protracted battles which saw the relief of both Imphal and Kohima and effectively eliminated their 15th Army. In June, Imphal was relieved and the stage was set for the advance into Burma in 1945.

Aided by a series of amphibious landings along the Arakan coast and the Chinese army's offensive in the north-east, the British moved relentlessly into Burma. Kalewa fell on 24 December, Nyaungu on 21 February and the main prize, Meiktila and its airfield in early March. A final desperate attack by the Japanese retook the airfield but they were soon beaten back. Mandalay fell and the Allies continued their drive south until Rangoon was taken on 3 May 1945. The war ended with the Japanese trying to regroup their still considerable forces in Burma.

See - Leonard Brown, Ron Clayton, Haydn Cocking, Jack Foster, Robert Harrison, Tom Kerridge, Fred Kirk, Philip Thompson

Castledyke and at Hull GREGG School, an independent commercial college. She was subsequently employed by J.C. Lee Chemists in George Street.

In October 1942, she was conscripted into the WAAF and completed her initial training at Morecombe in Lancashire. She was later posted to RAF North Coates - a Coastal Command station; the BPSO (Base Personnel Staff Office) at Avening Court in Gloucester which was a manor house requisitioned by the RAF for the storage of records; RAF Clifton at York - also a records office; and RAF Barnwood in Gloucestershire - yet another records office.

During the whole of her service she was engaged in clerical duties.

Information from

Beula Hammond

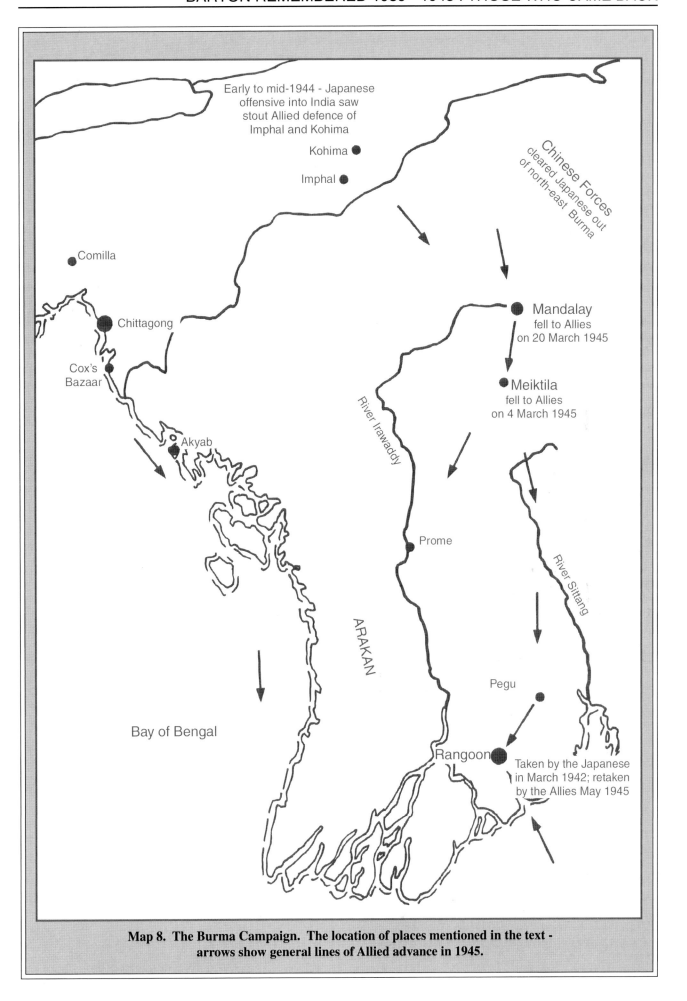

Early to mid-1944 - Japanese offensive into India saw stout Allied defence of Imphal and Kohima

Kohima ●

Imphal ●

Chinese Forces cleared Japanese out of north-east Burma

● Comilla

● Chittagong

Cox's
Bazaar ●

○ Akyab

Mandalay
fell to Allies
on 20 March 1945

● Meiktila
fell to Allies
on 4 March 1945

River Irawaddy

Prome

River Sittang

ARAKAN

Pegu

Bay of Bengal

Rangoon ●
Taken by the Japanese
in March 1942; retaken
by the Allies May 1945

**Map 8. The Burma Campaign. The location of places mentioned in the text -
arrows show general lines of Allied advance in 1945.**

Frank Milner

Corporal, 14908594
Royal Army Service Corps
Staff Clerk

Frank Revell Milner was born in 1926, the son of Mr George Francis and Mrs Nellie Milner of 2 East Acridge (now demolished), Barton-on-Humber. He attended the County School and subsequently worked as a clerk at Brown, Hudson and Hudson, Solicitors in Priestgate. For three years he was a member of the Barton Air Training Corps (see *Barton Remembered 1939-1945; Part Two, The Home Front,* pp 24-25) and hoped that when he reached 18 years of age he would be able to join the RAF. The Corps made regular visits to Elsham Wolds where they were shown around the base and joined the Lancaster crews on short pre-operational flights. On one memorable occasion he was flown to the very north of Scotland, westwards towards the Isles down to the Welsh border and then across England back to Elsham. The flight lasted for some 3½ hours. He attended an aircrew selection board at Scarborough where he was classified as PNB - fit for training as either a pilot, navigator or bomb aimer. Unfortunately, by the time he reached 18, the war was nearly over and the RAF was not needing any more aircrew.

Frank was very disappointed when, in January 1945, he was conscripted into the army and travelled to Fort

George near Inverness for initial training. He then did a six-week clerical training course at Loughborough Technical College after which he joined the RASC. His first postings were to Woking and Leeds. On VE-Day he was sent to Dunstable in Bedfordshire where he stayed until September 1945 when he was posted to Newcastle on overseas draft. From there he was sent to Liverpool and boarded the *MV Llangibby Castle.*

After three weeks he landed at Bombay where he stayed for two months before he was posted to Colombo in Ceylon (now Sri Lanka). From there he moved to Trincomalee where he was employed in clerical duties. His release from the services was long delayed because he had been conscripted late in the war and soldiers who had served for many years were being demobbed first.

From Trincomalee he was moved to Kandy - Admiral Mountbatten's wartime HQ. The unit was next moved back to Garrison HQ at Colombo where he stayed until December 1947 when he came home on a pre-release course at Welbeck Abbey. Here he did a six-week course in preparation for his demobilisation at Aldershot on 20 February 1948.

Information from

Frank Milner

Frank Milner.

Ken Milner

Flight Sergeant, 571919
Royal Air Force
Radio Instructor

Kenneth George Milner was born in 1922, the son of Mr George Francis and Mrs Nellie Milner of Scunthorpe. The family moved to Barton when he was two years old. He was educated at the Church School in Queen Street, at the County School in Castledyke and at Barton Grammar School.

He left school in 1937 when he was 15 years old and joined the RAF as an aircraft apprentice at RAF Halton in Buckinghamshire. From there he moved to RAF Cranwell and when he was 18 he went to RAF Scampton where he completed his electric and wireless training. There he flew as an instructor.

From Scampton he was sent to Canada to help train the many RAF personnel who were sent there during the war. In Canada they could complete their training flights safely distanced from the war in Europe. He stayed there for three years.

In late 1944 he returned to England and was stationed at various airfields still as a wireless instructor. He stayed in the RAF for a further seven years after the

Ken Milner.

war working on long-distance radio teleprinter communications between India, Singapore, Ceylon and the UK.

Information from

Ken Milner

Arthur Newbitt

Stoker First Class, KX 146080
Royal Navy
Stoker

Arthur Newbitt was born in 1902, the second son (of seven children) of Mr George and Mrs Sarah Ann Newbitt of 6 Hungate, Barton-on-Humber. He was educated at the Church of England School in Queen Street and along with his brother Ernest (see *Barton Remembered, Part One : Lest We Forget*, p 48) he was a member of the choir at St. Mary's church. As a small boy, he helped Carline the Bakers of Hungate delivering bread with their horse and cart. He was a keen footballer and played for various teams in the town before serving on the Committee of the Barton Town Football Club. He was always a keen gardener and had an allotment on the site of what is now the Humber Bridge viewing area car park.

On leaving school, he worked for a short time at the

Barton Cement Works at Ness Point before joining the staff of the North Lindsey and Howdenshire Electric Supply Company on East Acridge. This later became part of the Yorkshire Electricity Board and it was whilst he was working for them as a metre reader that he was called up in December 1941. On 3 December 1927, he married Emily Plaskitt the daughter of Emily Plaskitt who kept a shop at the bottom of Waterside Road.

He saw service at a number of shore bases before going to sea on the 5,450 ton *Dido* class cruiser *HMS Phoebe* in July 1943. This ship's main armament was eight 5.25-inch guns and she had a maximum speed of 33 knots. She had been built at the Govan yard in Glasgow between 1937 and 1940. During Arthur's period on this ship, he saw action in the Mediterranean escorting convoys to Malta and also took part in operations in the Aegean Sea.

In December 1943, he moved to *HMS Woolwich* and stayed on this ship until September 1945. This ship saw service in the Pacific under Lord Louis Mountbatten. This included a period in Ceylon from where he sent his family a 2lb tin of tea in a small wooden box. He was awarded the Italy Medal and the Burma Star.

He was eventually demobbed in January 1946 and in

Arthur Newbitt (left) with his brother George in Ceylon c.1944.

HMS Phoebe.

War Gratuity and Post War Credits of Wages received the princely sum of £60/12/-.

Information from

Norah Thompson (daughter)

Naval Historical Branch, Ministry of Defence

John Newbown known as Jack Newby

Petty Officer, JX313496/FX100093
Royal Navy/Fleet Air Arm
Ordinary Seaman/Air Fitter

John Edwin Newbown (frequently known as Jack Newby) was born in 1913, the son of Mr Herbert and Mrs Emily Newbown of Ings Lane, Barton-on-Humber. He attended St. Chad's School and on leaving worked variously in the Barton Brick and Tile Yards and on river barges. He was a Methodist. He married Olive Matthews in June 1938 and took up residence at 85 Ings Lane.

In November 1941, he joined the Royal Navy under the terms of the 1939 National Service Act. This act had been passed by Parliament on the first day of the war, 3 September 1939, and made all men between the ages of 18 and 41 liable for conscription into the forces. He undertook his initial training at *HMS Glendower* and subsequently served as an ordinary

John Newbown.

seaman on *HMS Pembroke* and HMS *Victory V* before, in May 1942, being sent for training as an air fitter in the Fleet Air Arm. By May 1943, he had become a leading air fitter and in May 1944, was promoted to the rank of petty officer and granted a Workshop Supervisory Certificate.

He served on a number of vessels - that on *HMS Vindex* and *HMS Campania* qualifying him for the 1939-1945 Star Ribbon and the Atlantic Star Ribbon. He did escort work on the convoys to Russia.

He was finally demobbed in January 1946.

Information from

Hilda Ashton (sister)

Sheila Drayton (daughter)

Charles Newton

Lance Corporal, 7635195
Royal Electrical and Mechanical Engineers
Fitter

Charles Henry Newton was born in 1914, the son of Mr John Henry and Mrs Melvina Newton of 5 Barraclough Lane, Barton-on-Humber. He was educated at St. Chad's School and the Technical College in Hull. He subsequently worked at Barraclough's Shipyard in Grimsby, maintaining the sloops, keels and cranes at the dock.

In June 1940, he volunteered to join the REME (Royal Electrical and Mechanical Engineers) and reported to Hillsea near Plymouth for initial training. At the height of the blitz, he was sent to London where the REME had taken over a garage as a maintenance depot looking after the many searchlights and anti-aircraft guns located in and around the capital. There the men worked all day maintaining the equipment and often all night carrying out essential repairs. Eventually lack of sleep took its toll and the medical officer gave the order for the men to be sent away for a well-earned rest.

Charles went to the REME dispersal centre at Chilwell near Nottingham and from there he was posted to a REME workshop at Kit Hill, Callington in Cornwall. There about 100 soldiers manned a REME workshop which looked after all the searchlights and anti-aircraft guns in Devon and Cornwall. Each man travelled around in a small pick-up truck visiting various sites to ensure that the equipment was working efficiently.

Whilst he was there in the winter of 1942-1943, he volunteered to make three trips across to occupied Europe. These were highly secret operations intended to prepare the way for the eventual invasion of Europe

by investigating possible landing places. They were undertaken in small, fast landing craft which carried a small Royal Navy crew, often a Commando, a number of men from the Reconnaissance Corps and one REME fitter. The fitter's job was to ensure that the motor cycles and small vehicles which were taken were in tip-top order. The boats sailed over and back during the hours of darkness and on arrival at the European coast, the Commandos and reconnaissance men would set off to investigate the German defences in the area. When their task was finished, they would dump their transport and dash back to the safety of England. Charles might set foot in occupied Europe but he did not go inland. His job was to handle any mechanical problems which arose. Many such expeditions were mounted during the period leading up to D-Day to ensure that wherever the Allies chose to land, the German defences on the beaches and in the nearby hinterland would be well known.

In 1943, Charles developed medical problems and was posted near to his home. He was stationed at the REME Workshop in New Holland (still known as 'The Camp') and there was part of the team responsible for the repair and maintenance of all the searchlights and anti-aircraft guns on both banks of the Humber. His medical condition did not improve and in December 1943, he was discharged from the army.

Information from

Charles Newton

Ron Newton

Seaman, JX 382496
Royal Navy
Patrol Service Seaman Gunner

Ronald John Newton was born in 1923, the second son of the Mr John Henry and Mrs Malvina Newton of 5 Barraclough Lane, Barton-on-Humber. He was educated at St. Chad's School and on leaving joined his father who was skipper of the Humber sloop *New Clee*. In the early years of the war, he continued working on the river carrying general cargo throughout the region.

In 1941, the *New Clee* was commandeered by the navy and used to store the equipment used by a former Lowestoft drifter - the *Ocean Gain* - to degauss **(3)** merchant ships. This work took place in all the Humber ports prior to ships sailing. Ships leaving the Humber passed over a wire laid across the river from Paul to Goxhill. The polarity of every ship which passed over this wire could be checked in an army base at Paul and if the degaussing was shown to be faulty, it was

Ron Newton (centre with cucumber) and the crew of *MMS 233*.

***BYMS 2079* in Lowestoft, 1946.**

Blowing up a magnetic mine off Lowestoft with *BYMS 2079* on extreme right.

ordered back to port and the degaussing procedure repeated - hopefully successfully.

In August 1942, he volunteered to join the Royal Navy and was sent to *HMS Collingwood*, a shore base near Portsmouth. There he did 12 weeks training in seamanship. From there he was drafted into the Patrol Service based at *HMS Europa* at Lowestoft. Soon afterwards he was transferred to the base ship, *HMS Eaglet*, at Birkenhead from where he was sent to the gunnery school at Southport and trained in the use of various guns with a bore of up to 4.5 inches.

Subsequently Ron was engaged in escort duties aboard *HMS Oracle* accompanying merchant vessels sailing in the Irish Sea between the Clyde and the Bristol Channel.

In June 1943, he was transferred to the wooden, single-screwed motor mine sweeper (MMS) *MMS 233*. (MMSs such as this were built at Clapson's Yard in Barton during the war years - see *Barton Remembered 1939-1945; Part Two, The Home Front*, pp 142-144) which had been built at Poole but was now based at Birkenhead. It was engaged in sweeping magnetic and acoustic mines in the Irish Sea between the Isle of Man and Holyhead.

In 1944 *MMS 233* travelled through the Caledonian Canal and sailed down to Sheerness. From there it proceeded to sweep for mines in the English Channel just after D -Day **(15)**. During one sweeping operation, he saw the PLUTO pipeline being laid between England and Boulogne. Later he was sent to sweep up the Belgian and Dutch coasts and for a while was based at Den Helder in northern Holland.

After this the ship sailed back to London for repairs. Shortly afterwards the war in Europe ended. Following a move to Lowestoft in late 1945, *MMS 233* was 'paid off' and Ron was transferred to the American-built Brooklyn Yard Mine Sweeper (BYMS) *BYMS 2079* and spent some months clearing mines in the North Sea - particularly those remaining off the Norfolk and Suffolk coasts. These ships were twin-screwed, far faster than the British-built vessels and better equipped with power-steering, ice-cream making facilities and a water-drinking fountain. The crew of about 30 men included one lieutenant, two sub-lieutenants, two petty officers and 25 men. The whole crew was on duty during sweeping operation in daylight but during darkness the ship was anchored in a suitably safe location - a bay or river estuary - and every crewman did a short watch.

Finally, in June 1946, he was demobbed and returned to Barton.

Information from

Ron Newton

Alf Pike

Lance Corporal
Loyal North Lancashire Regiment/Corps of
Royal Military Police
Infantryman, Traffic Control and General Duties

Alfred Pike was born in 1916, the son of Mr James William and Mrs Keturah Pike of 6 Dam Road, Barton-on-Humber. He attended the County School and on leaving worked variously at the Brick and Tile Works at Barrow Haven, on a local farm and in the Bonderising Shop at Hoppers Cycle Works.

In 1934 he joined the Loyal Regiment (North Lancashire) at Preston. He later moved into the Corps of Royal Military Police. He saw service in Palestine and Shanghai and was taken prisoner-of-war by the Japanese (along with 32,000 Indian, 16,000 British and 14,000 Australian soldiers) when Singapore fell in February 1942 **(9)**. He was held in captivity for 3½ years.

Information from

Wilf Pike (brother)

Ern Pike

Chief Petty Officer
Royal Navy
Gunnery Artificer

William Ernest Pike was born in 1915 the brother of Alf Pike, (qv). He attended the County School and on leaving was employed in the Tool Shop at Hopper's Cycle Works.

In 1942 he joined the Royal Navy at Portsmouth and served on *HMS Charity.* He took part in escort duties with the Atlantic convoys **(6)** and was part of the fleet of ships which bombarded the Normandy beaches prior to the landings on D-Day 1944 **(15)**.

His death in 1960 was caused in part by the wounds he suffered in the war.

Information from

Wilf Pike (brother)

Wilf Pike

Driver, 270681
Royal Army Service Corps
Driver

Wilfred Maurice Pike was born in 1921, the son of Mr James William and Mrs Keturah Pike of 6 Dam Road, Barton-on-Humber. He attended the County School and on leaving was employed as a farmhand by Mr W. Todd on his farm in Marsh Lane (the site of the present St. Peter's School). He also worked at two brick and tile yards, for Stamp's sloop owners, at Killingholme and immediately before he was called up at the Farmers' Company.

He reported to the RASC Training Unit at Sutton-in-Ashfield in May 1941. After a month's initial training he was transferred to the Drivers' Training School at Mansfield. On passing his driving test, he was moved to 182 AA Company RASC at Eccles near Manchester.

On Christmas Eve 1941, he was sent to Surrey awaiting transfer to the Far East. Later he moved to Chippenham in Wiltshire where he joined a general transport company and was given possession of a Bedford 3-ton truck. A few months later he was posted to a holding company in Woking from where he travelled to Liverpool and embarked on the troopship *The Monarch of Bermuda* which sailed to Cape Town. There he was transferred to another troopship - the

Wilf Pike.

Scythia - which took him to Ismailia. From there he travelled by rail to the RASC holding depot at Geneifa in Egypt and was attached to the 15 Tank Transporter Company. This company had three sections which each held 33 tank transporters. There was also a HQ section which included all the Company's clerks and diesel transporters. Here he became second driver on a 34-wheeled tank transporter capable of carrying anything up to a 30 ton Sherman tank. Wilf was responsible for the maintenance of the massive trailer, the driver looked after the motor part. Both of them lived on the lorry and had beds in the rear compartment.

When they travelled in small convoys - four or five lorries - they did their own cooking on Primus stoves which they carried. When they travelled in large convoys - anything up to 60 units carrying the tanks for a whole battalion - they had an accompanying cookhouse truck, diesel tanker and water carrier. The tank crews stayed in their vehicles during the journey and were required to drive them off the transporters on arrival at their destination. At night the convoy dispersed in the desert as an air raid precaution and the men often had to walk a considerable distance to get their evening meal. If you were unlucky, you might be required to mount a guard during the night. The drive wheels of the transporters were weighted down with tons of pig iron held in lockers underneath the beds.

The company moved forward and, after loading a brand-new tank onto its trailer, it moved into a position to the rear of El Alamein just prior to the big battle **(7)**. From then on he was employed moving damaged tanks to the repair depots and transporting new tanks to the war front to replace those which had been knocked out by Rommel's army. Some of these journeys involved moving a tank some 50 or more miles.

Wilf followed Montgomery's army across Egypt, Libya and through Tunisia until he finally ended up at Sfax in early 1943. Here, like many other soldiers, he succumbed to 'desert sores' which were caused by a constant diet of tinned food and a consequent lack of fresh fruit and vegetables. The cure was to cover one's body in an ointment called 'blue unction' which was applied with a shaving brush.

After the end of the North African Campaign, Wilf moved back to the base depot at Geneifa where he got four days leave in Cairo. From there his unit (without its transporters) moved to the port at Alexandria and boarded the Dutch ship *Nieuw Holland* which brought it back to England through the Mediterranean Sea.

He arrived at Greenock in December 1943 from where he was moved by train to Leigh-on-Sea in Essex. He got 14 days leave from there and came back to Barton carrying all his army kit.

On his return to Leigh, he and 15 Tank Transporter Company (without vehicles) were moved to Syston in Leicestershire. He was employed for some months moving new lorries from Ford's at Dagenham to various RAOC depots up and down the country. Eventually he was moved to Sefton Park near Liverpool where the Company was re-equipped with new, bigger tank transporters. These would carry one of the new 53-ton Churchill tanks.

Prior to D-Day, the Company moved to Weybridge in Surrey where the transporters were waterproofed so that they could land from a landing craft through sea water and onto the invasion beaches. From there the Company moved west into the New Forest and was parked up among the trees. It eventually moved to Southampton Common before it was carried over the Channel and landed on Gold Beach in Normandy in early July 1944 **(15)**. For three weeks the Company was parked up as the roads in the area were too congested.

Following the fall of Caen, the Company carried tanks eastwards. The journey through devastated Caen had to be undertaken without lights - a most hazardous experience!

After about six weeks in Europe, the Company found itself at Lens where the drivers were able to use the local pithead baths for their first proper ablutions since they had left England. From there, the Company took the Guards Armoured Division to Brussels. By December 1944, the unit had moved to Diest in Belgium - still moving different armoured units to the front.

From there the Company moved to Eindhoven and parked in the town's streets. There it picked up English Cromwell and Comet tanks and moved them to the Rhine crossing. The tanks were dropped off on the west bank and later taken over into Germany by their crews.

The Company later moved over the Rhine and when the war ended the unit was stationed on the Baltic at Timandorfer Strand - a peacetime seaside resort. From there it moved to Hamburg and the drivers spent some months as peacetime soldiers. On three occasions during this period, he drove a tank transporter down the autobahn to Duisburg to pick up parts of a gear-cutting machine. These were destined (via Hamburg) for delivery to David Brown's of Huddersfield as part of the war reparations demanded from the Germans. He later moved to an aerodrome outside Oldenberg near Bremen from where he was demobbed. In September 1946 he caught the Bremen to Hull ferry - the *Empire Liberty*. He landed on the pontoon outside the Albert Dock within sight of Barton but had to travel to York to pick up his demob suit.

Information from

Wilfred Pike

Walter Readhead

Gunner
Honourable Artillery Company
Driver

Walter Readhead was born in 1909, the son of Mr George and Mrs Mary Readhead of Flamborough, Yorkshire. On leaving school, he became a bus driver in Bridlington before moving to Barton in 1930 where he became a turf accountant. In 1933 he married Freda Watson at St. Mary's church in Barton.

In 1940 he was called up and reported to join the Honourable Artillery Company for initial training at Clacton. He later underwent training at Blackpool and in Scotland.

He landed in Normandy on D-Day **(15)** and subsequently fought his way across north-western Europe. He was in Holland on VE Day and the following piece which appeared in a local newspaper on 30 May 1945 relates Gunner Readhead's memories of the following day.

'BARTON MAN'S V-DAY IN HOLLAND

'"Frost" Dispelled by Cup of Tea

'For Gnr. Redhead [sic], of 21, Fleetgate, Barton-on-Humber, V-Plus 1 Day was "a bit of a frost."

'He mopped his perspiring brow as he made the confession and stared gloomily across Walcheren [Island].

'It might have been a slice of Bedfordshire or Canvey Island, without the music or the ice-cream man.

Walter Readhead.

'The radio told him that the end of the war was being celebrated in various ways, but he could hardly believe that the guns whose polished parts winked at him in the hot sunshine had said their last word.

'It was all so quiet.

'The villagers with their queer-looking headgear and wooden shoes stared at him, and he at them. They seemed content to stand and look at him and celebrate by waiting contentedly for something to happen. He wanted it to happen now, on this great day when the folks at home would be making whoopee.

'While he, one of the liberators, browned off while the world he had helped to clean up went mad with joy! Forgotten armies! They weren't all in Burma.

'The larks were trilling, solemn babies were staring at him; there were patriotic goldfish in the pond at his feet, their orange backs no longer solitary subterfuge symbols of "No surrender!" for the whole landscape fluttered with orange flags and streamers - but he wanted a bit more than all that.

'Then he got it.

'A tall square van lurched into sight, squelching over the soft grey mud. He wasn't forgotten! Britain had sent out her long arm from her tea parties, offering him a cup of tea and the sight of an English girl.

'It wasn't much, this could be a Salvation Army mobile canteen, but to Gnr. Redhead and his pals it was the symbol of being remembered on V-Plus 1 Day.

'He winked at the massive matrons in their voluminous black skirts and gave his biscuits to their round-eyed babies.

'The fierce snatch which they made at the offered tit-bits kicked him for a second somewhere inside his battle jacket. They'd heard these silent Hollanders had been short of food. He had noticed there were no young men about, though some had been seen returning from Germany with deep lines on their faces. Well, it was over. He couldn't believe it.

'But another cup o'char was in his hand, and Walcheren Island was as good a place as any to leave to its own business now.

'There were lines of green on the black earth, and the small boy in blue jerkin was too busy with the hoe to celebrate.

'Holland was putting her house in order.

'Seven years, they told him, must elapse before those miles of flooded fields would be producing crops again.

'But V-Plus 1 Day had come, and he had joined the tea party, sitting on a green bank beneath a windmill in Walcheren.'

Information from

Freda Readhead (widow)

Joyce Robinson

Corporal, 152600
Auxiliary Territorial Service
Radar Technician

Joyce Robinson is the daughter of Mr Arthur (he was wounded in WW1) and Mrs Elizabeth Robinson of 100 High Street, Barton-on-Humber. She was educated at the County School and Barton Grammar School and on leaving helped in her parents' drapery store in the High Street. She was a member of the Methodist Church Badminton Club.

In 1942, she volunteered to join the ATS. During her initial training at Northampton she was chosen to go forward for further instruction in radar maintenance and repair work. This took her to a Technical College in London where she underwent six months of instruction.

On completion of the course, she was posted to a REME workshop at Totton near Southampton and there she spent the rest of the war. She was one of a group of ATS technicians whose job it was to accompany a REME sergeant on visits to scattered sites in the area whenever a radar set broke down or required maintenance. There were 12 ATS ladies at the workshop and they were accommodated in a wooden hut of their own. On a site visit, which could be during the day or in the dead of night, the REME sergeant was accompanied by three members of the ATS group. When away from the workshop, Joyce and her companions ate where they could; she particularly looked forward to eating in American camps where the food was significantly better than that which was available to the British forces!

The radar sets, staffed by the ATS and a number of servicemen, were lined up along the south coast searching out raiding German aircraft and tracking Allied planes as they flew over the area. Each radar set was housed in a truck and was powered by its own petrol-driven generator.

Information from

Joyce Robinson

Joyce Robinson (centre) with colleague Paddy Wake (right) and driver prepare to go out to service a radar set in their truck.

Vic Robinson

Able Seaman, JX 274752
Royal Navy
Seaman

Victor George Harvey Robinson was born at Berwick on Tweed in 1916, the son of Mr Frederick and Mrs Mary Robinson later of 4 Green Lane, Barton-on-Humber. He was educated at the Church School and on leaving worked as a quarryman at Leggett's Quarry. This being a reserved occupation, he was not called into the services but volunteered to join the Royal Navy in June 1941. His employer at the quarry let it be known that any worker volunteering to join the services could be sure of a job there after the war ended.

He did his initial training at *HMS Collingwood* and afterwards served on a number of ships. From September 1942 until June 1945 he was aboard the destroyer *HMS Whitshed* which saw service in the Atlantic.

On 19 December 1943, the wife of the ship's captain wrote to Vic's wife Lillian:

'Dear Mrs Robinson,

'The wives of all who are serving on my husband's ship are so often in my thoughts and I would like to take this opportunity of wishing you a Happy Xmas from us both. Good Luck, & perhaps Peace in the Coming Year.

'Yours sincerely,

Victor and Lillian Robinson on their wedding day in 1940.

'Joyce Talbot.'

Vic was demobbed from the navy in January 1946 and on 7 August received £3/13/6d as a 'War Office Gratuity Salvage Award', presumably in payment for his efforts in helping salvage a damaged merchant ship at some unknown date during the war.

Information from

Laurie Robinson (son)

Ken Sempers

Sergeant, 950032
Royal Artillery, Army Catering Corps
Gunner/Cook

Kenneth Jack Sempers was born in 1919, the son of Mr Charles Richard and Mrs Ethel Sempers of Pasture Road (later Butts Road), Barton-on-Humber. He was educated at the County School and on leaving worked in his father's butcher's shop in George Street (opposite what is now Lindsey Relay). His main hobby was football and he played inside right in the local Thursday league.

In October 1939, he was called up with the Militia and reported to the Royal Artillery depot at Deepcut Camp between Aldershot and Purbright for initial training which included learning how to fire a howitzer. He stayed at this camp for some time training in the art of gunnery.

The destroyer *HMS Whitshed*.

19. Danish Gestapo HQ Precision Bombed

On 31 October 1944, 24 Mosquito aircraft answered a call from the Danish Resistance to bomb the Gestapo headquarters in Aarhus University in which building one of their members, Pastor Harald Sandbaek, was being tortured to breaking point in the hope that he would reveal to the enemy full details of the country's Resistance movement.

After flying at low level over the North Sea, the aircraft struck with commendable precision destroying archives relating to the Resistance movement, killing some 150 Germans and 20 Danish informers and setting the Pastor free. He was subsequently smuggled to Sweden and out of further harm's way.

See - Clarke Dunn

Sometime later, having learned of his experience as a butcher, he was transferred into the Army Catering Corps and was posted to Aldershot for training in the use and building of field kitchens. After this training he was posted to a Royal Marines unit at Margate from where he travelled to Towyn in North Wales for

exercises. From there they moved to Dalton-in-Furness before being sent to Belgium some time after D-day. The unit then fought its way through Germany and Ken was constantly building new field kitchens just at the rear of the front line and supplying meals to the fighting troops. The field cookers were fuelled with wood or oil.

His war service in Europe ended at Kiel where he stayed for some months before he was flown back to Shropshire for demobilization in May 1946.

Information from

Ken Sempers

Roland Shephardson

1770723
Royal Army Service Corps
Driver

Ken Sempers.

Roland Shepardson.

Roland Garton Shephardson was born in 1906, the son of Mr James and Mrs Elizabeth Annie Shephardson at Marsh Farm, Barton-on-Humber - now the North Lincs Sailing Club. On leaving school he worked for a time for his father before moving to nearby Earle and Sons at their clay workings.

At the outbreak of the war he joined the Home Guard, but on 20 February 1942 he enlisted in the army. After his initial training he was placed in 762 Company of the Royal Army Service Corps. He was stationed at various places in Cornwall before he was posted overseas as a driver.

Roland served in Iraq, Egypt (he was at El Alamein (7)), Libya, Algeria, Egypt, Sicily and Italy. He was at the Anzio landings (13) and also served in Gallipoli. At one stage he drove Montgomery who he described to his daughter as a 'small, slightly built man with a clever brain.' He was slightly wounded on one occasion and on another his life was saved by a colleague when their Jeep caught fire. He also contracted malaria and was very ill for a time.

His daughter vividly remembers that all the family (Roland's wife and five daughters) all received a silver chain and cross when he was serving in Italy. Unfortunately these gifts presented Mrs Shephardson with a problem as she had to save hard to pay the duty required.

He was demobbed on 2 November 1945.

Information from

Kathleen North (daughter)

Arthur Sobey

Corporal, 4808137
7th Battalion Lincolnshire Regiment, 102 Light
AA Regiment, 3 Battalion Parachute Regiment
Machine Gunner

Albert Arthur Sobey was born in 1920, the son of Mr Albert and Mrs Beatrice Sobey of Hewson's Lane, Waterside Road, Barton-on-Humber. He was educated at St. Chad's School and the County School. On leaving he was employed in the Machine Shop at Hopper's Cycle Works, at the Cement Works at South Ferriby and finally by Holst and Co which was building an oil tank depot beside the Humber on the Ferriby/ Winteringham parish boundary. Just before he joined the forces, he signed on in Hull as a merchant seaman for a three-month voyage to West Africa. He was a member of Barton Toc H which met in Chapel Lane and the Wesleyan Methodist church in Waterside Road.

Arthur Sobey.

In June 1940, he was called into the forces and travelled to Nottingham to join the 7th Battalion of the Lincolnshire Regiment and complete his initial training. From there the Battalion moved to various locations on the Lincolnshire Coast. Arthur was based at Sandilands near Sutton-on-Sea where he undertook coastal defence duties. In mid-1941, the 7th Battalion was disbanded and Arthur was transferred into the 336 Battery, 102 Light Anti-Aircraft Regiment based at Withernsea and Chester. The Battery was initially given a single Bofors gun on which to train but later at Hertford was completely armed.

At this point, early in 1942, Arthur volunteered to transfer into the Parachute Regiment. He was sent to Ringway Airport at Manchester for training. Here recruits trained by jumping from obsolete, twin-engined Whitley bombers. He was given his Wings in June 1942 and posted to the A Company, 3rd Battalion of the Parachute Regiment at Bulford near Salisbury. The Battalion held some 450 paratroopers in four companies (HQ, A, B, and C) plus a number of supplementary staff such as cooks, clerks, mechanics, and armourers.

A period of training preceded the Battalion's move to North Africa in November 1942 (11). His Battalion dropped at Bone Aerodrome near Algiers which was at the time held by Singhalese troops under the control of the Vichy Government. They put up little resistance and the airport was taken with a single British casualty. The 3rd Battalion joined the British 1st Army under General Alexander and was used at various points in the front as the Army moved eastwards towards Tunis.

The Germans final surrendered in April 1943 at which time Arthur was in the front line and was present when German and Italian soldiers surrendered to the paratroopers.

A period of further training near Sousse followed until in July 1943 he was dropped from a C47 Dakota at Catania on Sicily **(12)**. The Battalion was required to take the bridge over the River Simeto which it did and held until reinforcements came through in the drive to the north-east. When Sicily was finally taken, the Battalion returned to Sousse for rest and training.

On 9 September, the Battalion took part in Operation *Slapstick* - the seaborne landing of the 3,600 men of 1st Airborne Division at Taranto, the great naval base in the 'instep' of Italy. This move was intended to secure the port as a base from which to supply troops advancing up the eastern flank in Italy and also ensure that no Italian warships should fall into German hands. When the Paras landed, there were no Germans to be seen and what Italian defenders there were never fired a shot and cheered the British as they came ashore. (Bartonian Harold Bell was killed during the landings when his ship hit a mine - see Chapter 4). From Taranto they pushed up north through Altamura, Barletta and Bari. Here they stopped for a while but were soon after recalled to Algiers and then came back to England by sea.

At Christmas 1943 they took up station at Spalding in Lincolnshire and were there training until September 1944. On Sunday 17 September 1944 Arthur's Battalion, along with the whole Airborne Division, took off on the flight to Arnhem **(17)**. He landed at 13.30 at Ginkelheath, seven kilometres west of the Bridge. The Battalion formed up at its rendezvous point marked by a red smoke flare and at about 14.30 was ordered to move off up the main road to Arnhem. At first it met little resistance but, at about teatime, German self-propelled guns and half-track troop carriers appeared. These were quickly dealt with and the Battalion continued to advance. It was then decided that A Company (some 110 men under the command of a Major) should take up defensive positions for the night. ('A bad mistake' says Arthur.) When the time came to move off at about 5.30 next day, the Germans had formed their defences and the Company had to fight its way towards the bridge.

It got as far The Pavilion on the river bank, about half a mile downstream of the bridge where the advance came to a halt in the face of the 9th and 10th German Panzer (Tank) Divisions. Arthur's A Company was quickly surrounded and forced to surrender.

From Arnhem, he was marched some 12 miles to Appledorn where he was put on a train which took him Stalag 11B, a British prisoner-of-war camp near Limberg. There he was a member of a working-party which marched daily to a nearby steel works to perform labouring duties. At one point his work was deemed unsatisfactory and he was fired! He remained there until March 1945 when the whole camp was formed up to begin a march to the east out of the way of the advancing Allied armies. His column stopped the first night in a warehouse and the next morning the German guards, sensing danger, one by one disappeared. A cloud of dust on the western horizon heralded the arrival of an American armoured column. Arthur was free!

The group was told to march westwards and that day arrived at Hildesheim which was in American hands. The freed prisoners were fed and flown out to England on the 2 July 1945 in Dakotas which were landing at the nearby airfield bringing in supplies.

He landed at Cheshunt where, following documentation, he was sent home on six week's leave. He eventually reported back to a station near Horsham in Sussex from where he went on a clerical course prior to demobilisation.

He was finally demobbed from the War Office in Whitehall in July 1946.

Information from

Arthur Sobey

Fred Sobey

Able Seaman, PJX399412
Royal Navy
Gunner

Fred Sobey.

Frederick Henry Sobey was born in 1924, the son of Mr Albert and Mrs Beatrice Sobey of 11 Hewson Lane, Barton-on-Humber. He was educated at the County School and was subsequently employed as a farm worker by Mr Todd of Marsh Lane. He attended the Methodist Church.

In January 1942 he volunteered to join the Royal Navy and was trained as a gunner. He served at *HMS Glendower* (Butlin's, Pwllheli) and undertook special training in connection with the D-Day landings **(15)**.

Information from

Fred Sobey

George Stamp

Sapper/Lance Corporal, 2064032
Royal Engineers, Royal Artillery, Corps of Military Police
Sapper, Gunner, Military Policeman

George Alexander Stamp was born in Hull in 1913, the son of Mr Cyril and Mrs Nellie Stamp of 7 Queens Avenue, Barton-on-Humber. The family moved to Barton when he was an infant. He attended the County School and on leaving trained as a bricklayer with Stamp and Sons of Brigg Road. He worked on the Hull Savings Bank (now the St. John's Ambulance HQ) in Fleetgate and at the Catholic Church. He played 2nd trombone in the Barton Town Band.

In 1938, he joined the Barton Company of the Territorial Army at its headquarters in Butts Road and was trained as an arm controller on the unit's searchlight. He was called into the Regular Army when war was declared in 1939 and, like the rest of the Barton 'Terriers', was sent to the New Waltham area. The unit was later moved to Northumberland but in 1940-1941, George was called out of the army and sent to London to use his building skills in the repair of houses which had been damaged in the blitz **(6)**. Later he was sent to Hull on similar work before being called back to London.

In June 1942, when the worst of the Blitz was over, he rejoined the army and was sent to Fleetwood to train as a driver in the Royal Artillery. In October 1942 he boarded the *Awra,* an ex-refrigerated banana boat, in which he sailed to the Middle East via the USA, South Africa and Aden. On New Year's Eve 1942 he landed at Port Said **(7)**. From there he was sent for training at the Heliopolis base near Cairo before being attached to a heavy anti-aircraft unit near Benghazi. He stayed there for some six months driving a lorry which supplied food and water to many army, navy and air force units in the area.

His next move was to a HQ unit near Haifa where he spent six months driving officers on their duties. The intention was to move the unit through Turkey but permission from the Turkish government was never received.

In December 1944 he was posted to Port Said where he was transferred into the Corps of Royal Military Police and he there acted as a driver on various patrol duties. Here he was promoted to the rank of lance corporal.

After sailing back to Liverpool, he was finally demobbed from Aldershot in January 1946.

Information from

George Stamp

Barton Territorials in the Waltham area manning searchlights.
Back: Len Brown, Bob Blyth, ? Snow (Brigg).
Front: George Stamp, John Bilton, Jack Dean, Geoff Sanvig.

Clifford Stockdale

Private, 14791788
Royal Army Medical Corps
Medical Orderly

Clifford Rowland Stockdale was born in 1926, the son of Mr George (who was a stretcher bearer in WW1 and who won the Military Medal) and Mrs Laura Stockdale of 15 Beck Hill, Barton-on-Humber. He went to the Church School in Queen Street. On leaving he was employed first as errand boy at Kirkby's Stores in Market Lane and later at Melia's Stores off Dam Road. In 1941 he went to Jubb's Whiting Works in Castledyke West. He attended the Primitive Methodist Sunday School in Queen Street and was a member of the Barton Boys' Club.

On 29 June 1944 he was conscripted into the army and reported to the Maryhill Barracks in Glasgow for initial training. From there he was transferred to No 1 PDC (Physical Development Centre) at Hereford before being posted back to Glasgow for more training. He was next sent to the RAMC Depot at Boyce Barracks, Crookham, near Aldershot. There he did eight weeks RAMC training in ward and field work to become a nursing orderly. His next posting was to 9 Company Military Hospital at Colchester where he looked after sick members of the local garrison and was sometimes called out in an ambulance to pick up soldiers who had been sent home from the BLA (British Liberation Army) fighting on the continent.

In March 1945, he came home on embarkation leave before he travelled to Liverpool where he boarded the troopship *Medina Victory* which sailed in convoy to Gibraltar. From there she sailed alone to Port Said in Egypt.

His first posting in North Africa **(7)** was to join 131 General Military Hospital at Tobruk. This was a former Italian military hospital which had been taken over by the Allies and was now caring for any sick British troops based in North Africa as well as sick Italian prisoners-of-war housed in a nearby camp. Here he was first engaged on ward work but was later moved to the hospital canteen. He was initially assistant to the corporal but when his superior was sent back to England Clifford took over the responsibility of running the kitchen.

Whilst in the army, Clifford spent a lot of time amusing his fellow soldiers in concert party performances. He whistled and played the harmonica.

In January 1946 he had the option of a class B release which he took and one month later he arrived back in England and was demobbed from Colchester.

Information from

Clifford Stockdale

Allen Thompson

Sergeant, 14765304
Royal Army Medical Corps
Hospital work and administration

Allen Robert Thompson was born in 1926, the son of Mr John William and Mrs Betsy Thompson of 12 Marsh Lane, Barton-on-Humber. The family later moved to live at 13 Market Place, Barton. He was educated at the Church School in Queen Street and when he left in May 1941 was employed as a solicitor's clerk at T A Denby's in Whitecross Street. He was a member of the St. John Ambulance Cadets, the Barton Boys' Club and the local Air Training Corps. Early in the war he acted as an ARP messenger. He formed a dance band - 'The Melody Makers' - which played at weekly dances in Barrow-on-Humber in aid of the Red Cross and for dances at the Royal Artillery anti-aircraft camps at Barrow Haven and East Halton. The band gave its services free of charge and the army provided the transport to get it to their venues.

Allen (standing) and Philip Thompson. Deolali India September 1945.

129

In May 1944 he joined the army at the New Barracks in Lincoln where he underwent 10 weeks primary training. From there, in July 1944, he was posted to the Royal Army Medical Corps depot at Crookham in Hampshire and in October to No 1 Company RAMC at Cambridge Military Hospital, Aldershot.

In May 1945, he embarked on *MV Sobieski* at Greenock and arrived in RAMC depot, Deolali, Bombay, India in July. He was posted to the 22nd British Casualty Clearing Station at Uruli Plain outside Poona. This unit, a mobile, tented establishment, was not operational when he arrived as it had recently been withdrawn from Burma with General Slim's 36 Division pending the formation of a force to invade Japan. Following the bombing of Hiroshima and the Japanese surrender, this force was disbanded.

In September 1945 the unit was disbanded and he returned to the depot at Deolali and worked in the Orderly Room there pending a new posting. (By doing this he hoped to avoid the period of limbo known as 'In Transit'.) He was promoted to corporal and there, somewhat amazingly, met his brother Philip (qv) on leave from his unit in Malaya.

In March 1946, he was posted to Embarkation HQ in Bombay as a Sergeant working under the Port Medical Officer. He was responsible for the supplies sent to Troopship Hospitals and for transferring incoming patients who needed hospital treatment to the BMH (British Military Hospital) in Colaba, Bombay. Not infrequently ships at Bombay, fully laden with troops ready to return to the UK, had to be boarded and all the passengers inoculated when it was found that some noxious disease had broken out in the Suez Canal area. Another memory of his work in Bombay is that when he was required to visit a troopship anchored offshore, the journey was made in an antiquated steam launch - somewhat like the *African Queen* - crewed by two elderly Indians. In windy weather the voyage was hair-raising but after a late evening crossing with a medical officer a more seaworthy craft was requisitioned.

Eventually, Allen was able to take a leave in England, sailing home on the *Georgic* and returning on the *Brittanic*. On arriving back in India he found that someone else had taken his job and so, in December 1946, he was transferred to the BMH in Delhi. In March 1947, he moved to the BMH in Calcutta and from there returned to the UK for demobilization at York on 8 February 1948.

Information from

Allen Thompson

Philip Thompson

Corporal, 7401990
Royal Army Medical Corps
Medical Laboratory Assistant

Philip John Thompson was born in 1922, the son of Mr John William and Mrs Betsy Thompson of Barrow Haven. The family moved to 12 Marsh Lane when Philip was two years old and in 1933 to 'The Book Shop', Market Place, Barton. He attended the Church School in Queen Street from 1928 until 1936. He sang in the choir and was an altar server at St. Mary's and St. Peter's churches. He was a member of the Barton Meccano Club (see below), St. John's Ambulance Cadets and the Boy Scouts. On leaving school he worked for Leslie Walker who ran the Chemist's Shop in High Street (now Lloyd's).

(The Barton Meccano Club met in a room at the rear of the Oddfellows' Hall. It was authorised by Hornby Ltd and its leader was Fred Burton whose father had a grocery business in Whitecross Street. Club members made Meccano models which were judged and marks were awarded. Philip won a medal for the consistently high quality of his models. The club usually had a float in the Barton Carnival on which the best models were displayed.)

Philip was conscripted into the army in December 1941 and reported for initial training to the RAMC Depot at Crookham in Hampshire. Three months later he was posted to 143 Field Ambulance at Martin Manor, Horncastle - a small hospital with about 20 beds, an operating theatre and casualty reception department. The hospital treated the sick and injured from the various regiments stationed in the area. As there were various battle schools using live ammunition in the vicinity, there was never a shortage of patients. The first patient Philip dealt with had had his hand blown off by a grenade which he had held on to instead of throwing. On another occasion eight patients arrived suffering from gas poisoning. Someone had unintentionally included a gas grenade in a batch of smoke grenades. The hospital's staff lived in very basic accommodation in the nearby grange with no lighting, heating or beds. They had to sleep on a blanket on the wooden floor and shaved in cold water in darkness. Light relief was variously provided by route marches, the provision of ambulance services for soldiers on military exercises, and periods of detachment to Bracebridge Military Hospital at Lincoln.

In early January 1943, Philip was posted to Moorland School, Leeds and from there to Liverpool to board the *SS Volendam* bound for an unknown destination. The ship initially sailed to the Clyde to join a convoy which called first at Freetown before progressing round the Cape and putting in at Durban. There he camped on Clairwood Racecourse and whilst there, he spent

No 43 Indian Field Laboratory staff, Jorhat, July 1944. Philip Thompson is standing on the extreme right.

one Sunday, most impressed, watching Zulu dancing in Durban Stadium. Later he embarked on *SS Cap Norte* (a captured German ship) and sailed to Bombay. There he reported to the RAMC Depot at Deolali prior to being posted to the BMH (British Military Hospital) at Ambala where he underwent training as a medical laboratory assistant. In October 1943 he was sent to the BMH at Lahore to complete his training and there he celebrated his 21st birthday working until 11 pm! In November he was posted to the Deccan District Laboratory at Secunderabad where he found the testing and post mortem work most interesting.

In April 1944, Allied forces were very hard pressed on the Burma Front and Philip was posted to Comilla from where, along with other medical staff and infantry units, he was to have been dropped by parachute into the besieged town of Kohima (which had no airfield). However, just as they were assembled ready for take off the operation was cancelled, the infantry were sent to other parts of the front and Philip eventually made his way by paddle steamer and Jeep to BMH Shillong. From there he was posted to 45 Indian General Hospital at Jorhat, not far from Kohima, where he arrived in the middle of an air raid **(18)**. There he worked in 43 Indian Field Laboratory in the hospital compound. This hospital was housed in bamboo huts and the staff were treating sick and wounded Chindits

- groups of Allied soldiers who were operating behind the Japanese front lines. As well as usual battle wounds, cases of typhus, malaria and dysentery were common place. Nearby there was an American airbase from where supplies were flown 'over the hump' into China. He found the personnel at the base very kind to the patients bringing in books and games to keep them occupied. They also took off-duty staff to film shows at their open-air cinema. Philip visited a leper colony on the road to the airfield and was made very welcome by the staff.

On 6 August 1945, he was sent to a concentration area near Ranchi prior to embarkation for the invasion of Malaya. On 27 August, he was given 14 days leave which allowed him to visit his brother Allen (qv) who was at the RAMC Depot at Deolali. He stayed at the nearby naval barracks and met his brother in off-duty hours. He was recalled by telegram and on arriving back in camp was sent to Calcutta to embark on the *SS Dunera* bound for Malaya. The ship docked at Singapore and he then went over to Johore Bahru where he was part of the force which took over the civilian hospital. Unfortunately, the unit's equipment was on another ship which had landed at Port Swettenham half way up the Malay peninsular and Philip was sent to organise a convoy to bring it back to Johore. He spent Christmas Day in the home of a

131

Chinese pharmacist who worked at the hospital.

In March 1946 he was admitted to his own hospital with abdominal infestation. Shortly afterwards, he was given a place on a RAF repatriation ship and arrived back in England in April. After four weeks disembarkation, leave he was sent for a three month spell on Guernsey where he worked in an ex-German hospital. Following this he travelled back to England on a destroyer and was posted to the military hospital at Chester. He was demobilized from York in October 1946.

Information from

Philip Thompson

Audrey Varah (later Walton)

Captain, 263976
Auxiliary Territorial Service
Special Wireless (known as 'Y') Service

Audrey Mary Varah was born in 1912, the daughter of Canon WE and Mrs M Varah of The Vicarage, Barton-on-Humber. She was educated at St. Hilda's school in Whitby and later at Hull University where she read mathematics but did not graduate. At the outbreak of the war she was working as a secretary in London.

She joined the forces in March 1942 and after her initial training was posted to Uxbridge Searchlight Battery. At the end of 1942, she was selected for officer training. After being commissioned in 1943, she was posted as a subaltern to No 3 ATS Special Wireless 'Y' Wing at Kedleston Hall in Derbyshire. In February 1944, she was promoted to the rank of Junior Commander (Captain) and was posted to No 7 ATS 'Y' Wing at Beaumoor, Woodhouse Eaves, Leicestershire.

The 'Y' service was a massive, secret wireless interception service whose members, along with volunteer radio 'hams', listened into and wrote down on paper all enemy radio signals. Many of these were in the *Enigma* cypher which was used by the German armed forces. Audrey and her companions provided the raw material which was forwarded to Station X, the GCHQ (Government Communications Headquarters) at Bletchley Park 50 miles north-west of London. There, some 10,000 men and women were engaged in the decipherment of the *Enigma* and other enciphered signals. The most valuable information gained - codenamed 'Ultra' - was forwarded to a restricted number of politicians and military leaders and proved of enormous value when planning Allied operations or countering Axis threats. During the period of the Normandy landings, much time and many lives were saved as Bletchley Park could inform Eisenhower and Montgomery of the enemy's dispositions and intentions. Unfortunately, at the time of the Arnhem airborne landings, 'Ultra' warnings that two panzer divisions were in the area were ignored - with tragic consequences.

In June 1945, by which time the war in Europe was over, she was posted with a small ATS party to a 'Y' station near Bangalore in southern India as part of the build-up of forces for the continuing conflict with Japan.

Soon after her arrival in India the war ended and on 23 August 1946, she married her commanding officer, Lt Col Gordon Walton. She was finally demobilised in May 1946.

Information from

William Varah (brother)

Richard Walton (son)

Audrey Varah and Brigadier Akehurst (who 'gave her away' on 23 August 1946).

Edmund Varah.

Edmund Varah

Corporal
Royal Army Pay Corps and The Princess Louise
Kensingtons
Brigade Support Group - heavy mortars,
machine guns etc.

Winfrid Edmund Varah (Audrey's brother [qv]) was born in 1916 and was educated at Worksop College. Before the war, he was employed in banking and thus on joining the forces he was put into the Pay Corps. Later, however, he transferred into the Princess Louise Kensingtons and served as an NCO in North Africa **(7)** and Italy **(12)** with the Brigade Support Group of the 1st Army. He was wounded slightly but not seriously enough to be evacuated.

Information from

William Varah (brother)

Bill Varah MC

Corporal, 14405855
Durham Light Infantry
Major, 300419
2nd Battalion Lincolnshire Regiment and 2nd
Battalion East Yorkshire Regiment
Platoon Commander/Company Commander

William Oswald Varah (Audrey's brother [qv] was born in 1924. He was educated at the Church School in Barton, De Aston School at Market Rasen, Durham School and London University. On leaving, he was employed as a temporary teacher at St. Chad's School in Waterside Road. His hobby was the study of local history and natural science and he was a member of the Home Guard at both Durham School and in Barton. He attended St. Mary's and St. Peter's churches in Barton.

In 1942 he volunteered to join the army and, after initial training at Brancepeth Castle in County Durham, he went on to serve as a corporal in the Durham Light Infantry at Barnard Castle.

In 1943 he went on an officer training course at Barmouth in North Wales and was commissioned into the 2nd Battalion of the Lincolnshire Regiment based

Bill Varah.

in Scotland. Unfortunately, he was injured on the last D-Day rehearsal exercise and, after hospital treatment, convalesced in Scotland.

Following his recovery he was posted first to Northern Ireland and then to Pickering. He rejoined 3rd British Infantry Division as a member of the 2nd Battalion of the East Yorkshire Regiment in Europe as a platoon commander. He was wounded in Germany on the push to Bremen and was awarded the Military Cross.

After hospital treatment in Brussels and Lille, he rejoined the East Yorks and served with it as a company commander during the troubles in Palestine and Egypt.

He was demobbed in mid-1947.

Information from

William Varah

Charles Watkinson.

Charles Watkinson

Flight Lieutenant, 171374
No 201 Squadron, No 204 Squadron, Coastal
Command Flying Instructors' School
Royal Air Force
Squadron Pilot and Flying Instructor

Charles Herbert Watkinson was born on 29 July 1920 at 34 Marsh Lane, Barton-on-Humber. He attended the Church School in Queen Street and the Barton Grammar School (1931-1936). Subsequently he worked in Brigg Road offices of Hopper's Cycle Works, as a tilemaker on the Humberbank and in the Meat Supply Depot (slaughterhouse) in Cottage Lane.

In 1940 he volunteered to join the RAF and was accepted for aircrew pilot/observer training, initially in Torquay but later in Rhodesia (on Tiger Moths) and Heany, near Bulawayo (on twin-engined Oxfords). After gaining his pilot's 'Wings' he was sent to George in South Africa where he did further navigation and reconnaissance training.

On returning to England in 1942, he married Edna Towle at St. Mary's church before being posted as a second pilot/navigator on Sunderland flying boats of No 201 Squadron, based at RAF Castle Archdale, Lough Erne in Northern Ireland. His duties involved convoy escort and other patrols in the North Atlantic.

In December 1942, he was transferred onto the Captains' course at Invergordon and in April 1943 flew from RAF Pembroke Dock with a ferry unit taking flying boats to Bathurst and Dakar in West Africa. Here his new flying boat was handed over to the Free French forces and he brought an old one back to England. Later he acquired a new flying boat of his own and, whilst based with No 204 Squadron at Bathurst, was

employed on convoy escort duties, anti-U-boat patrols and reconnaissance duties in the Atlantic.

On 12 August 1943 he was ordered to take off at 0630 hours in Sunderland H/204 to search for a missing British Liberator which had attacked a U-boat and subsequently gone missing. His plane did a 'creeping line ahead' search in the relevant area and eventually sighted the Liberator's dinghy with seven men aboard. Survival packs were dropped and contact was made with a nearby naval vessel *HMS Clarkia* which was asked to pick up the survivors. Later it was discovered that the occupants of the dinghy were, in fact, not the crew of the Liberator (who had all perished when the plane crashed into the sea), but the U-boat captain and members of his crew who had abandoned the submarine after it had been struck by the Liberator's depth charges and had, luckily for them, discovered the dinghy floating nearby. A later account of the action, given by Klemens Schamong, the U-boat's captain, resulted in Flying Officer Trigg, the pilot of the Liberator, receiving a posthumous Victoria Cross.

After some 800 hours of flying duty, he was sent home and was posted to operational training units at Invergordon and Bristol on an instructors' course. After qualifying, he was posted to the Coastal Command Instructors' School at St. Angelo near Enniskillen. By now he had been promoted to the rank of flight lieutenant.

At the end of 1945, he was seconded to BOAC before being demobbed in April 1946.

Information from

Charles Watkinson

Harold Welch

Private , 4343414
1, 2 and 5 Battalion, East Yorkshire Regiment
Infantryman

Harold Welch was born in 1916, the son of Mr Herbert and Mrs Florence Welch of 45 Pasture Road, Barton-on-Humber. He attended the County School and subsequently worked in the Polishing Department at Hopper's Cycle works and was a member of the social club. His hobbies were football (he played for Barton Town Boys) and he was a member of the Victory Club Fishing Section.

In 1935 he travelled to Beverley and joined the East Yorkshire Regiment. After initial training at Beverley, he was transferred to its 1st Battalion and posted to Bombay in India where the British army was engaged in internal security duties. Whilst serving there he caught malaria.

Having completed his seven years as a regular soldier, he had the choice of either going on to Burma with the 1st Battalion or coming back to the UK to join the 5th Battalion which was training for Operation *Overlord* - the invasion of Europe. He chose to come home. Early on the morning of 6 June 1944, Harold's battalion was part of the first wave which, along with the 6th Battalion of the Green Howards, landed near la Rivière on Gold Beach in Normandy **(15)**. Jumping from the landing barge into water up to his neck, and seeing his Beach Landing Officer (Captain Cocking) dead, he gave up all hope! The Battalion, after advancing up the beach under heavy enemy fire, made its way inland for three days before being relieved. After about three days rest it moved inland again until, within sight of Caen, Harold was taken. He was part of a night patrol attempting to capture a German prisoner for interrogation when the party came under machine gun fire. Harold took shelter under a big bramble bush and after laying there for three days and nights, was seen by a German soldier and taken back to the enemy lines.

After being held for some time in a prisoner of war compound, he was eventually transported back to Germany in a cattle truck. There he was put in prison camp Stalag 8B which was occupied by about 7,000 other British soldiers - some of whom had been there since Dunkirk. From there he was sent every day,

including Sundays, to work as a forced labourer in a German coal mine. The food was poor - usually dry bread and watery soup - and everyone eagerly awaited the arrival of the Red Cross parcels which contained milk, tea, sugar, butter, cigarettes, pipe tobacco and writing materials. The German army guards were capable of rough treatment.

As the Allies advanced across northern Europe in 1945, he was force-marched eastwards into Poland but in the face of the advancing Russians, the group turned round and headed back into Germany. Eventually, after walking some 800 miles, on occasions through deep snow, the Americans caught up with his group of prisoners and he was a free men again. After spending a period with the Americans, he was handed over to the British army who flew him to France. A bout of malaria saw him detained in an American army hospital where he spent a fortnight living in some luxury.

In autumn 1945, he flew back to England and landed at Aylesbury, Bucks where the WRVS was on hand to take care of the returned prisoners-of- war. Eventually he went back to his battalion at York from where he was demobbed.

He was one of the prisoners-of-war who attended the dinner given by the Barton UDC in late 1945 - see back cover of this book.

Information from

Harold Welch

Margaret West (later Gouldthorpe)

Private, W/161517
Auxiliary Territorial Service
Operation Fire Control

Margaret West was born in 1921, the daughter of Mr John and Mrs Mary West of 32 Marsh Lane, Barton-on-Humber. She attended the Church School and on leaving was employed in a children's creche in Hull and later as a nanny at Swanland. She played tennis on Hopper's Club court which was situated at the rear of Butts Road.

In April 1942, she was conscripted into the ATS and did her initial training at Neville's Cross in Durham. From there she was posted to the Cottesmore Kennels (home for two packs of hounds) near Oakham in Rutland. This was at that time the Headquarters of the 41 Searchlight Regiment. Whilst there she volunteered to join a course on the wireless wing which took place at nearby Ashwell. This proved to be training in the use of radar sets on anti-aircraft gun sites to detect enemy aircraft. She passed the course with a

Margaret West.

mark of 81% and was then sent to the 516 Heavy Anti-Aircraft Battery of 511 Regiment, Royal Artillery based at Sheffield. The Battery had four guns and a radar tracking unit staffed by ATS ladies. Its job was to protect the vital steel works in the Sheffield area.

When warned of the approach of enemy aircraft, the radar team of six ladies operated a transmitter and a receiver. The transmitter - with two operators - sent out a radio pulse. When the pulse hit an enemy aircraft, it was reflected back to the ground and was picked up by the receiver located in a nearby field. The receiver was managed by four people. One determined the bearing and another range. Margaret operated the equipment that measured the vertical angle of the aircraft above the horizontal. With the range and the angle of elevation known, the height could be calculated. The fourth person, 'No 1' - a corporal - reported the details to an underground control room which plotted the position of the enemy aircraft and reported that information to the nearby anti-aircraft guns. The trackers were able to distinguish an Allied aircraft from a German one because friendly planes transmitted an extra signal known as IFF (Identification Friend or Foe) which was picked up on the radar screens. Whilst tracking an enemy aircraft with these early radar sets, it was necessary to rotate the whole receiver - a sensation which was often found to be

somewhat uncomfortable. However, during Margaret's stay at Sheffield, the radar sets were being constantly improved. Also in the team at Sheffield were a number of ATS visual spotters, plotters, cooks and clerks. The ladies lived in Nissen huts located near to the guns.

From Sheffield, Margaret's battery was moved by troop-train, usually at night, to various other locations. These included various sites on the north bank of the Humber including the Costello Playing Fields in Hull, Meaux, Spurn Point and Sutton. Whilst they were at Hull, Margaret and some of her colleagues were sent to look around a captured German U-boat in Hull Docks.

Just before D-Day, the Battery was moved to Bungay near Beccles in Suffolk. On D-Day itself Margaret was not on duty but stood outside watching the hundreds of American aircraft which were flying over on their way to Normandy. The radar sets were then being used to track Allied aircraft on their way back to base.

She was finally moved back to Sheffield and she was there on VE Day. Following a Victory Parade, the Lord Mayor gave a reception for the service men and women. By the end of the war, the radar units were housed in long buses with the receiver and transmitter in the one vehicle. A rotating dish aerial on the top of the bus allowed the seated lady receivers to remain stationary and not have to suffer, as previously, the discomfort of being continually rotated.

In December 1945, Margaret married Donald Gouldthorpe (qv - on leave from Italy) and so was demobbed in early 1946.

Information from

Margaret Gouldthorpe

Clifford Winship

Able Seaman, CJX376410
Royal Navy
Mechanic

Clifford Winship was born in 1924, the son of Mr Arthur William and Mrs Annie Amelia Winship of 27 Dam Road, Barton-on-Humber. His hobbies were shooting and football. He attended St. Chad's School and on leaving was employed on keels, sloops and motor boats on the Humber. He has vivid memories of sailing in the Humber in the early years of the war - he was tied up in the harbour at Hull during the massive raids on the city in May 1941. Shortly after that, whilst travelling to Immingham to pick up a cargo, his boat's engine broke down outside the dock in the middle of the British minefield at the entrance to the dock. He

Clifford Winship in April 1943.

was eventually picked up by a Royal Navy rescue vessel and taken into Immingham. The boat was towed into the dock later. Sailing in the Humber at this time was particularly hazardous after the Germans had dropped mines into the river. A black flag flown from a mast on Victoria Pier in Hull warned the vessels on the river of this danger.

He volunteered to join the Royal Navy in 1942 and did his training at *HMS Ganges* at Ipswich. From there he went to *HMS Daedalus* at Lee-on-Solent near Portsmouth from where he was transferred to motor launches and rescue boats running out of south coast ports. Their main job was to rescue anyone in distress in the English Channel, particularly airmen whose planes had ditched into the sea. When not on this work, they were used to collect dummy torpedoes which had been dropped from aircraft on torpedo-dropping exercises.

From there, in 1943, he moved to Campbelltown in NW Scotland where he was engaged in patrol work in the North Atlantic, Irish Sea and Scottish Lochs. Again this was largely search-and-find duties wherever and whenever necessary. The boat in which he sailed was a high-speed motor launch with about 10 crew members. In charge was a RNR lieutenant, Lawrence Atkinson, a former trawler skipper from Grimsby. Clifford's job was as ship's mechanic in the engine room but when necessary he had to undertake other duties such as manning the ship's guns - two twin

Lewis guns and/or two twin Brownings. These were used to fire at enemy aircraft or ships. The ships also carried rifles and hand grenades.

He remained in Scotland until the end of the war and was demobbed from this base in May 1946.

Information from

Clifford Winship

Roy Winship

Sergeant, 1620555
Royal Air Force
Flight Mechanic/Engines
Merchant Navy
Engineer

Roy Winship was born in 1922, the son of Mr Harold and Mrs Grace Winship of 1 Queen Street, Barton. He was educated at the Church School and on leaving was apprenticed by Isaiah Grassby, Engineer, of Queen Street, Barton.

On 6 July 1942, he joined the RAE and did a period of training at St. Andrew's in Scotland. He eventually qualified as a flight mechanic specializing in engines and went on numerous bombing raids over Germany.

Roy Winship.

SS Samwy at Tocopilla, Chile in November 1945. Note gun on the raised platform behind the bow, presumably manned by DEMS gunners - see Jim Clayton (cv).

By 1944 he felt that he could no longer undertake further raids on civilian targets and on 12 October in that year he was 'temporarily released from regular Royal Air Force Service ... to take up civil employment with The Merchant Navy.' He was 'subject to recall to regular service as and when required'.

In October 1944 he was listed in the 'Merchant Navy Reserve Pool' and on 10 November he joined the crew of the *SS Auretta* in Hull as 5th Engineer. The ship belonged to WH Cockerline and Co, Ltd, Steamship Owners and Brokers of Filey, Yorkshire. On 27 February 1945, Cockerline informed Mrs Winship that Roy's ship had been 'sunk by enemy action' but that they were pleased to inform her that 'Mr Winship is safe and in port on the Continent.' In *Lloyd's War Losses Second World War* it is recorded that the ship was sunk on 25 February 1945 by 'mine or submarine' whilst on a voyage from London to Antwerp. The War Loss Card for the *Auretta* further records that the ship was 'mined at 7.45 am GMT on 26 February in 51 23 30 N, 244 E, and sank in 51 24 6 N, 2494 E., with the masts showing above water ... *Auretta* had sailed from London on 24 February and passed Southend on 25 February'. There were 46 survivors including seven gunners (presumably DEMS gunners - see Jim Clayton [cv]) who were landed at Ostend. Soon afterwards Roy returned home to Barton where he slept solidly for 24 hours!

Roy's Certificate of Discharge records that on 19 April 1945 he sailed from Immingham as 4th Engineer on the Bank Line Ltd merchantman, *SS Samwy*. He was issued with an identity card in New York on 4 June

and a 'Short Period Ship's Crew Pass' in Calcutta on 15 September. The ship berthed in Buenos Aires, Argentina in October and at Tocopilla, Chile on 15 November 1945. He finally left the ship in Liverpool in February 1946. He appears to have been discharged from the Merchant Navy in May 1946 'to resume former employment in the Brick and Tile Making Industry.'

Information from

Margaret Evison (sister)

Claire Leyland (daughter)

Principal Reference Librarian, Guildhall Library, London

George Wright

Private/Gunner, 4806657
8th Battalion Lincolnshire Regiment, Argyll and Sutherland Highlanders, Royal Artillery
Batman/Infantryman

George William Wright was born in 1913, the son of Mr George and Mrs Alice Wright of Goxhill. The family moved to Barton in 1935.

He joined the Lincolnshire Regiment on 20 June 1940 and, after initial training at Stores Park, joined the 8th Battalion in which he served as a batman at various stations in Norfolk. When the 8th Battalion was split up he was transferred into the Argyll and Sutherland

George Wright.

Highlanders at Strensall Barracks, York.

In 1944 he landed on Gold Beach in Normandy **(15)**, a few days after the invasion of 6 June. From there he travelled across Northern Europe into Germany constantly on the move but always somewhat behind the front line. Towards the end of the war he was transferred into the Royal Artillery.

In January 1946 he was demobbed from York.

Information from

George Wright

Chapter Four

Addenda to Parts One and Two

Addendum to Part One - Lest We Forget

In 1997 the Barton-on-Humber Branch of the WEA published its *Barton Remembered 1939-1945; Part One, Lest We Forget* which gave detailed biographies of the 53 men and women from the town who gave their lives during the Second World War. Additional information was included in the Addendum to Part Two of the series, *The Home Front*, pp 169-171, published in 1998. Since then further details have become known about Harold Bell, Donald Hewitt, Kenneth Houghton and Ralph Watkin.

Harold Bell

It is now known that Harold Bell died whilst taking part in Operation *Slapstick*, the Allied landings of 3,600 British paratroopers of the 1st Airborne Division at Taranto, southern Italy, on 9 September 1943. Arthur Sobey (see above) was also present at these landings and was in the boat alongside that in which Harold Bell was sailing. Harold's boat hit a mine.

Information from

Arthur Sobey

Donald Hewitt

The Commonwealth War Graves Commission has recently put details of all those men and women who died in WW2 onto the Internet. The only Donald Hewitt who appears on their list is 4986425 Private Donald Hewitt, 5 Battalion, Wiltshire Regiment who died on 8 March 1945, aged 21. He was the son of Thomas and Florence Hewitt of Scunthorpe and is buried in the Reichswald Forest War Cemetery in Germany. An appeal in the pages of the Scunthorpe Telegraph for further information about Donald and/or his parents produced no new information. This might well be the man commemorated on our town's War Memorial but until further information is forthcoming a definitive biography of Donald Hewitt cannot be produced.

Kenneth Houghton

Flying Officer, 55226
Royal Air Force
Navigator/Pilot

Barton Remembered 1939-1945; Part One, Lest We Forget, p 44 recorded that Kenneth Houghton was '... shot down on a bombing raid over Germany. He

subsequently escaped from his prisoner-of-war camp [sic] and made his way back to England ...'

The following information was provided by Mr J. Scott of Chilwell, Nottinghamshire who, in late 1998, read a piece appealing for information about Kenneth Houghton which the author had placed in the RAFAs Magazine *Air Mail* in 1995. He is able to provide much more detail about the 'escape' (which was technically an 'evasion') -

'I first met him [ie Kenneth Houghton] at Boscombe Down where we were both involved in the testing of the first Manchester aircraft. [A short-lived twin-engined bomber that was developed into the four-engined Lancaster.] This was towards the end of 1940 when we had both completed a tour of duty of operations in Hampden aircraft; Ken with 83 Squadron and myself with No 44(Rhodesia) Squadron. He was a navigator at that time. After testing had been completed we, along with about six other air crew and ground crew support, were posted to Waddington where we reformed No 207 Squadron. Further trials continued and in February 1941 operations commenced. Ken subsequently crewed up with Pilot Officer L.A. Plaskell and it was he with whom he was flying on the night of 13/14 October 1941 in Manchester L7373 when they were intercepted and shot down by a German Me110 night fighter. Ken and Arthur Smith managed to bale out (the aircraft had caught fire) but sadly the pilot and the rest of the crew were killed when the Manchester crashed near Louvain [in Belgium].

'From then onwards the only news that filtered through was that Smith, who had been badly burnt before baling out, was picked up by German soldiers and extremely well-treated by them) and that Houghton had managed to escape capture and was able to make his way to Switzerland.

'I was looking out of the window in the Mess at Bottesford (207 Squadron had moved there) and someone tapped me on the shoulder - it was Ken Houghton and by now it was about August/September 1942! Ken then told me his amazing story.

'After hiding after the aftermath of the crash (the Germans had thought that Smith was the only survivor), by lying up during the day and travelling by night, he was able to make his way to the Swiss border where he gave himself up to the authorities as an evader and then gave his parole (his word not to escape). He was allowed to look for a job and eventually found work in a bank [It may be remembered that his father was manager of Barclay's Bank in Barton High Street - was there a connection there?]. In the meantime he had been able to obtain identity papers which described him as "DEAF, DUMB AND MENTALLY RETARDED". Thus equipped and with the money he had been able to save, he again contacted the Swiss authorities, withdrew his parole and began his epic journey from Switzerland through France and so to the Franco-Spanish border. He travelled mostly by train and at one time was in a carriage packed with German troops! His "status" as an idiot was never questioned and he was able to reach the border without incident. There he met a Polish escaper and the pair were conducted across the border by members of the French escape organisation and then embarked on what was to be the most gruelling part of the journey. They had little money and only a small amount of food; water was a constant problem. Travelling on foot during the Spanish summer tested their endurance to the limit and they chose to walk in the early morning and evening. There was always the fear that they might be picked up by the local police, consequently they holed up during the day.

'Eventually they reached Portugal where they were held by the police until the British Embassy came to their aid. After a few days rest arrangements were made for them to fly to the UK on one of the few available air services.

'Ken was a slightly built person but his courage and determination must have been immense. After returning to the UK he trained as a pilot and flew with Transport Command. It was a great sadness that I heard that he had lost his life in an air accident at Lydda in Palestine. The war was over and he deserved more than this tragic end. Arthur Smith survived the war but he never knew about Ken's adventures and subsequent death for about 45 years; he always thought he was the sole survivor of the Manchester crash.'

Information from

J. Scott (RAF friend)

Ralph Watkin

Flight Lieutenant, 116992
No 180 Squadron, Royal Air Force
Navigator

The short biography of Ralph Watkin which appeared in Part One of this series was largely based on

information provided by Les Morrison of the Historical Branch RAF. Nothing in that biography and no-one spoken to by the author could definitely identify him and connect him with Barton-on-Humber. Once again a search of the Commonwealth War Graves Commission Internet site revealed that only one man named Ralph Watkin died in WW2. As Les Morrison had already shown, he was 116992 Flight Lieutenant Ralph Watkin RAFVR of No 180 Squadron who died on 22 January 1943, aged 30. He was the son of Ralph and Gertrude Watkin and wife of Phyllis Watkin, all of Hull. The Editor of the Hull Daily Mail kindly printed my letter asking anyone who knew Ralph Watkin, his wife or parents to contact me.

First to reply was Ralph's cousin, Joyce Ward, who confirmed that following his marriage to Phyllis Bird at some date before 1939, Ralph had moved to Barton to work at Elswick Hopper's Cycle Works. She further informed me that the couple had had a son, Keith. I was delighted when, a few days later, Keith Watkin contacted me and was able to confirm that all my information was correct. Later still, Malcolm Mann wrote and informed me that he is collecting information on all the men and women from Hull who died serving their country in WW2 and was able to supply more information.

Ralph Watkin was the son of Ralph Watkin of Hull who was well-known in legal circles being clerk to the Hull County Court Judge. He was called up at the outbreak of war when he was a resident of Barton-on-Humber and working at Hopper's Cycle Works. He was a keen athlete and footballer and a member of the Barton Boys' Club. After completing his RAF training he was posted to Bomber Command and completed over 40 flights including the first daylight raid on Cologne early in 1941.

Ralph was killed in action on 22 January 1943 aged 30 years flying aircraft Mitchell II - FL212 EV-A on Operation *Ghent*. Take-off was at 1355 hrs from Foulsham UK, to attack the Purfina and Sinclair oil facilities alongside the Ghent-Terneuzen Canal. (Although Ghent is given as the target, Purfina was in the village of Ertwelde-Rieme, whilst the Sinclair plant came within the area of Evergem.)

The aircraft was hit by flak in the starboard engine and later shot down by a German Focke Wulf Fw190 flown by Uffz Vorhaurer of 11/JG1 and crashed into the sea at 1500 hours at Basseveilde (Oost Vlaanderen) 9km north east of Eeklo, Belgium, where all five crew are still buried in the communal cemetery.

Operation *Ghent* was undertaken by 23 Bostons, 18 Venturas and 12 Mitchells (all US-built twin-engined bombers) of Nos 98 and 180 Squadrons. The Bostons and Venturas attacked airfields in France while the Mitchells carried out the first raid by this new type of aircraft on the oil facilities. Two Venturas and three Mitchells were lost, including the aircraft of Wing

Commander C.C. Hodder, Officer Commanding No 180 Squadron, and Ralph Watkin.

Ralph's wife moved back to Hull during the war. Ralph and the rest of the crew of the fated aircraft are remembered on the Runnymede Memorial.

Information from

Maurice Barrick (military researcher)

Malcolm Mann (military researcher)

Joyce Ward (cousin)

Keith Watkin (son)

Addendum to Part Two - The Home Front

In 1998 the Branch published *Barton Remembered 1939-1945; Part Two, The Home Front*. I am grateful to many readers who have provided the corrections which are listed below:

p 10   There were three women on duty at the Report Centre, six nights each week (with Saturday off) from 11 pm until 8 am the following day. During the last few weeks of the war the duty extended from 11 pm until 12 noon. Women who worked there included Mildred Marsden, Bessie Shucksmith and Joan Mather.

p 92   Sixth from the left on the back row was Raymond Emmerson, not Ernison.

p 98   Seventh from left on back row is Joyce Needham who was the daughter of Andrew Needham, the landlord of the Steam Packet Inn in Fleetgate.

p 102   The names of those who attended the POWs' Party at the White Swan hotel in 1945 is incomplete. A photograph of the event and a full list of those who attended can be found on the back cover of this book.

p 114   Among the teachers listed at the bottom of column 2 is Eric Sykes. This should read William Clucas Sykes, the teacher who succeeded Harry Boulton as Headmaster at the Grammar School.

p 115   The unknown teacher, third from the left on the front row, was Agatha McGaw, an exchange teacher from the United States.

p 118   The fourth boy from the left is Royce Foster not Stan Doughty.

p 151   Five lines down in right hand column. George Mager (not Major) owned two shrimp boats - *Spendrift* and *Venture* both of which were usually moored at Barrow Haven, one below the railway station and the other opposite.

p 165   The caption under the photograph should read: Tim (Cecil) Burkitt, on the left, and Ron Earle of South Ferriby loading loaves into Earle's van (property of Edward Earle and Sons) for sale in the Ferriby village shop.